Monahan

1997

AN INTRODUCTION
TO THE NATURE AND NEEDS
OF STUDENTS WITH
MILD DISABILITIES

ABOUT THE AUTHOR

Carroll J. Jones received her Ph.D. in Special Education Administration and Learning Disabilities from Kansas State University, and her M.Ed. in Reading and B.A. in Elementary Education are from the University of Arizona. Doctor Jones has spent the last decade involved in special education teacher training at small, primarily rural colleges.

As a Professor at Lander University, Doctor Jones designed one of the first B.S. degree programs in South Carolina for training teachers of students with mild disabilities that resulted in triple certification (elementary, early childhood, and special education). Currently, she is involved with the implementation of that program and piloting a special education portfolio monitoring system to track acquisition of special education competencies among preservice teachers. Her current research interests involve teaching styles of preservice teachers. Doctor Jones has published seven special education textbooks, five of these books, and the current book are part of a series regarding the education of students with mild disabilities.

AN INTRODUCTION TO THE NATURE AND NEEDS OF STUDENTS WITH MILD DISABILITIES

Mild Mental Retardation, Behavior Disorders, and Learning Disabilities

By

CARROLL J. JONES, PH.D.

CHARLES C THOMAS • PUBLISHER, LTD.
Springfield • Illinois • U.S.A.

Published and Distributed Throughout the World by

CHARLES C THOMAS • PUBLISHER, LTD.
2600 South First Street
Springfield, Illinois 62794-9265

© *1996 by* CHARLES C THOMAS • PUBLISHER, LTD.

ISBN 0-398-06711-2 (cloth)
ISBN 0-398-06712-0 (paper)

Library of Congress Catalog Card Number: 96-28091

Printed in the United States of America
SC-R-3

Library of Congress Cataloging-in-Publication Data

Jones, Carroll J.
   An introduction to the nature and needs of students with mild
disabilities : mild mental retardation, behavioral disorders, and
learning disabilities / by Carroll J. Jones.
      p.   cm.
   Includes bibliographical references (p.   ) and index.
   ISBN 0-398-06711-2 (cloth). — ISBN 0-398-06712-0 (paper)
   1. Mentally handicapped children—Education—United States.
2. Learning disabled children—Education—United States.   3. Problem
children—Education—United States.   I. Title.
LC4631.J66   1996
371.92'82—dc20   96-28091
                                                                      CIP

To Jordan

FOREWORD

We have spent at least the last fifty years in Special Education carefully identifying and defining who our population of students is, what makes them unique from other children, and how they best learn. Now, in this time of emphasis on including all students in the mainstream classroom, we may be in danger of forgetting the very differences in children which made them need special attention in the first place. In her characteristically clear and concise way, Carroll Jones reminds us who these students are we so often lump together under the label "mildly handicapped." She reminds us that students who have mild retardation, who have a learning disability or who are behavior disordered do have similarities, but they also exhibit significant differences which have bearing on the way they learn. Dr. Jones gives us a valuable, in-depth profile of each of these three disability areas, complete with historical, theoretical, and learning perspectives.

This is not a methods book. It was not intended to be, because there are a number of useful methods books available for our choosing. Rather, this is a book which allows us to explore the ways in which each of these categories of students has been treated in the past and to explore a highly readable and useful analysis of what learning characteristics they display now that cause them to be identified as mentally retarded, learning disabled, or behavior disordered. It is not until we **know our learners** that we can plan the best ways to help these learners learn and grow.

This is a book that will prove very useful to special and general educators, alike, both at the pre-service and in-service levels. Teachers who will be serving in inclusion classrooms need to understand the students with disabilities under their care and what makes them learn differently from those sitting next to them. Teachers who will be serving in pull-out or self-contained classrooms need to be very familiar with why their students needed to be separate. Particularly useful to all teachers is the final chapter comparing and contrasting the mildly handicapped categories of learners according to cognitive, social/emotional, and academic learning characteristics (the latter across all school age levels). Dr. Jones provides a chart which will be invaluable to teachers and prospective teachers alike who want help in understanding the unique natures of their students with disabilities.

VIRGINIA J. DICKENS
Professor
Fayetteville State University

PREFACE

The critical lack of special education teachers for students with mild disabilities has resulted in the creation of teacher preparation programs in generic special education or mildly handicapping conditions. Some of these programs focus on commonalities among the high incidence categories as if all students with mild disabilities experienced the same learning rates, learning characteristics, and academic and social problems completely ignoring the categorical aspect. Some of these teacher preparation programs have a totally categorical focus as if there were no commonalities among the high incidence exceptionalities. Regardless of the focus of the program, there are few to no textbooks written which meet the program demands with introduction course textbooks separate from methods course textbooks.

This book, *An Introduction to the Nature and Needs of Students with Mild Disabilities: Mild Mental Retardation, Behavior Disorders and Learning Disabilities,* was designed as the foundation or introduction textbook for a Generic Special Education B.S. degree program with a cross-categorical focus. The text includes an overview (Chapter 1) of students at-risk for academic failure. The remainder of the text is divided into three categorical units—students with mild mental retardation, behavior disorders, and learning disabilities. The first chapter of each unit (Chapters 2, 5, 8) provides a historical overview of the various categorical areas including the historical background of services in Europe, early to current services in the United States, and landmark legislation and litigation relevant to each categorical area, and definitions and classification systems. The second chapter of each categorical unit (Chapters 3, 6, 9) provides an overview of the theoretical, psychological, and philosophical models including contributions of primary theorists regarding etiology, diagnosis, and treatment of each categorical area. The third chapter in each unit (Chapters 4, 7, 10) provides a categorical overview of learning perspectives including cognitive, academic, social, emotional, and self-concept characteristics. Chapter 11, the last chapter, provides a comparative analysis of the similarities and differences among the cognitive, learning, and social characteristics of students with mild mental retardation, behavior disorders, and learning disabilities.

Thanks to my colleague Dr. Virginia Dickens at Fayetteville State University for continuous support and suggestions. Thanks to Porter Wideman Palmer, a special education resource teacher in Newberry, South Carolina, for reading rough drafts; and to Lisa Hiott, special education pre-service teacher, for proofing the bibliography. This book is dedicated with much love to our young grandson, Jordan, through whom everything is new again!

C.J.J.

CONTENTS

AN INTRODUCTION TO
THE NATURE AND NEEDS
OF STUDENTS
WITH MILD DISABILITIES

Chapter 1

INTRODUCTION: AT-RISK
CHILDREN AND YOUTH

Many of today's pressing social problems, such as poverty, homelessness, drug abuse, and child abuse are factors that place children and youth at-risk in a variety of ways (Helge, 1991, v).

Magnitude of the Problem
Students with Mild Disabilities
Students Declassified "EMR"
Students with Cultural and Linguistic Differences
Students from Poverty Environments
Substance Exposed Students
Medically At-Risk Students
Summary

The most significant problem facing the public schools today is the education of perhaps 20 to 30 million at-risk children and youth whose concerns may often require the interrelated interventions of social welfare, special education, bilingual education, medical treatment, and psychological services. The magnitude of the problem is too great to be remedied by educational intervention alone. At-risk infants, children, and youth are not only at-risk for school failure and dropout, but also, for social, emotional, behavioral, and life problems.

Some startling similarities exist among the cognitive, social, emotional, and behavioral characteristics of mildly disabled students and the various other categories of at-risk children and youth. Noncompliance, difficulties in language and communication, problems in social relationships, and difficulties exercising judgment and making decisions are all behaviors that appear to be associated with at-risk students (Stevens & Price, 1992). A significant portion of the students served in high incidence special education programs exhibit problems due to at-risk life conditions.

3

MAGNITUDE OF THE PROBLEM

A Phi Delta Kappa study of students at-risk indicated 33%–40% of the K–12 school population were at-risk for academic failure (Frymier & Gansneder, 1989). In 1991, large numbers of students functioned below grade level and were at high risk for dropout (Kominski & Adams, 1992):

Age	6–8 years	9–11 years	12–14 years	15–17 years
Total	21.8%	28.1%	31.4%	34.8%
White	22.2%	27.2%	28.7%	32.0%
Black	21.1%	33.3%	46.1%	48.0%
Hispanic	21.9%	35.6%	38.5%	48.6%

The 1992 average public high school graduation rate nationwide was 71.2 percent of students enrolled (The 1995 World Almanac, 1994). Graduation rates in 1992 ranged from high rates in Minnesota (89.2% graduation rate), Iowa (87.6% graduation rate), and North Dakota (85.5% graduation rate) to low rates in South Carolina (58.1% graduation rate), Texas (56.0% graduation rate), and Louisiana (52.9%, the lowest graduation rate) (The 1995 World Almanac, 1994). These figures indicate that the high school dropout rate ranges from 10.8 to 47.1 percent; however, the reported national average for 1990 high school dropouts is 11.2 percent (The Chronicle, 1994).

Though categories of at-risk children and youth are often overlapping and exact prevalences extremely difficult to determine, the following estimates may help indicate the magnitude of the problem:

5 million	Children and Youth with Disabilities (OSEP, 1994)
1 million	Depressed and Suicidal Youth (Guetzloe, 1991)
7.5 million	Children and Youth Declassified "EMR"
20 million	Minority Children and Youth (1993 World Almanac)
13.9 million	Poor Children and Youth (1995 World Almanac)
1.6 million	Homeless Children and Youth (1993 World Almanac)
730,000	Runaway Children and Youth (1993 World Almanac)
17 million	Rural Children and Youth (1990 Bureau of Census)
350,000	Born Substance-Exposed (Widerstrom et al., 1991)
3–4 million	Lead-Exposed Children (Needleman, 1992)
1–2 million	Abused Children and Youth (US Dept. of Health, 1993)
3–5,000	HIV/AIDS Children and Youth (1993 World Almanac)
290,000	Premature/Low Birth Weight Infants (Kids Count, 1993).

STUDENTS WITH MILD DISABILITIES

According to the 16th Annual Report to Congress, 5,170,242 children and youth (birth through age 21 years) received special education services in school year 1992–93 (OSEP, 1994). Approximately 93 percent of all disabled students fall into the mildly disabled categories of learning disabled (51.1%), speech and language impaired (21.6%), mildly mentally retarded (11.5%), and behaviorally disordered or emotionally disabled (8.7%) (OSEP, 1994). These children and youth by virtue of their diagnostic label and demonstrated need for special education services are recognized as being at-risk for academic failure and school dropout, social and emotional problems, adaptive behavior problems, and adult life problems.

Mildly disabled students appear to be at extreme risk for school dropout even though they are receiving special educational services. During the 1991–92 academic year 57.4 percent of special education students exited with a diploma or certificate. However, 49,434 disabled students, or 22.4 percent of all special education students, dropped out of school and another 39,733, or 15.8 percent, were labeled status unknown and were probably dropouts (OSEP, 1994). Numerous studies indicate high dropout rates for mildly disabled students consistent across locations (suburban, rural, urban) as follows (OSEP, 1994):

	Dropout	*Unknown*
Learning disabled	21.3% (28,257)	17.7% (23,409)
Speech/language impaired	20.1% (1,633)	27.5% (2,230)
Mentally Retarded	19.6% (7,650)	10.5% (4,099)
Emotionally Disturbed	35.0% (11,894)	29.9% (9,995)

The evidence to date suggests that mildly disabled students are particularly prone to dropping out of school. Additionally, students living in states with minimum competency-test requirements for graduation are at greater risk for dropout than those in states without such requirements.

Since disabled children and youth experience significant anxiety and depression, it is not surprising that they are at high risk for suicide. Children and adolescents with emotional and behavioral disorders and other disabling conditions are at greater risk for suicide behaviors than youngsters without disabilities (Guetzloe, 1991). Among the U.S. population suicide is the fifth leading cause of death among children ages 5–14 years and the third leading cause of death among 15–24 year-olds (Vital

Statistics, 1989). The number of suicide attempts in the United States annually may range from 500,000 to 1 million (Guetzloe, 1991).

STUDENTS DECLASSIFIED "EMR"

A significant number of students at-risk for educational failure, school dropout, and social and emotional adjustment problems are children and youth whose IQ falls within the 70–85 range. Students with IQs in this range who formerly were classified as having borderline or mild retardation became nonretarded due to changes in American Association on Mental Retardation (AAMR) IQ guidelines in 1973 (Grossman, 1973). According to the 1961 AAMR definition, almost 16 percent of the population were identified as mentally retarded from a psychometric perspective, while the 1973 definition considered less than 3 percent of the population as mentally retarded (Patton et al., 1990).

These students with IQs 70–85, declassified in response to parental demands and court rulings for equal educational opportunity, comprise about 85 percent of the formerly mildly retarded or educable mentally retarded students. These students no longer qualify for special education services yet progress at about 75 percent of the rate of average students, so are marginal achievers. Due to both low IQ and low achievement, they do not meet the severe discrepancy requirement of learning disability classification.

The probability of these declassified students graduating from high school has been significantly reduced by new policies that require minimum competency testing requirements which these students often cannot meet (MacMillan et al., 1988). This at-risk, but no longer disabled, population appears to contribute disproportionate numbers of students to the dropout statistics (MacMillan et al., 1991). Ironically, this low "average" functioning 13 percent of the school population or approximately 6.2 million children ages 3–17 contribute significantly to the lower standardized test score averages nationwide that have prompted legislators to initiate minimal competency testing and demand school reform.

STUDENTS WITH CULTURAL
AND LINGUISTIC DIFFERENCES

Ethnic minority students constitute approximately 31 percent of the general school population or 20 million children and youth under age 18 years (The 1993 World Almanac, 1992). Currently, approximately 6 million Americans ages 5–17 years (13.9%) speak non-English languages at home and over half of these speak Spanish (The 1993 World Almanac, 1992). Spanish speakers make up the largest group of bilingual students in the United States, while the smallest minority population, American Indians, is made up of more than 500 tribes with over 200 different languages (McDonald, 1989).

Nationally, the population growth rate of Americans between 1980 and 1990 increased at an overall rate of 9.8 percent with the white population increasing at the rate of 6% while minority populations increased cumulatively at a rate of 211.9 percent (Black, 13.2%; American Indians, 37.9%; Asian, 107.8%, and Hispanic, 53%) (The 1993 World Almanac, 1992, 388). Projections indicate that by the year 2000, minority students will comprise 40 percent of the public school population (Ramirez, 1988) and 46 percent by 2020 (Pallas, Natriello & McDill, 1989).

Though minority children function at all levels of intellectual ability from subaverage through gifted ranges, language differences derived from cultural diversity (e.g., Spanish) and language differences from nonstandard language cultures (e.g., Black English) may place them at-risk for academic and social difficulties in school (Hardman et al., 1990). Linguistically different students are at high risk for academic failure and school dropout because they are faced with learning a second language simultaneously with receiving academic instruction in that language.

Some children have handicaps as well as language differences; it is not always easy to distinguish between those children whose learning and communication problems are due to disabilities and those who are solely in need of instruction in English (Heward, 1996). A very high percentage—perhaps as high as 41 percent—of all special education students are from culturally divergent backgrounds (Bedell, 1989). Estimates suggest that there are about 1 million culturally and linguistically different exceptional (CLDE) students who have limited English proficiency and learning problems and/or behavior disorders (Boca & Cervantes, 1989). CLDE students are significantly at-risk for educational failure due to disabilities, limited English proficiency, and often to living in environments of poverty. In 1990, only 42 percent of Hispanic teens graduated from high school by age 19, compared to 61 percent of African-American teens, and 73 percent of white teens (1993 World Almanac, 1992).

STUDENTS FROM POVERTY ENVIRONMENTS

Children who live in environments of poverty are at extreme high risk for academic failure, school dropout, unemployment, and adult lives that perpetuate the culture of poverty. The overall poverty rate for U.S. children under age 18 years is 21.9 percent or 13.8 million American children (8,321,000 or 16% of white and 4,637,000 or 46% of black), and over half of these children are living in female single-parent households (The 1995 World Almanac, 1994). "Nationwide, children living in poverty increased 22% in the 1980s" (The 1995 World Almanac, 1994, 383). Forty-nine states and the District of Columbia have double digit poverty rates for children under age 18 years with 14 states and the District of Columbia having poverty rates that include a quarter to a third of the total number of children in their state (The Chronicle Almanac, 1992).

The overriding concern is not the reduced financial income level itself, but the correlates of poverty—inadequate environments, undernutrition, lack of medical care, and negative psychological impact on families and children. A primary effect of undernutrition is the reduction of nutrients necessary for normal growth and development, social and cognitive learning, and sensorimotor functioning; thus, poverty results in increased risk to children for developmental delay including physical, neurological, and cognitive impairments (Peterson, 1987). Poor medical care including poor prenatal care results in higher rates of prematurity and low birth weight, and increased infant mortality, as well as increased susceptibility to infection and disease. Poverty and the child-rearing methods associated with it contribute to the number of youth identified as emotionally and behaviorally troubled (over 20% of some inner-city populations) (Recer, 1989).

Estimates of the number of homeless people varies considerably; however, according to the Children's Defense Fund, as many as 4 million of the nearly 34 million poor may be homeless, including 1.6 million children (Burns, 1991). Estimates indicate that from 730,000 to 1 million young people run away each year, 25 percent of whom are considered homeless (Council of Scientific Affairs, 1989). The National Network of

Runaway and Youth Services estimates that there are 1.3 to 2 million street youth in this country (Kerr, 1989).

MIGRANT CHILDREN AND YOUTH

Migrant children and youth are multiply at risk for academic failure, school dropout, social and behavioral problems, and adult work-related and social problems. The infant mortality rate for migrants is 125 percent higher than the national average (Platt et al., 1991). Migrant working effects an estimated 2 to 3 million people each year, with approximately 628,150 children under age 21 years, 80 percent of whom are Hispanics from Mexico (National Commission on Migrant Education, 1992 cited in Pindus et al., 1993).

Since the majority of migrant workers live in poverty, their children exhibit similar behaviors and problems as other homeless children and youth. Migrant children underperform all other groups: educational attainment averages fourth or fifth grade, only 12 percent of those who start school graduate from high school, and 20 percent never enroll in school (Barresi, 1982). By second grade, 50 percent of migrant students nationally are already below grade level, compared with 19 percent of the general population (MESA, 1989). School dropout estimates among migrant children have been estimated to be as high as 90 percent (Platt et al., 1991). Few migrant children are served in special education classes due to high levels of mobility and to their status as culturally, racially, and economically diverse population.

RURAL CHILDREN AND YOUTH

The incidence of childhood poverty is higher in nonmetro than metro communities (Garrett et al., 1994). By 1990, the nonmetro childhood poverty rate stood at 21 percent compared with 18 percent for metro children (Bureau of Census, 1991 cited in Garrett et al., 1994). A disproportionately high number of the 17,666,519 rural children and youth (ages 0–19 years) (National Bureau of Census, 1990) are at risk for academic and social failure, and school dropout due to a multiplicity of interacting factors: poverty and related concerns of inadequate housing, poor nutrition, and health concerns; minority status (e.g., Hispanic migrants, American Indians on reservations, Southern black communities); lack of English proficiency; female-headed households, unemployment;

lack of opportunity. The average dropout rate for small and rural schools may be 40–50 percent (Phelps & Prock, 1991).

PRENATAL SUBSTANCE EXPOSED

Children who have been exposed prenatally to alcohol and/or drugs have a wide range of resultant effects from severely multihandicapping conditions to mild-moderate effects. The estimated percentage of infants exposed to legal and illegal substances before birth includes the following: (1) cocaine, 2–3 percent; (2) marijuana, 3–12 percent; (3) cigarettes, 38 percent; and (4) alcohol, 73 percent (Gomby & Shiono, 1991). The risks and effects of substance exposure are often compounded by numerous prenatal and postnatal home and family risk factors including the correlates of poverty—inadequate housing, poor medical care, and inadequate nutrition. Maternal abuse of substances during pregnancy places the fetus and later the child, at-risk for a variety of medical, neurological, neurodevelopmental, and behavioral difficulties (Zuckerman, 1991). In addition, chronic substance abuse is associated with an increased incidence of neglect or abuse of children.

Prenatal Alcohol Exposed

The effects of excess alcohol consumption during pregnancy are quite predictable causing low birth weight, mental and physical retardation, heart defects, and facial disfigurement known as Fetal Alcohol Syndrome (FAS). This condition has been accepted as the leading preventable cause of mental retardation in the western world (Burgess & Streissguth, 1992). Almost 5% of all birth defects or nearly 5000 infants born in the United States each year have been affected by prenatal exposure to alcohol (Mussen et al., 1990).

A child who has some of the physical characteristics of FAS, but not all of the characteristics, has Fetal Alcohol Effects (FAE). Unfortunately children and adolescents with FAE may be just as severely affected as those with FAS (Burgess & Streissguth, 1992). For every child born with FAS, ten other children may be born with FAE or approximately 50,000 FAE children born each year (National Clearinghouse for Alcohol Information, 1985). Most identified cases of FAS in North America come from sites where the majority of mothers are black or Indian, or where socioeconomic status (SES) is low (Abel & Sokol, 1991). Although studies have demonstrated the average IQ of students with FAS to be approximately 65 to 70, the range is between IQ 30 and 105 (Burgess & Streissguth, 1992). FAS and FAE are lifelong disabilities caused by prenatal brain damage.

Prenatal Drug and/or Nicotine Exposed

Drugs known to produce fetal damage include LSD, heroin, morphine, cocaine, and prescription drugs as anticonvulsants and antibiotics (Peterson, 1987; Batshaw & Perret, 1986). The number of drug exposed newborns increased from 4 to 5 percent of total newborns in 1985 to 15 percent, or 350,000, in 1988 (Widerstrom et al., 1991). Cocaine and methamphetamine taken during pregnancy appear to have similar effects including intrauterine growth retardation, decreased head circumference, preterm delivery with fetal distress, and anemia (Widerstrom et al., 1991). Of children exposed prenatally to substances, 2 to 17 percent will display congenital malformations at birth; some will display mental retardation, seizure disorders, cerebral palsy, and/or physical anomalies (Poulsen, 1991).

Substance exposed children show uneven neurologic maturation, which is displayed through their difficulty in modulating and regulating their own behavior; and when their capacities to self-regulate are overwhelmed, they may lose impulse control and display disorganized and/or inappropriate behavior (Poulsen, 1991). By age three, 30 to 40 percent of substance-exposed children display mild to severe delays in language development, attention problems, and self-regulation (Burgess & Streissguth, 1992).

Pregnant women who smoke cigarettes are at greater risk of having a premature baby with complicating developmental problems, retarded growth of the fetus, lower newborn birth weight and lower resistance to illness (Hetherington & Parke, 1986). The Environmental Protection Agency (1993) released the results of a study that indicated secondhand smoke was responsible for 300,000 cases of bronchitis, pneumonia, and other ailments in infants. Between 20 and 40 percent of the incidence of low birth weight can be explained by smoking and the decrease in weight is directly related to the number of cigarettes smoked daily (Finegan, 1985). Thus, substance-exposed children may be exposed to the effects of several substances in utero, simultaneously increasing the negative at-risk factors.

Lead Exposed Students

Lead poisoning is the Number One environmental problem facing American children (Brody, 1993). It has been estimated that 16 percent of all American children have blood lead levels in the neurotoxic range (Agency for Toxic Substances and Disease Registry, 1988); 3–4 million children are being exposed to concentrations of lead that could compromise their cognitive and social development (Needleman, 1992). In some cases over 50 percent of students in special education classes are lead poisoning victims (Kimball, 1994).

Lead exposure may be a significant cause of cognitive impairments, learning disorders, behavioral problems, and school failure (Kimball, 1994). Lead exposure is associated with poor language skills and increased risks of reading disability; and the child's ability to pay attention, inhibit distraction, and resist impulses (Needleman, 1992). Exposure to lead, even at doses too small to produce symptoms, is associated with impaired neurobehavioral functioning (Needleman & Bellinger, 1991), and neuropsychological problems (Kimball, 1994). Studies also suggest that low lead levels can cause behavioral abnormalities in young children, particularly undue aggression; and young children absorb far more lead than adults exposed to the same levels, and absorption is highest among those with iron deficiency, a problem especially prevalent among poor children (Brody, 1993). Children suffering from exposure to lead have an average IQ four to eight points lower than unexposed children, and they run four times the risk of having an IQ below 80 (Eitzen, 1992). Early lead exposure has been associated with a sevenfold increase in the risk of failing to graduate from high school (Needleman, 1992).

OTHER MEDICALLY AT-RISK STUDENTS

During the 1992–93 school year there were 118,975 children and youth diagnosed orthopedically impaired (52,921) and other health impaired (66,054) (OSEP, 1994), and all of these children are at high risk for academic, social, behavioral, and adaptive life problems. Numerous other youth including physically, sexually, and emotionally abused; HIV positive; premature and/or low birth weight infants are diagnosed disabled, and are at high risk for current and future academic, social, behavioral, and adaptive life problems.

Abused Children and Youth

Child abuse is a term used to describe emotional or psychological injury, negligence, nonaccidental physical injury, and sexual molestation of children by caregivers (Zirpoli, 1995). Over 1,767,673 cases of confirmed or suspected abuse were reported in 1991 (U.S. Dept. of Health and Human Services, 1993), but the actual incidence is probably much higher. Over 50 percent of all children abused are school-aged and the types of substantiated maltreatment include the following: neglect, 45.9 percent; physical abuse, 24.4 percent; sexual abuse, 15.5 percent; emotional maltreatment, 5.9 percent (US Dept. of Health and Human Services, 1993). The Council of Scientific Affairs (1989) estimated that between 730,000 and 1.3 million youth run away each year. A significant portion of runaways in one study indicated physical abuse (36.5%); sexual abuse (30.5%) (Sherman, 1992).

It is estimated that persons with disabilities are four times more likely than their nondisabled peers to be sexually abused (Muccigrosso et al., 1991). A significant body of research since the 1960s substantiates that child abuse is a known cause of physical and mental handicapping conditions. A survey using 2,771 preschool children with developmental disabilities revealed that 11.2 percent acquired the disability as the result of known abuse (Cohen & Warren, 1987).

Identifying physical and sexual abuse symptoms among developmentally delayed individuals is often difficult because some children engage in self-abusive behaviors and some disabled children are prone to accidental injury from falls. Numerous developmentally delayed children and youth have not mastered self-help behaviors, so require very personal assistance in toileting, bathing, and dressing which might be misinterpreted. Some physically disabled students require assistance with procedures such as catheterization which require touching the genitals.

Prematurity and Low Birth Weight

In 1990, 289,418 babies or 7 percent of all babies born that year, came into the world at-risk because of low birth-weight (Kids Count, 1993). Almost 13 percent of African-American babies were born low birth-weight in 1990, a rate more than twice the low birth-weight rate of white or Hispanic babies (Kids Count, 1993). Infants born prematurely are developmentally and physically immature and their size and weight are inappropriate for gestational age. Premature infants are at-risk for jaundice, intraventricular hemorrhage, hyalin membrane disease, and cardiovascular disorders. Low birth-weight in a full-term baby indicates improper growth of the fetus during gestation. Low birth weight babies are more vulnerable than normal weight babies to mental retardation, developmental difficulties such as delays in walking or talking, growth problems, and central nervous system disorders. Many preventable maternal factors are associated with low birth weight: inadequate prenatal care, poor nutrition, smoking, alcohol and/or drug abuse, teen mother.

SUMMARY

In the public schools today large numbers of students are functioning below grade level, approximately one-fourth of the children ages 6–11 years and one-third of the youth ages 12–17 years. Among these children and youth functioning below grade level are mildly disabled students with deficits in cognitive and reasoning skills, difficulties in language and communication, problems in noncompliance and behavioral problems, social relationships, and emotional liabilities which interact to make learning in the classroom difficult. There are significant numbers of children and youth who exhibit many of the same characteristics as students diagnosed mildly disabled including students declassified "EMR," language minority students, poor children, substance exposed children and youth, and children who were premature and/or low birth weight infants.

UNIT 1
STUDENTS WITH MILD
MENTAL RETARDATION

Chapter 2

HISTORICAL PERSPECTIVES
OF MILD MENTAL RETARDATION

Not until 1975 and the passage of P.L.94-142, the Education for All Handicapped Children Act, was the issue of educating all students with mental retardation formally addressed on a national level (Beirne-Smith, Patton & Ittenbach, 1994, 42).

Historical Background of Educational Services
    The Beginning: 1800–1900
    Early MR Services in the United States
    Disillusionment: Early 1900s–1920s
    Gradual Renewed Interest: 1920s–1950
    The Political Years: 1950s–Present
Definitions of Mental Retardation
    Models of Definitions
    AAMR Definitions
Classification of Mental Retardation
    Historical Classification of MR: Behavioral System
    Current Classification of MR: Functional System
Summary

According to the *Sixteenth Annual Report to Congress,* a total of 533,715 students with mental retardation ages 6–21 years or 11.5 percent of all students with disabilities were served during school year 1992–93 (U.S. Dept. of Educ., 1994). This number includes children and youth with mental retardation at all functioning levels (mild, moderate, severe, profound). Since 1976–77 when children and youth with mental retardation comprised 24.9 percent of the total population of students with disabilities compared to the current 11.5 percent, there has been a significant decrease in children and youth identified mentally retarded (U.S. Department of Education, 1994).

HISTORICAL BACKGROUND OF EDUCATIONAL SERVICES

There has always been exceptional children, but there has not always been special education services to address their needs (Hallahan & Kauffman, 1994, 25). Throughout history, definition and treatment of individuals with mental retardation has always been swayed by the socio-political trends of the times, and by current knowledge about mental retardation (Morrison, 1988).

The Beginning: 1800–1900

Until the end of the 18th century there were extremely few references to mental retardation in the medical literature (Kanner, 1964). The majority of physicians and professional educators felt that efforts to educate the idiot were futile. The documented history relating to special education is found primarily in the early 1800s with European physicians who attempted to discriminate and to educate "idiotic" and "insane" children (Patton et al., 1990). Previously, the most society had offered exceptional children was protection in an asylum (Hallahan & Kauffman, 1994).

Interest in mental defectives began to flare up in the first half of the 19th century, spreading from France and Switzerland to the rest of the civilized portion of Europe and to the United States of America (Kanner, 1964). In France Philip Pinel's focus on moral management, elimination of physical abuse and chains, gentle treatment, and a broad array of medical, psychological, and educational services in a humane living environment for mentally ill fanned the enthusiasm for a "cure" for both insane and idiots (Scheerenberger, 1983). In 1842, Johann Jakob Guggenbuhl (1816–1883), a Swiss physician, began the first recognized residential facility for mentally retarded persons (cretins), whom he believed could be cured through proper health programming (e.g., good diets, mountain air, baths, massages, physical exercise) and training (e.g., set routines, sensory training, memory activities, language programs) (Kanner, 1964; Scheerenberger, 1983).

Jean Marc Itard

A French physician, Jean Marc Itard was an authority on diseases of the ear and on the education of students who were deaf, and is the person to whom most historians trace the beginnings of special education as we know it today (Hallahan & Kauffman, 1994). The contributions of Itard have been recognized as among the most visible landmarks in the development of education and treatment programs for disabled people (Hardman et al., 1990). Itard and his student, Edouard Seguin, who later became a famous educator of idiotic children in Europe and in the United States, pioneered a number of revolutionary instructional procedures in their teaching efforts that are still evident in our education and special education programs today:

1. **A Developmental Approach to Instruction:** Intervention based on the interaction of biological/genetic characteristics and the physical environment; and determining the individual's functioning level in the normal developmental sequence.
2. **Individualized Instruction:** Instruction based on the characteristics, needs, and functioning levels of the individual.
3. **Sensory Stimulation:** Intervention based on the remediation of deficits in basic sensory systems including vision, hearing, tactile, kinesthetic, smell, and taste.
4. **Systematic Instruction:** A sequence of instruction based on beginning with real-life and concrete tasks at the child's functioning level and building gradually to more abstract concepts or ideas.
5. **Functional-Life Curriculum:** Curriculum that focuses on developing independent living skills within the immediate environment (e.g., self-care, recreation/leisure activities, social communication, and academic instruction related to daily life) (Hardman et al., 1990).

John Langdon Down

The physician to the Asylum for Idiots at Earlswood, England, John Langdon Down advanced the cause of mental retardation and the need for treatment and special education, and provided the first major separate classification and comprehensive description of the Mongoloid individual (later called Down syndrome) (Scheerenberger, 1983). Down encouraged the prevention of mental retardation by the temperate use of alcohol, promoting good mental and physical health among parents, sound practices of prenatal care, and proper care of children at home and school (Scheerenberger, 1983).

Like most experts of the 19th century, Down was not an advocate of "mainstreaming", but advocated the residential institution as the proper place to educate mentally retarded children (Scheerenberger, 1983). Down proposed a comprehensive curriculum including physical activities to ensure strength and coordination; intellectual training including senses, basic self-care, use and value of money, gardening, and vocational training; speech and language training; moral training including obedience, and right from wrong (Scheerenberger, 1983).

Maria Montessori

As director for the Orthophrenic School for the Cure of the Feeble-Minded in Rome from 1899–1901, Maria Montessori implemented many of Seguin's ideas on the physiological method (Scheerenberger, 1983). "For her times, Montessori held many unusual views on children. She believed, for example, that youngsters had an amazing ability to concentrate, that they preferred repetition, order, freedom of choice, work over play, and silence. Also, even they had a strong sense of personal dignity" (Scheerenberger, 1983, 86). Upon publication of her first educational book in 1909, *The Method of Scientific Pedagogy as Applied to Infant Education and the Children's Houses,* Montessori's reputation spread throughout the world (Scheerenberger, 1983). Over the next 30 years, Montessori schools were established world-wide.

Early MR Services in the United States

Prior to the 19th century, there was no public or private facility for the care of retarded children on the North American continent (Kanner, 1964). During the early days of special education (mid-1800s to early 1900s), enthusiasm ran high that many retarded persons would be "cured", thus, the first institutions were schools and treatment centers. Early institutions had a large proportion of inmates of the higher grade or improvable class of idiots. The goal was to educate them so they would be capable of supporting themselves (Sloan & Stevens, 1976). Initially, those individuals who were not capable of profiting from an educational system were not admitted to the institutions. Early workers with the higher level retardates held high hopes that the retardates would be elevated intellectually to the average level of individuals in society at large (Sloan & Stevens, 1976).

Edouard Seguin

Known as the father of special education for the mentally retarded, Edouard Seguin was the great reformer of institutional programming for the mentally retarded (Scheerenberger, 1983). He immigrated to the United States in 1848, and assisted in the development of a number of early institutions including Samuel Gridley Howe's program, the Institution for Feeble-minded Youth at Barre, Massachusetts before establishing his own school (Scheerenberger, 1983).

Seguin's book, *Idiocy and Its Treatment by the Physiological Method,* was published in 1866 (Beirne-Smith et al., 1994). "Though many educational and psychological theories have been introduced pertaining to the education and training of mentally retarded children during the twentieth century, none has had the impact of Seguin's physiological method" (Scheerenberger, 1983, 78). Underlying all of Seguin's efforts in terms of psychological and educational principles was the very firm conviction that most idiots could be relieved in more or less complete measure of their disabilities by the physiological method of education (Scheerenberger, 1983).

The physiological method was aimed at developing the senses and training certain motor movements which would then become functional (Sloan & Stevens, 1976). Seguin was convinced that the physiological method and moral treatment were applicable to all retarded youngsters regardless of their level of retardation, though much of his energy was devoted to those more severely retarded (Scheerenberger, 1983). His approach involved five steps: (1) training the muscular system, (2) training the nervous system, (3) educating the senses, (4) acquiring general ideas, and (5) developing the ability to think in abstract terms and acquiring a strong understanding and practice of moral (social) precepts (Scheerenberger, 1983, 79).

As a consequence of Seguin's ideas regarding the benefits of the physiological methods of teaching, early institutions were founded on the principle that the mentally retarded could be trained so they would function at a higher level than their existing level of performance. This led to the concept of institutions as schools and training centers, rather than asylums or custodial facilities (Sloan & Stevens, 1976). Seguin established a day school, the Seguin Physiological School for Feeble-Minded Children in New York City devoted to the care and education of idiotic and feebleminded children, and spent most of his lifetime developing methods of training and educating the idiot and the feebleminded (Sloan & Stevens, 1976).

> Seguin's theory of education and its application was encompassing, ranging from passive exercises for the nonambulatory child through academic training and vocational placement for the more capable individual. His curriculum was quite contemporary in nature: learning involved perception, imitation, coordination, memory, and generalization (Scheerenberger, 1983, 79).

Samuel Gridley Howe

A physician well known for convincing his contemporaries that the training and education of the feebleminded was a public responsibility, Samuel Gridley Howe began the Perkins Institute and Massachusetts School for the Blind in 1832 and established the Massachusetts School for Idiots and Feeble-Minded Youth in 1855 (Kanner, 1964). Howe believed mentally retarded could be improved, but he did not claim to "cure" them (Scheerenberger, 1983).

The American Association on Mental Deficiency

In 1876, Seguin was elected the first president of The Association of Medical Officers of American Institutions of Idiotic and Feebleminded Persons later to be renamed The American Association on Mental Deficiency (Beirne-Smith et al., 1994). Interest during the first decade of the organization centered around the development of institutions, etiology and prevention, and educational methods used with idiots (Sloan & Stevens, 1976). In 1886, "the Association" drafted a resolution indicating that the effects of alcohol accounted for a large number of idiots in institutions, and that the sale of alcohol should be repressed (Sloan & Stevens, 1976). During this period, marriage of close relatives (1st cousins) was considered a cause of idiocy.

Isaac Kerlin, Superintendent of the Pennsylvania Training School and the first Secretary of "the Association," reported there was a relationship between crime, poverty, and idiocy (Sloan & Stevens, 1976). In 1876, he strongly urged the development of institutions in the belief that mentally retarded persons should not be placed and neglected in insane asylums, penal institutions, or almshouses (Scheerenberger, 1983).

Initially, institutional programs were educational, and intended to serve school-age (CA 6 to 16 or 18 years) youth with mental retardation (Scheerenberger, 1983). By 1890, the school facilities of the 1850s evolved into large institutions intended to serve four groups of residents on the "colony plan": (1) teachable, (2) helpless, deformed, epileptic, (3) male adults who had passed school-age and were not self-supporting, (4) adult females kept under careful custody (Scheerenberger, 1983). The colony plan, adopted throughout the country included a training school as well as an industrial, custodial, and farm department. This method provided the cheapest as well as the wisest method, utilizing the labor of the mentally retarded residents, who could not compete with skilled laborers (Scheerenberger, 1983).

Disillusionment: Early 1900s to 1920

Prior to and including the early 1900s, the population referred to as mentally retarded were moderately to severely retarded persons who differed significantly from the norm. In a period when most people were illiterate, there was no concept of mild retardation as we know it today. Careworkers of the retarded in institutions became disillusioned as they began to realize that these moderately to severely retarded persons could not be "cured" nor could they reach "normalcy". "Institutions originally designed to serve as training facilities from which individuals would leave to return to community settings now began to assume a new custodial role" (Patton et al., 1990, 12).

A dramatic change in attitude regarding the mentally retarded and their place in society occurred during the early 1900s. "A change from concern for caring about individuals who had special needs to one for protecting society from them was evident" (Beirne-Smith et al., 1994). Since normalcy was not attainable through intensive training, then life-time commitment in institutions was considered best for both the feeble-minded and for society. In his 1901 AAMD President's address, W.A. Polglase supported the adoption of a policy for the segregation and life-long detention of all defectives, the restriction of marriage of the unfit, and legalizing the operation of asexualization (Sloan & Stevens, 1976). The thrust of the Eugenics movement was to control the number of feebleminded through selective breeding, and many states enacted sterilization laws during the early 1900s for such purposes (Beirne-Smith et al., 1994). Sterilization of the "feebleminded" was continued in some states until the 1970s (Haring et al., 1994).

In 1905, M.W. Barr published a book, *Mental Defectives — Their History, Treatment and Training,* which was the first comprehensive book on mental retardation since Seguin's work almost four decades previously (Sloan

& Stevens, 1976). Barr proposed the first classification system of retarded persons based on education and the methods of training needed for the different levels of feeblemindedness (Sloan & Stevens, 1976).

In 1905, Alfred Binet and Theodore Simon developed a mental scale of intelligence to be used in French schools to screen those students who were not benefiting from the regular classroom experience and who might need special education (Patton et al., 1990). The intelligence scale allowed mental functioning to be divided into various categories. Binet and Simon created a new definable category of retardation, known to us today as "mild retardation" (Patton et al., 1990, 16). Henry Goddard translated the Binet-Simon scales into English in 1911, and in 1916, Louis Terman of Stanford University refined the mental scales into the instrument known as the Stanford-Binet Intelligence Scale (Beirne-Smith et al., 1994). In 1914, Kuhlman discussed the "intelligence quotient" or mental age divided by chronological age, as a truer index of intelligence (Sloan & Stevens, 1976).

By the early 1900s, institutions began to take a custodial role rather than training role and the populations were increased in some instances to more than 1,000 patients. "The matter of caring for epileptics was unresolved; most states included them with the feebleminded, but some states established colonies for epileptics" (Sloan & Stevens, 1976, 59). In 1919, the "Association" recommended that defective delinquents who have criminal tendencies should not be placed in institutions for the feebleminded, but should have special provision for custody and care (Sloan & Stevens, 1976).

Gradual Renewed Interest: 1920s–1950s

Special education as a bona fide professional field took a tremendous step in 1922, when Elizabeth Farrell established the International Council for the Education of Exceptional Children, now Council for Exceptional Children (Patton et al., 1990). By 1923 there were special classes in 171 cities in the United States with an enrollment of nearly 34,000 MR students; and 56 state institutions with a population of 50,000 individuals (Sloan & Stevens, 1976).

The years between 1930 and 1950 saw few advances directly affecting the mentally retarded. The 1930s was a period of expansion of institutions for mentally retarded as well as the expansion of sterilization laws. In 1932, "the Association" changed its name to the American Association on Mental Deficiency (Sloan & Stevens, 1976). Wallace, 1930 President of AAMD, recommended that school for the feebleminded be extended to 12 months and that the institution school should be training the lowest mental levels (Sloan & Stevens, 1976). He also recommended that the special classes should train the moron level by coordinating the areas of academics and social skills with hand training activities (i.e., playground, agricultural), and field trips to community-based factories and stores (Sloan & Stevens, 1976).

Wallace advocated establishing a state social service department under the state authority for mental retardation (Sloan & Stevens, 1976). This program would supervise those individuals who had received little training in special classes or institutional schools; organize an employment bureau; visit homes or places of employment; and assist in recreational activities. Wallace presented a program that included identification, registration, education, supervision, and segregation (Sloan & Stevens, 1976).

Marianne Frostig, a psychiatric social worker and rehabilitation therapist in Austria and Poland who emigrated to the United States in 1938, had a strong influence on the development of special education in her work with retarded, delinquent, and learning disabled children (Patton et al., 1990). She was interested in visual perception as highly related to the child's ability to learn to read. *The Frostig Developmental Test of Visual Perception* (DTVP) was designed to assess visual perception and the *Frostig Program for the Development of Visual Perception* was a remediation program (1964).

Several important contributions to the diagnosis of mental retardation included Arnold Gesell's (1928) *Infant Development Scales,* Edgar Doll's (1935) *Vineland Social Maturity Scale,* and David Wechsler's (1949) *Wechsler Intelligence Scale for Children.* Research centers were established at several major institutions serving the mentally retarded: Letchworth Village in New York, Vineland Training School in New Jersey, and the Wayne County Training School in Michigan (Sloan & Stevens, 1976). Research results such as that by Skeels and Dye (1939) began to influence public perception of mental retardation as they indicated that an inadequate environment could be a cause of mental retardation (Patton et al., 1990).

Over the years, social attitudes toward people with retardation have changed from fear and revulsion to tolerance and compassion. One of the most significant influences on the changing of opinions regarding mental retardation was the development of parent organizations such as the National Association for Retarded Children (NARC), now known as the Association for Retarded Citizens (ARC). This organization through the years has advocated for retarded persons, functioned as lobbyists, provided services, promoted research, and coordinated the efforts of its members in politically effective ways (Beirne-Smith et al., 1994).

By 1950, the nation had had a physically disabled president, Franklin Delano Roosevelt; WWII was over, and many families had disabled members; and there was a heightened sensitivity to the needs of the disabled (Beirne-Smith et al., 1994). By 1952, 46 of 48 states had enacted legislation for educating students who were labeled mentally retarded, however, this legislation often excluded children functioning within the moderate to severe ranges of mental retardation (Patton et al., 1990).

The Political Years: 1950s to Present

In 1961, with the establishment of the President's Panel on Mental Retardation to serve as a guide and source for national policy formation, President Kennedy set into motion thirty-plus years of significant progress in services for persons with mental retardation and other disabilities. Legislation and litigation over the past thirty years has resulted in free appropriate public education in the least restrictive environment, due process, and civil rights for all persons with disabilities.

Major Legislation and Landmark Litigation

Major legislation and landmark litigation affecting individuals with mental retardation includes the following:

Legislation		*Litigation*	
1953	Vocational Rehabilitation Act	1954	*Brown v. Board of Education*
1963	The MR Facilities Construction Act	1970	*Diana v. State Board of Education*
1965	Elementary & Secondary Education Act	1972	PARC
1968	HCEEP	1972	*Mills v. BOE*
1973	Vocational Rehabilitation Act Amendment	1972	*Larry P. v. Riles*
1975	P.L.94-142 (EHA)	1979	*New York State ARC v. Carey*
1983	P.L.98-199	1979	*Armstrong v. Kline*
1984	Perkins Vocational Education Act	1984	*Marshall et al., v. Georgia*
1986	P.L.99-457	1989	*Daniel R.R. v. State BOE*
1986	Amend. to Vocational Rehabilitation Act	1992	*Greer v. Rome City School District*
1990	P.L.101-476 (IDEA)	1993	*Oberti v. Board of Education of Clementon*
1990	Americans with Disabilities Act	1993	*Connecticut ARC v. State Board of Education*
1992	Reauthorization of Vocational	1993	*Statum v. Birmingham Board of Education*
	Rehabilitation Act	1994	*Sacramento School v. Holland*

Major Legislation: 1950—Present

In the twenty years between 1963 and 1983, Congress passed 116 acts or amendments that provided support for mentally retarded persons and their families in the areas of education, nutrition, rights, and social services including Social Security benefits, transportation, and vocational rehabilitation (Scheerenberger, 1987).

Vocational Rehabilitation Act. In 1953, Congress attempted to meet the employment needs of adult mentally retarded persons with the passage of the Vocational Rehabilitation Act (P.L.84-566). This act requires that the state vocational agencies subsidize vocational rehabilitation for mentally retarded persons. The Act was amended in 1963 to lower the age of eligibility and to offer greater financial assistance (P.L.88-214) (Scheerenberger, 1987).

Public Law 88-164. The Mental Retardation Facilities and Community Mental Health Centers Construction Act of 1963 authorized the establishment of thirteen mental retardation research centers to study mental retardation and related aspects of human development (Scheerenberger, 1987).

Elementary and Secondary Education Act. In 1965, the Elementary and Secondary Education Act (ESEA) (P.L. 89-10), authorized federal financial assistance to local education agencies to help meet the special needs of educationally deprived students. ESEA amendments granted federal funds to state and local agencies for educating children and youth with disabilities (P.L.89-313, Title I, 1965 and P.L.89-750, Title VI, 1966). In 1967, ESEA amendments created regional resource centers for evaluation of children and youth with disabilities and services for children and youth with deaf-blindness (P.L.90-247) (Haring et al., 1994).

HCEEP. In 1968, Congress passed P.L.90-538 establishing the Handicapped Children's Early Education Program (HCEEP), the first federal special education program aimed specifically at young children with disabilities and their families (Hallahan & Kauffman, 1994). HCEEP funded model demonstration projects for delivering experimental educational programming for young children with disabilities and their families, and produced curriculum materials, assessment devices, and parent training materials (Hallahan & Kauffman, 1994).

Vocational Rehabilitation Act of 1973. Section 504 of the Vocational Rehabilitation Act Amendments of 1973 marked an important shift from permissive to mandatory legislation in stating that persons with disabilities could not be excluded from any program or activity receiving federal funds simply on the basis of their handicapping condition (Haring et al., 1994). The purpose of this Act was to ensure a broad array of services that would enable individuals with disabilities to secure gainful employment by removing all barriers, not just physical or architectural (Hallahan & Kauffman, 1994). Later amendments in 1978 established a community service employment program, provided for independent living and rehabilitation services for the severely disabled, and merged rehabilitation and developmental disability acts into one legislative package (Scheerenberger, 1987).

P.L.94-142 (EHA). This landmark bill, Education for All Handicapped Children Act (PL94-142), later renamed Education of the Handicapped Act (EHA), was passed on November 29, 1975, and is the most sweeping statement this nation has ever made about rights of children with disabilities to full educational opportunity. Key components of the legislation included the following: free appropriate public education (FAPE), least restrictive environment (LRE), Individual Education Programs (IEPs), due process rights, nondiscriminatory evaluation, and related services.

Developmental Disabilities Assistance Act (1978). The Developmental Disabilities Assistance Act provided a functional definition of developmental disabilities as well as finding funding to assist persons who demonstrate problems in major life functioning areas (Patton et al., 1990).

P.L.98-199 (1983). This amendment to EHA extended a variety of discretionary grants and established new programs for transition of secondary students and evaluation of services as well as financial incentives to expand services for children from birth to 3 years of age (Haring et al., 1994).

The Carl D. Perkins Vocational Education Act (1984). This Act aimed to provide quality vocational education to underserved groups and to encourage improvement of vocational educational programs (Haring et al., 1994).

P.L.99-457 (1986). An amendment to EHA, P.L.99-457 mandates educational services through the public schools for children with disabilities ages three to five beginning 1991–1992 (Shea & Bauer, 1994). This law lowers the age requirements of P.L.94-142 to the new age category and requires schools to serve young children not previously served by most school districts. Incentive grants to state and local education agencies, also, provide services to infants and toddlers (ages birth through 2 years) with disabilities. A large number of children served under this law have developmental delays and/or moderate or severe mental retardation.

Amendments to the Rehabilitation Act (1986). Amendments to the Vocational Rehabilitation Act emphasized importance of transition and post-secondary education programs and added supported employment services for people with severe disabilities to traditional vocational rehabilitation programs (Haring et al., 1994).

PL101-476 (1990). An additional amendment to EHA, PL101-476 mandated several important changes in the law (PL94-142) that specifically affected individuals with mental retardation. The name of the legislation was changed from the Education of the Handicapped Act (EHA) to Individuals with Disabilities Education Act (IDEA) to focus on the wide age span of individuals served under this legislation (Haring et al., 1994). A major addition to IDEA was the requirement for transition services to aid movement from the school to post-school adjustment. The Individual Transition Plan (ITP) becomes part of the IEP and must be implemented no later than age 14 or 16 years. IDEA, also, added two new handicapping categories, traumatic brain injury and autism, for which the schools must provide specific programming. Individuals with these handicapping conditions generally have moderate or severe disabilities.

ADA (1990). The Americans with Disabilities Act (ADA) guarantees equal opportunities and access to more than 40 million Americans with various disabilities. ADA is known as the Civil Rights Act for persons with disabilities ensuring nondiscrimination in a range of activities including employment, transportation, public accommodations (e.g., accessibility to restaurants, stores, offices, businesses and services), state and local government, and telecommunications (Haring et al., 1994).

Reauthorization of Rehabilitation Act (1992). The reauthorization of the Vocational Rehabilitation Act of 1973 allowed easier eligibility for vocational rehabilitation services for individuals with severe disabilities, and addressed interagency linkages for transition services (Haring et al., 1994). Section 504 includes detailed regulations regarding building and program accessibility. Under Section 504 the student (e.g., ADHD, severe allergies, chronic asthma, temporary disabling conditions) is not required to be in need of special education services to receive 504 classroom modifications. Section 504 requires a written plan describing placement and services to be provided, although a formal IEP is not required. Section 504 does not provide additional funds (LDA Newsbriefs, 1995).

Litigation: 1950–Present

Litigation played a major role in gaining a free appropriate public education for disabled children and youth. Court rulings impacted public opinion and were influential in effecting the contents of forthcoming legislation. Many court rulings in pre-1975 cases mandating free appropriate public education, nondiscriminatory evaluation of minority students, and due process of parents formed the framework of P.L.94-142, the Education for All Handicapped Children Act (EHA). Among the landmark cases during that period were Brown v. Board of Education (1954), Pennsylvania Association for Retarded Children (PARC) v. Pennsylvania (1972), Mills v. Board of Education (1972), and Larry P. v. Riles (1972).

Litigation following the passage of P.L.94-142 sought to interpret the letter of the law. Many of the cases dealt with students with moderate and severe retardation, rather than mild retardation. Some of the landmark cases included: NYARC v. Carey (1979), Armstrong v. Kline (1979), Marshall et al., v. Georgia (1984). Some court cases regarding interpreting least restrictive environment from IDEA requirements include the following: Daniel R.R. v. State Board of Education (1989), Greer v. Rome City School District (1992), Oberti v. Board of Education of the Borough of Clementon School District (1993), Connecticut Association for Retarded Citizens v. State of Connecticut Board of Education (1993), Statum v. Birmingham Public Schools Board of Education (1993), and Sacramento City Unified School District v. Holland (1994). In general, courts today require uncontroverted proof from the schools that inclusion is not feasible, whereas, in the past courts were willing to accept the judgment of school officials at face value with little evidence to support their position (Osborne & Dimattiu, 1994).

Brown v. Board of Education (1954). Efforts to integrate minorities had both direct and indirect bearing on the movement for integrated education of students with disabilities (Haring et al., 1994). In Brown v. Board of Education, the Supreme Court ruled against "separate but equal" education for black and white children. The court affirmed that education was not a privilege but a right of all Americans which could not be deprived except by due process of law. "Parents of children with disabilities observed the success of the civil rights movement and used it as a blueprint for their own activities" (Smith, Finn & Dowdy, 1993, 6).

Diana v. State Board of Education (1970). This class action suit was filed by parents of Mexican-American students to challenge placement in classes for students with educable mental retardation on the basis of invalid IQ testing (Henley et al., 1993). The court ruled against discriminatory testing, and ruled that Mexican-American and Chinese students should be tested in their native language for eligibility for special education services (Smith et al., 1993).

PARC (1972). Pennsylvania Association for Retarded Children v. Pennsylvania (1972) was a class action suit filed on behalf of all children with mental retardation in Pennsylvania who were seeking equal access to free public education. In a consent decree, Pennsylvania agreed to provide appropriate educational services to children with mental retardation (Beirne-Smith et al., 1994). The PARC decision emphasized the due process rights of parents to review and challenge placement decisions regarding their children (Henley et al., 1993).

Mills v. Board of Education (1972). This case was filed by parents of students with mental retardation to gain access to public education programs. In Mills v. Board of Education, District of Columbia (1972), the court ruled that children with disabilities had a right to equal access to educational programs (Smith et al., 1993). The court, also, ruled that schools could not use limited finances as a reason for denying programs to students with disabilities.

Larry P. v. Riles (1972). This case was filed on behalf of black children in California who had been placed in classes for students labeled educable mentally retarded to challenge testing procedures (Haring et al., 1993). The court's decision resulted in the requirement to stop using standardized IQ tests in California to place black students in classes for mentally retarded, to eliminate the disproportionate number of black children in EMR classes, and to retest every black student in EMR classes to determine appropriate placement (Smith et al., 1993). In 1992, the judge rescinded the ban on IQ tests indicating the decision was too broad (Haring et al., 1994).

New York State ARC v. Carey (1979). The court ruled that retarded children with hepatitis-B may not be placed in separate, self-contained programs in New York City schools (Haring et al., 1994). Thus, students with mental retardation, even those with hepatitis-B, must be provided an education in the least restrictive environment.

Armstrong v. Kline (1979). This case was filed by parents of a student with disabilities denied summer programming. The court ruled in favor of the parents and required schools to provide extended school year programs (summer programs) to students with disabilities who would regress significantly without summer programs (Smith et al., 1993).

Marshall et al. v. Georgia (1984). This case considered whether the overrepresentation of African-Americans in special classes was discriminatory. The judge ruled that lower socio-economic conditions rather than discriminatory assessment and placement practices was the reason African-American students were placed in programs for students with mild mental retardation (Henley et al., 1993). This was the first court case that highlighted the need to include a measure of adaptive behavior within the classroom as part of the criteria for determining mild retardation (Henley et al., 1993).

Daniel R.R. v. State Board of Education (1989). In the case of a boy with Down syndrome, an appeals court developed a two faceted test to determine whether a placement is appropriate and consistent with the concept of least restrictive environment (LRE): (1) determine whether education in a regular classroom with supplementary aids can be achieved satisfactorily, and (2) if not, determine whether the child has been mainstreamed to the maximum extent appropriate (Haring et al., 1994; Beirne-Smith et al., 1994). The court found that under IDEA, a child with disabilities must be educated in a regular classroom if the child can receive a satisfactory education there, even if it is not the best academic setting for the child (Arnold & Dodge, 1994).

Greer v. Rome City School District (1992). In the case of a 10-year-old girl with Down syndrome, the parents rejected the school district's recommendation for placement in a self-contained classroom outside the neighborhood school and requested regular classroom placement. The court held for the parents indicating that before the school district determines that a child with disabilities should be educated outside of the regular education class, it must consider whether supplemental aids and services would permit satisfactory education in the regular class. The school district failed to consider the whole range of supplemental aids and services including the resource room and itinerant instruction (Arnold & Dodge, 1994). The court indicated that a district may not decline to educate a disabled child in a regular classroom because it costs more than educating in a self-contained classroom. However, the court went on to indicate that the school district cannot be required to provide a student his/her own full-time teacher even if this would mean she/he would get a satisfactory education in the regular classroom (Arnold and Dodge, 1994).

Oberti v. Board of Education of the Borough of Clementon School District (1993). In the case of Rafael Oberti, an 8-year-old child with Down syndrome with severely impaired intellectual functioning and communication skills, and highly disruptive behavior, the school proposed placement in a self-contained program. The court supported the parents' request for full-time regular education because the school did not consider the whole range of supplemental aids and services including resource rooms and itinerant instruction before attempting a self-contained placement, failed to attempt to modify the regular education program to accommodate a child with disabilities, and failed to document including the child in school programs with nondisabled children to the maximum extent appropriate (Arnold & Dodge, 1994).

The court indicated that three factors must be considered in determining whether a disabled student can be educated satisfactorily in a regular classroom with supplementary aids and services: (1) the school district must attempt to accommodate the student in a regular class and attempt to modify the curriculum, (2) the school must consider regular class benefits academic and nonacademic for the student, (3) the school must consider the effect of the inclusion of the disabled student on the education of other children in the regular education classroom (Arnold & Dodge, 1994).

Connecticut Association for Retarded Citizens v. State of Connecticut Board of Education (1993). Parents of four students with mental retardation sought a class action suit claiming their children and all children with mental retardation had been inappropriately denied special education instruction in regular classrooms. The court denied the class action request stating that IDEA requirements must be considered case-by-case (Arnold & Dodge, 1994).

Statum v. Birmingham Public Schools Board of Education (1993). The court rejected the school district's recommendation for a change of placement during the school year from regular education kindergarten placement (with accommodations) to a self-contained program for a 7-year-old girl with physical disabilities and severe profound mental retardation. The court determined that the burden of proof was on the school district and they had failed to demonstrate that the student could not be satisfactorily educated in the regular education setting, and failed to illustrate how a self-contained program would enhance the student's education (Arnold & Dodge, 1994).

Sacramento City Unified School District v. Holland (1994). Preferring full inclusion, parents rejected the school district's proposal that 9-year-old Rachel H., a child with an IQ of 44, spend half of her school time in a special education classroom and half in a regular education classroom. The court indicated IDEA creates a strong preference for mainstreaming, imposing on the school district the burden of proof that the child cannot be mainstreamed (Arnold & Dodge, 1994). The court indicated that under IDEA, a child with disabilities must be educated in a regular classroom if the child can receive a satisfactory education there, even if it is not the best academic setting for the child, if the child gains nonacademic benefits (Arnold & Dodge, 1994).

The court proposed four factors to be considered in determining the placement of the disabled child: (1) the educational benefits of placing the child in a full-time regular education program, (2) the nonacademic benefits of such a placement, (3) the effect the child would have on the teacher and other students in the classroom, and (4) the costs associated with the placement (Arnold & Dodge, 1994).

DEFINITIONS OF MENTAL RETARDATION

"Mental retardation generally refers to delayed intellectual growth and is manifested in inappropriate or immature reactions to one's environment and below average performance in the academic, psychological, physical, linguistic, and social domains" (Patton et al., 1990, 33).

Models of Definitions

Defining mental retardation is often an interdisciplinary process that depends on the philosophical or psychological perspective of the professionals. Historically, there are four major models or perspectives used in preparing definitions of mental retardation: (1) Medical Model, (2) Behavioral Model, (3) Educational Model, and (4) Functional Model.

Medical Model

The earliest contributions to the field of mental retardation were made by physicians who defined mental retardation in terms of physical and organic deficits (Morrison, 1988). Those children classified as mentally retarded in the early days of special education, early 1800s to early 1900s, were moderately and/or severely mentally retarded. They required specialized educational, psychological, and medical services to maximize their potential.

Reviews of the etiologies of the population of students with severe and multiple disabilities revealed that approximately 75 percent of the cases were due to some type of organic or biomedical cause (Snell, 1983). These biomedical causes are factors that relate to biologic processes, such as genetic disorders or nutrition including chromosomal disorders (i.e., Down syndrome, Fragile X); inborn errors of metabolism (i.e., amino acid disorders); disorders of brain formation (i.e., hydrocephalus, spina bifida); inborn errors of metabolism (i.e., PKU, carbohydrate disorders); injuries, infections; environmental influences (i.e., maternal malnutrition, thalidomide) (Grossman, 1983).

Behavioral Model

The behavioral perspective does not focus on uncovering underlying constructs such as defective intelligence or biological abnormalities because these are not educationally relevant; more importance is given to a person's observable interactions with the environment (Patton & Polloway, 1990). The focus is on observable behavior in different settings.

Tredgold was the chief advocate of using social competency as the sole diagnostic criterion of mental deficiency (Patton et al., 1990). He rejected educational and intellectual measures as criteria of "arrested" mental development and maintained that the inability to adapt to the environment, to live independently, was the best criterion (Morrison, 1988). In 1937, Tredgold defined "mental deficiency" as a state of incomplete mental development of such a kind and degree that the individual is incapable of adapting himself to the normal environment of his fellows in such a way to maintain existence independently of supervision, control, or external support (Patton et al., 1990). However, Tredgold did not give any indication of the criteria to be employed in coming to such a distinction (Morrison, 1988).

Bijou (1966) recommended that developmental retardation be treated as observable, objectively defined stimulus-response relationships without recourse to hypothetical mental concepts such as "defective intelligence" and hypothetical biological abnormalities such as "clinically inferred brain damage." Thus, an individual with mental retardation is one who has a limited repertoire of behavior shaped by events that constitute his history (Morrison, 1988).

Educational Model

Educators have not traditionally used specific IQ cut-offs, but rather assessments of the best match between a child's functioning level and the program offerings (MacMillan, 1989). Educators usually use the terms "educable mentally retarded," "trainable mentally retarded," and "severely disabled" (MacMillan, 1989).

An educational perspective was taken by the Council for Exceptional Children-Mental Retardation (Kidd, 1979). The Council's Committee on Terminology and Classification proposed the following definition as one that would be more educationally functional:

> Mental retardation refers to subaverage general human cognitive functioning irrespective of etiology(ies), typically manifested during the developmental period, which is of such severity as to markedly limit one's ability to (a) learn, and consequently to (b) make logical decisions, choices, and judgments, and (c) cope with one's self and one's environment (Kidd, 1979, 2).

Functional Model

The 1959 AAMR definition of mental retardation formally included the importance of functioning (Heber, 1959). The requirement that subaverage intellectual functioning must be reflected by impairment in one or more of the aspects of adaptive behavior (maturation, learning, and social adjustment) indicated that the existence of intellectual limitations alone was not sufficient for a diagnosis of mental retardation (Morrison, 1988). These limitations must result in a functional impairment in adaptive behavior in order for mental retardation to exist.

The 1992 AAMR functional definition of mental retardation is concerned with the individual's difficulty in learning and performing daily life skills. Personal capabilities in which there must be a substantial limitation are conceptual intelligence (IQ below 70 or 75), practical intelligence (ordinary activities of daily living), and social intelligence (understanding social expectations and socially appropriate behavior) (Luckasson et al., 1992). "Mental retardation is present when specific limitations affect the person's ability to cope with ordinary challenges of everyday living in the community. If the intellectual limitations have no real effect on functioning, then the person does not have mental retardation" (Luckasson et al., 1992, 13).

AAMR Definitions

"Since its founding in 1876, the American Association on Mental Retardation (AAMR) has led the field of mental retardation in understanding, defining, and classifying the phenomenon of mental retardation" (Luckasson et al., 1992, ix). The definition of mental retardation has undergone several changes with major educational ramifications (Morrison, 1988). "Three major components have consistently (with certain revisions) appeared in all of the AAMR definitions: subaverage general intellectual functioning, impairments in adaptive behavior, and manifested during the developmental period" (Morrison, 1988, 142). The AAMR's first edition of a manual on definition was published in 1921 and the 9th and most current edition was published in 1992.

1933 and 1941 AAMR Definitions

In 1933, Edgar Doll specified that three essential elements were necessary for a diagnosis of feeblemindedness: (1) social inadequacy, (2) low intelligence, and (3) mentally arrested development (Sloan & Stevens, 1979). In the 1941 AAMR manual, Doll indicated that a definition of mental retardation should include six elements: (1) social incompetencies, (2) due to mental subnormality, (3) which has been developmentally arrested, (4) which obtains at maturity, (5) is of constitutional origin, and (6) is essentially incurable (Sloan & Stevens, 1976). In 1957, the AAMR published the 4th edition of the manual which provided an etiological classification system (Luckasson et al., 1992).

1959 AAMR Definition

Two dramatic changes to the AAMR definition of mental retardation were included in the 1959 manual: (1) raising the IQ ceiling to one standard deviation below the mean (an IQ of 85 or below), and (2) the formal introduction of an adaptive behavior criterion (Luckasson et al., 1992). The 1959 definition specified that adaptive behavior deficits in maturation, learning, and social adjustment were associated with low IQ. According to the 1959 AAMR definition of mental retardation "almost 16 percent of the general population could have been identified as mentally retarded from a purely psychometric perspective" (Beirne-Smith et al., 1994, 69). "As a result of professional criticism, court actions (e.g., Diana, 1970; Larry P., 1971), and socio-political concerns over the disproportionately high minority enrollments in EMR classes, the AAMR revised its definition of mental retardation in 1973 (MacMillan, 1989).

1973 AAMR Definition

The 1973 AAMR definition of mental retardation published in the 6th edition of the *Manual on Terminology and Classification in Mental Retardation* represented a significant change from the 1959 definition. The 1973 changes in definition included the following: (1) Lowered the IQ ceiling to two standard deviations below the mean (IQ of 70 or below), (2) Inserted the word "significantly" before the term "subaverage general intellectual functioning," (3) Raised the limit of the developmental period from age 16 to 18 years, and (4) Omitted the borderline level of retardation (IQ of 70 to 85) (Luckasson et al., 1992, ix). These definitional changes reduced the number of individuals labeled mentally retarded to 2.28 percent of the general population (Beirne-Smith et al., 1994). "The 1973 revision of the definition resulted in a reduction by more than 85 percent of the number of individuals who could be identified as mentally retarded" (Beirne-Smith et al., 1994, 69).

The 1973 AAMR definition of mental retardation was incorporated into P.L.94-142, the Education for All Handicapped Children Act, as the federal definition of mental retardation (Beirne-Smith et al., 1994):

> Mental retardation refers to significantly subaverage general intellectual functioning existing concurrently with deficits in adaptive behavior, and manifested during the developmental period (Grossman, 1973).

Adaptive behavior was defined as effectiveness or degree with which the individual meets the standards of personal independence and social responsibility expected of his age and cultural group (Grossman, 1973). These standards of age-appropriate behaviors included the following: (1) Infancy and early childhood: sensory-motor skills development, communication skills, self-help skills, and socialization; (2) Childhood and early adolescence: application of basic academics in daily life activities, the application of appropriate reasoning and judgment in mastery of the environment, and social skills; and (3) Adolescence and adult life adaptive behavior: vocational and social responsibilities and performances (Grossman, 1973).

1977 and 1983 AAMR Definitions

The seventh edition (1977) of the *Manual on Terminology and Classification in Mental Retardation* included a series of relatively minor corrections and changes, and the eighth edition (1983) further clarified that the upper IQ range for the diagnosis was a guideline and with clinical judgment could be extended to approximately IQ 75 (Grossman, 1983).

1992 AAMR Definition

The 1992 AAMR definition of mental retardation introduces a functional model as the conceptual basis of the definition stating:

> Mental retardation refers to substantial limitations in present functioning. It is characterized by significantly subaverage intellectual functioning, existing concurrently with related limitations in two or more of the following applicable adaptive skill areas: Communication, self-care, home living, social skills, community use, self-direction, health and safety, functional academics, leisure, and work. Mental retardation manifests itself before age 18 (Luckasson et al., 1992, 5).

The significant changes in the 9th edition of the AAMR manual, *Mental Retardation: Definition, Classification, and Systems of Supports* "reflect a changing paradigm, a more functional definition, and a focus on the interaction between the person, the environment, and the intensities and patterns of needed supports" (Luckasson et al., 1992, x). The paradigm change eliminates the practice of classifying students with mental retardation according to the level of severity of their problems based primarily on IQ scores (i.e., Mild, IQ 55–67; Moderate, IQ 40–55; Severe, IQ 25–40; Profound, IQ below 25) (Hallahan & Kauffman, 1994).

In the 1992 definition, a single diagnostic code of mental retardation is used if the person meets the three criteria of age of onset, significantly subaverage abilities in intellectual functioning, and limitations in two or more adaptive skill areas (Luckasson et al., 1992, 24). A profile is developed of needed supports in four dimensions: Dimension I: Intellectual Functioning and Adaptive Skills, Dimension II: Psychological and Emotional Considerations, Dimension III: Physical, Health, Etiology Considerations, and Dimension IV: Environmental Considerations (Luckasson et al., 1992, 25). The new paradigm then classifies students according to the level of support that is needed to function as completely as possible: Intermittent, Limited, Extensive, Pervasive (Luckasson et al., 1992).

CLASSIFICATION OF MENTAL RETARDATION

Historically, there have been a number of proposed classification systems of mental retardation, the majority of these systems are based on intellectual ability and social competence. The AAMR presents two separate classification systems—a medical classification and a behavioral/functional classification. The medical classification (etiologies) views mental retardation as a manifestation of some underlying disease or medical condition (Heber, 1959). The behavioral system classifies on the basis of measured intelligence and adaptive behavior (Baumeister, 1967).

Historical Classification of MR: Behavioral

In 1905, Barr proposed a system of classification based on education and the methods of training needed by different levels of feeblemindedness (Sloan & Stevens, 1976). Barr's system essentially was composed of three levels of feeblemindedness: *Idiot and Idio-Imbecile* who required education in self-help areas and asylum-care; *Moral Imbecile* (mentally and morally deficient) who were trainable in industrial occupations, manual arts, and simple intellectual arts for a long apprenticeship and colony life under protection; *Backward or Mentally Feeble* who required special training and environment due to slow mental processes and were trained for a place in the world (Sloan & Stevens, 1976).

At the 33rd annual meeting of the American Association for the Study of Feebleminded in 1909, H.H. Goddard presented a paper in which he proposed the terms IDIOT, IMBECILE, and FEEBLEMINDED, each with three subdivisions low, middle, and high, that were tied to Binet test scores (Sloan & Stevens, 1976). In 1910, the "Association" adopted a classification system based on Goddard's recommendation that provided three classes of feeblemindedness: IDIOT, IMBECILE, and MORON (Sloan & Stevens, 1976).

Several classification systems have been proposed since the adoption of the 1910 classification system including the following:

	IDIOT	IMBECILE	MORON	BORDERLINE
Terman, 1916	IQ 24	IQ 25–49	IQ 50–69	IQ 70–79
AAMR, 1934	IQ 20	IQ 20 to 49	IQ 50 to 69	
Wechsler, 1958	IQ 20	IQ 25 to 49	IQ 50 to 69	IQ 70–79

In 1952, the Committee on Nomenclature and Statistics of the American Psychiatric Association proposed a three level classification system:

(1) Mild — functional vocational impairment, IQ 70–85;
(2) Moderate — functional impairment requiring special training and guidance, IQ 50–70;
(3) Severe — functional impairment requiring custodial or complete protective care, IQs below 50 (Garrison & Force, 1965).

In 1959, the three-part classification system was abandoned in favor of a five-part structure based on the number of standard deviations from the mean. The new terminology was introduced to avoid the negativism that had surrounded earlier classifications (Scheerenberger, 1987). These five categories specified by the AAMR included the following:

Profound MR (-5 SD)	IQ -20
Severely MR (-4 SD)	IQ 20–35
Moderately MR (-3 SD)	IQ 36–51
Mildly MR (-2 SD)	IQ 52–67
Borderline (-1 SD)	IQ 68–84 (Heber, 1959).

In 1973, the category of Borderline level was eliminated from the AAMR guidelines, retaining the four categories and IQ ranges: mild, moderate, severe, profound (Grossman, 1973). The 1983 AAMR classification system expanded many of the scores to a range:

Mild MR	IQ 50/55 to 70
Moderate MR	IQ 35/40 to 50/55
Severe MR	IQ 20/25 to 35/40
Profound MR	IQ Below IQ 20 (Grossman, 1983).

CURRENT CLASSIFICATION OF MR: FUNCTIONAL SYSTEM

In 1992, the AAMR system for classification of severity levels of mental retardation abandoned the traditional levels. Rather than requiring classifications into four levels of mental retardation (mild, moderate, severe, profound) a single diagnostic code is used. "The person is either diagnosed as having or not having mental retardation based upon meeting the three criteria of age of onset and significantly subaverage abilities in intellectual functioning and two or more adaptive skill areas" (Luckasson et al., 1992, 34).

The new system of classification subclassifies the intensities and pattern of support systems into four levels (e.g., intermittent, limited, extensive, pervasive) (Luckasson et al., 1992). The AAMR intensities of supports as applied to adaptive skill areas are defined as follows:

INTERMITTENT: Supports on an "as needed basis." Characterized by episodic nature or short-term memory supports needed during transitions.

LIMITED: An intensity of supports characterized by consistency over time, time-limited but not of an intermittent nature.

EXTENSIVE: Supports characterized by regular involvement (e.g., daily) in at least some environments and not time-limited (e.g., long-term support and long-term home living support).

PERVASIVE: Supports characterized by their consistency, high intensity, provided across environment; potential life-sustaining nature (Luckasson, 1992, 26).

Under the current AAMR (1992) classification system, a diagnosis may state: (1) John is a person with mental retardation who needs limited supports in functional academics and leisure; (2) Mary is a person with mental retardation who needs extensive supports in communication, social skills, self-direction, and functional academics. This functional AAMR definition, then, abandons IQ based levels of mild, moderate, severe, and profound to focus on the level of support needed in adaptive behavior areas. However, since the P.L. 94-142 definition utilizes the 1973 AAMR definition, the current definition may require considerable time to phase into usage.

SUMMARY

The history of services to mentally retarded persons is a progression from infanticide or abuse to the current focus on free appropriate public education (FAPE). Jean Itard, the father of special education, and Edouard Seguin, famous educator of MR, pioneered a number of revolutionary teaching methodologies including task analysis, individualized instruction, sensory stimulation, structured settings, and behavior management.

Legislation and litigation have been very important in the field of special education to gain rights for persons with disabilities. Landmark legislation was passed in 1975 with the passage of P.L.94-142, the Education for All Handicapped Children Act, which addressed the issue of educating all students with disabilities regardless of severity of condition. Amendments have changed the name of the law to Individuals with Disabilities Act (IDEA) which focuses on functional skills.

Historically, there are four major models or perspectives used in preparing definitions of MR and in designing treatment/education: medical model, behavioral model, educational model, and functional model. The development of the intelligence scale by Binet and Simon helped professionals to divide MRs into categories and to create a new category "Mild Retardation." The definition of MR has undergone numerous changes but has consistently retained three aspects — subaverage general intellectual functioning, deficits in adaptive behavior, and manifested during the developmental period. The 1973 AAMR definition of mental retardation, written into P.L.94-142 as the federal definition of MR, classified individuals as mild, moderate, severe, profound. The 1992 AAMR definition of MR abandons those IQ based diagnostic labels, and classifies students according to the amount of adaptive behavior support needed — Intermittent, Limited, Extensive, Pervasive.

Chapter 3

THEORETICAL PERSPECTIVES OF
MENTAL RETARDATION

*There being in our opinion no contemporary, comprehensive psycho-
logical theory which is superior to all others in its relevance to mentally
retarded children, it is probably well to use many different sets of concepts
in considering the processes of psychological development (Robinson &
Robinson, 1965, 276).*

Historically, the major perspectives that provide definitions, etiology, treatment, and education of individuals with mental retardation have evolved from five theoretical models—medical, developmental, behavioral, cognitive, and functional. The medical model of mental retardation has long been concerned with etiology, treatment, and prevention. The developmental, behavioral, cognitive, and functional models of mental retardation involve various learning theories or sub-areas of psychology which grew out of the field of philosophy in the late 1800s. This separation of psychology from philosophy was initiated by Wilhelm Wundt's experimental approach to psychology (Gredler, 1992).

MEDICAL MODEL OF MENTAL RETARDATION

The medical model of mental retardation appears to focus on three separate but interrelated perspectives—physiological psychology, personality theories, and physiological etiology (i.e., neurology, genetics, chromosomal anomalies). Early research in physiological psychology focused on the human being from a physiological standpoint. Personality theorists sought information on the personality and self-concept, while physicians and neurologists sought the physiological etiology of mental retardation and the use of psychopharmocology to modify behavior.

Physiological Psychology

The medical model of mental retardation can be traced to Wilhelm Wundt's 1874 text on physiological psychology (Gredler, 1992). This small branch of medical psychology contributed significantly to the physiological understanding of the sense organs, reflex physiology, perception, and human conduct, and led to a greater reliance upon experimental methods (Turner, 1982). Wundt, the founder of experimental psychology, first referred to this new psychology as "physiological psychology" (Turner, 1982). Physiological psychology arose from efforts to solve certain philosophical problems concerning the nature of knowledge and the relation between mind and body (Bijou & Ribes-Inesta, 1972). The experimental methods used physiological techniques to examine the body-mind complex that comprises a human being (Humphrey, 1968). With Pavlov's discovery and development of knowledge of the conditioned reflex, it became possible to investigate the universal function of the brain (Anokhin, 1968). Wundt's first four books dealt with the topics of psychobiology and behavior, sensation and psychophysics, perception and cognition, feelings and language (Woodward, 1982).

The medical model of educating individuals with mental retardation can be traced to Jean Itard, Edouard Seguin, and Maria Montessori, physicians in the mid-1800s and early 1900s who began modern techniques of care and education of retarded children. After the publication of his book in 1866, Seguin became famous both in Europe and in the United States for using the physiological method of teaching mentally retarded individuals which focused on sensory stimulation and training of motor movements that Seguin believed would permit undamaged areas of the brain to take over the functions of damaged areas (Sloan & Stevens, 1976).

Samuel Howe, a Boston neuropsychiatrist introduced Seguin's "physiological method" to the United States when he became director of the first facility for the mentally retarded in this country (Sloan & Stevens, 1976). Thus, early institutions were founded on the belief that individuals with mental retardation could be trained to function at a higher level, perhaps even cured, and accepted only those individuals who were likely to profit from training.

Personality Theories

Personality refers to the recurring, long term aspects of behavior that characterize individual differences among people (Cromwell, 1967). Few personality theorists have been concerned with the affective characteristics (i.e., emotions, self-concept) of retarded individuals. Generally psychological theorists accept the dynamic point of view which indicates that the personality system is in constant change and anything that "interferes with normal personality growth or with emotional or physical well-being is likely to interfere with intellectual functioning" (Robinson & Robinson, 1976, 148). Accordingly, mentally retarded individuals are likely to be retarded in social maturity, experience limited ability to cope with the demands of their environment, and may exhibit serious behavior problems. Meaningful decisions regarding planning the retardate's personal, social, and educational development depends on understanding the individual's personality.

Personality Development

Since the individual with retardation is slow in personality development as well as intellectual development, it is important to determine his/her level of development compared to nonhandicapped individuals. According to Cromwell (1967), the development of the personality involves five stages or phases: (1) basic boundary discrimination, (2) intact hedonic functioning, (3) conceptual motivation system, (4) effective interpersonal functioning, and (5) awareness of cultural expectations.

Basic boundary development of an infant involves the differentiation of boundaries of the self, the thought processes, and the basic elements of goal and threat in the environment (Cromwell, 1967, 70). Children who are undeveloped or deficient in boundary discrimination experience difficulty with reality contact, body identification, object relations, ability to relate or respond, perceive danger, and interpret meaning from facial expression (Cromwell, 1967). During the second stage in personality development, the intact hedonist, the child's behavior becomes oriented toward achieving immediate gratification and avoiding unpleasant circumstances. The child on the hedonistic level does not even conceive of personal responsibility and control except for limited situations or on occasions when others point this out to him/her (Cromwell, 1967). For the retarded child or for the normal child who is retarded in personality development, the phase of intact hedonism may persist longer than in the child who is developing normally (Cromwell, 1967).

As the child moves toward his/her teens and into the third phase of personality development, she/he learns to respond to conceptualized goals rather than to immediate gratification, becomes more aware of the acceptability and the shortcomings of his own actions, becomes motivated to approach success and avoid failure (Cromwell, 1967). Since the success-failure motivational system develops in parallel with mental age, retarded children are expected to be behind in this development compared with other children of the same chronological age (Cromwell, 1967). During this stage, the most frequent response to prolonged situations of failure or anxiety is to decrease effort (Cromwell, 1967).

Once the conceptual motivation system has developed, a part of this conceptual development becomes focused on interpersonal functioning (Cromwell, 1967). Interpersonal functioning refers specifically to empathy, the ability of an individual to conceptualize the feelings, attitudes, and motives of another. "Children with impairment in basic boundary development, hedonism, or conceptual motivation will develop interpersonal functioning in only a very limited way" (Cromwell, 1967, 76). Individuals with retardation experience significant difficulty understanding empathy and usually assume that the feelings of others are like their own (Cromwell, 1967).

The fifth phase of personality development includes the development of cultural functioning. Individuals with mental retardation seldom reach this level of development.

> Deficits in cultural development will be observed when a child (or adult) chronically steals, lies, disobeys rules, is destructive, has no concept of the welfare of people in general, or shows no guilt or anxiety about any violation except when threatened with personal punishment as a direct consequence (Cromwell, 1967, 77).

Early Personality Theories

Early approaches to personality theory included two major perspectives: goal approach behavior and threat-avoidance behavior (Cromwell, 1967). The goal approach to personality theory included classification by (1) mental disorders (e.g., paranoid schizophrenia, anxiety neurosis), (2) trait theory (e.g., honesty, compulsivity, etc.), and (3) need theory (e.g., biological and psychological needs) (Cromwell, 1967). The threat-avoidance or psychoanalysis approach includes classification by (1) defense mechanisms (e.g., projection, repression, physical avoidance, etc.), (2) threat objects (e.g., fear of female authority figures, school phobia, anxiety, etc.), and (3) personal constructs (e.g., intelligence and social competence) (Cromwell, 1967).

Psychoanalysis. The best known dynamic theory of personality development, formulated by Sigmund Freud in the 1940s, indicated that at any time in life a person has only a limited quantity of psychophysiological energy (Robinson & Robinson, 1976). Although Freud did not deal directly with the problems of the intellectually retarded, according to this theory an individual with retardation would have a smaller amount of psychical energy available for higher mental processes because of the unusual amounts of energy which are required to master routine daily tasks and to sustain life (Robinson & Robinson, 1976). "Since such basic processes tend to usurp his energy, the subnormal child has limited power at his disposal for self-control, for understanding the world about him, and for mastering the skills which society requires of him" (Robinson & Robinson, 1976, 288).

Psychoanalysts would indicate that the most infantile structure, the id, is theoretically the same in the subnormal and in the normal child, but the more mature structures, the ego and the superego, fail to develop properly in the individual with mental retardation (Robinson & Robinson, 1976). As a result of his defective ego, the person with retardation is seriously disabled in his ability to handle the demands of the id and the superego in the context of the real world. The child with mental retardation may have great difficulty in controlling his aggressive impulses and be less able than normal children to utilize their self-evaluative ability. "Because his ego is unable to consider alternative forms of action, the retarded child is relatively less flexible in behavior than is the normal child" (Robinson & Robinson, 1976, 286). When the child with retardation reaches school age, his/her defective ego extends its field of operation to relationships with peers; to failure in academic work; to failure in relationships with classmates; and she/he suffers deep and crippling injuries to self-esteem and to basic security (Robinson & Robinson, 1976).

AAMR Etiology of Mental Retardation

Under the medical model, mental retardation is the manifestation of some underlying disease or medical condition (Heber, 1959). Physicians or neurologists presumably can establish that there is actual disease or pathology of the brain which results in mental retardation (Baumeister, 1967). One of the best-known early classifications of etiology of mental retardation was proposed by Tredgold (1952): primary amentia (i.e., genetic, chromosomal) and secondary amentia (i.e., damage occurring later to the fetus at childbirth or from infant infection) (Craft, 1979).

The etiology of mental retardation has, historically, been divided into two broad categories—biological causes and psychosocial causes, however, this distinction no longer stands (Luckasson et al., 1992). Biological or pathological causes have traditionally been most often associated with moderate, severe, and profound retardation (Patton & Polloway, 1990). Pathological factors can be identified in from 60 percent to 75 percent of cases where the individual's IQ falls below 50 (McLaren & Bryson, 1987).

The psychosocial or unspecified environmental causes of mental retardation have been associated with mild mental retardation (Polloway & Patton, 1990). With the 1973 change in definition of mental retardation, reducing the intellectual functioning level of the mild category to IQ 50 to 70, the traditional assumption that causation in most mild retardation is psychosocial or environmental no longer holds true as 25 percent to 40 percent of all cases of mild retardation have an identifiable cause (McLaren & Bryson, 1987).

1983 AAMR Etiology Classification

The 1983 American Association of Mental Retardation medical classifications of biological causes of mental retardation focused primarily on a single cause that could be determined by observation of the noxious agent or from symptoms and syndromes typical of the disease as follows:

1. *Infections, Intoxicants, and Teratogens:* Rubella, congenital syphilis, Rh blood incompatibility, bacterial & viral infections, drugs, smoking, caffeine, lead, alcohol.

2. *Trauma or Physical Agent:* Hypoxia, irradiation, birth injury, postnatal trauma, anoxia. (Anoxia is one causative agent in more than 18% of cases of mild mental retardation; trauma and neglect are causative factors in 15% of the cases of mild mental retardation (McLaren & Bryson, 1987).

3. *Metabolism or Nutrition:* Carbohydrate disorders (galactosemia, hypoglycemia); amino acid disorders (phenylketonuria), endocrine disorders (hypothyroidism, Prader-Willie syndrome); lepid storage diseases (Tay Sachs); metabolic disorders (Lesch Nyhan syndrome).

4. *Gross Prenatal Brain Disease:* Neurofibromatosis, tuberous sclerosis, tumors, Huntington's chorea, Sturge Weber.

5. *Unknown Prenatal Influence:* Cerebral malformation, microcephalus, hydrocephalus, anencephaly, meningomyelocele (spina bifida).

6. *Chromosomal Abnormality:* Down syndrome, Klienfelter syndrome, Cri-du-Chat, Fragile X syndrome.

7. *Gestational Disorder:* Prematurity, postmaturity, low birth weight.

8. *Psychiatric Disorder:* Psychosis or other psychiatric disorder with no evidence of cerebral pathology.

9. *Environmental Influences:* Psychosocial disadvantage, sensory deprivation, severe neglect. (Approximately 25% of all American preschool children live in poverty, Kids Count, 1993).

10. *Other Conditions:* Blindness, deafness (contributing factors), mental retardation with ill-defined or unknown etiology. (Grossman, 1983; Cartwright et al., 1989, 232; Patton & Polloway, 1990, 207).

1992 AAMR Etiology Classification

The current AAMR classification is a multiple-risk-factor approach which includes biomedical, social, behavioral, and educational factors over three time periods—prenatal onset, perinatal onset, and postnatal onset (Luckasson et al., 1992). The *biomedical factors* relate to biologic processes, such as genetic disorders or nutrition; *social factors* relate to social and family interaction such as stimulation and adult responsiveness; *behavioral factors* relate to potentially causal behaviors, such as dangerous (injurious) activities or maternal substance abuse; and *educational factors* relate to the availability of educational supports that promote mental development and the development of adaptive skills (Luckasson et al., 1992). This etiological system is highly organized and coded for specificity in diagnosis.

A brief outline of the 1992 AAMR biomedical etiological categories of mental retardation with common examples follows:

I. Prenatal Causes:
   A. Chromosomal Disorders: Down syndrome, Fragile X syndrome.

    B. Syndrome Disorders: Neurofibromatosis, Tuberous Sclerosis, Muscular Dystrophy, Prader-Willie syndrome.

    C. Inborn Errors of Metabolism: Phenylketonuria, Galactosemia, Lesch-Nyhan syndrome.

    D. Developmental Disorders of Brain Formation: Spina Bifida, Hydrocephalus.

    E. Environmental Influences: Intrauterine Malnutrition; Drugs, Toxins, Teratogens (e.g., Thalidomide, Fetal Alcohol Syndrome); Maternal Diseases (e.g., Diabetes, Maternal PKU, Hypothyroidism).

II. Perinatal Causes:

    A. Intrauterine Disorders: Toxemia/Eclampsia; Maternal Hypertension, Anemia, Diabetes; Abnormal labor and Delivery (Premature, Breech); Multiple Gestation.

    B. Neonatal Disorders: Hypoxic-Ischemic Encephalopathy, Intercranial Hemorrhage, Neonatal Seizures, Respiratory Disorders (Hyaline Membrane Disease), Infections (Meningitis, Encephalitis-Herpes, Cytomegaloviris), Head Trauma at Birth, Metabolic Disorders (Hypoglycemia, Hypothyroidism), Nutritional Disorders.

III. Postnatal Causes:

    A. Head Injuries.

    B. Infections: Encephalitis (Herpes, Measles, HIV), Meningitis, Fungal Infections, Parasitic Infestations (Malaria), Slow or Persistent Virus Infections (Measles, Rubella).

    C. Demyelinating Disorders.

    D. Degenerative Disorders: Rett syndrome, Poliodystrophies, Huntington's disease, Parkinson's disease.

    E. Seizure Disorders: Infantile Spasms, Myoclonic Epilepsy.

    F. Toxic-Metabolic Disorders: Intoxications-Lead, Mercury, Metabolic Disorders.

    G. Malnutrition.

    H. Environmental Deprivation: Psychosocial Disadvantage, Child Abuse and Neglect.

    I. Hypoconnection Syndrome (Luckasson et al., 1992, 81–91).

Though there were numerous variations of the medical model, several aspects were severely criticized by professionals:

1. The overriding concept that mental retardation was an "illness" or "disease" with the subsequent tendency to treat developmentally disabled individuals as "sick" persons.

2. The emphasis on medical treatment to the neglect of the residents' total developmental needs.

3. The pronounced tendency to foster dependence among residents as a result of the "healer-patient" relationship, plus an almost abnormal fear that a resident may hurt himself or herself or come into contact with a communicable disease.

4. The frequent prognosis that the resident was so retarded that only custodial or skilled nursing care was required, which readily became a self-fulfilling prophecy (Scheerenberger, 1987, 122).

These criticisms of the medical model paired with the fact that information collected by investigators operating within the medical model typically provide little direction to those involved in educational programming efforts led to the rise of the other models of mental retardation. The medical model continues to be influential in diagnosis and medical treatment of mental retardation, but not influential in educational programming.

DEVELOPMENTAL MODEL OF MENTAL RETARDATION

Developmental psychology, the foundation of the Developmental Model of Mental Retardation, is the field of psychology concerned with the physical (biological) and psychological changes that take place throughout life from conception to death (Peterson, 1991). Experts in child development have organized human capabilities into four major developmental domains which include most of the skills and capabilities that children normally acquire: communication, affective-social, cognitive, and sensorimotor (gross and fine motor, perceptual motor) (Neisworth & Bagnato, 1987).

There are two major focuses of the developmental model: (1) the age-based view, and (2) the stage-based view. The age-based view, based on chronological age, is still the most common way to describe normal development (Wyne & O'Connor, 1979). The age-based view determines normal development by observing the behavior of one-year-olds, two-year-olds, and so on. The age-based concept provides a set of developmental norms that are useful as benchmarks against which children and infants can be compared. These norms or benchmarks have been most appropriate in the assessment and observation of physical maturation and motor development (Wyne & O'Connor, 1979).

The stage-based concept of development is based upon an unvarying sequence of stages of developmental growth. The focus is on a system that simultaneously accounts for physical, intellectual, and personality development. The stage-based theory conceives of development as being more closely dependent on the sequence of growth than on the passage of time (chronological growth) (Wyne & O'Connor, 1979). The stage-based concept provides a rationale as well as a structure for observing and studying qualitative changes in child and infant development (Wyne & O'Connor, 1979).

Major Developmental Theorists

Early roots of developmental psychology can be found in the works of Locke, Rousseau, and Darwin. John Locke helped to create the notion of childhood, and emphasized the idea that prior experiences shape our subsequent actions (Peterson, 1991). Jean-Jacques Rousseau influenced developmental psychology with his beliefs that children were qualitatively different than adults, and that development consisted of a passage through discrete stages (Peterson, 1991). Darwin pioneered the first explicit child research technique in developmental psychology, the infant biography, a journal of daily observations of a given child's behavior (Peterson, 1991). Gesell was among the most famous age-based developmental psychologists. Many of the subsequent developmental psychologists including G. Stanley Hall, Sigmund Freud, Erik Erikson, Jean Piaget, and Lawrence Kohlberg proposed stage theories of development. An American developmental psychologist, G. Stanley Hall (1844–1924) indicated that there were five stages in a lifespan: infancy, childhood, youth, adolescence, and adulthood (Peterson, 1991). Hall is credited with being the first psychologist to describe the developmental stage of adolescence (Peterson, 1991).

Arnold Gesell: Age-Based Development

Among the most influential age-based developmental psychologists was Arnold Gesell, who established the famous Institute of Child Development at Yale University during the 1930s, and who was the first to try to convince educators that growth and development occurred in an unvarying sequence (Sprinthall et al., 1994). His research and precise observations of children published in numerous books included extensive tables specifying what a child should be able to do at each chronological age, infancy through early childhood. The Gesell Institute has published a series of seven books for parents based on developmental skills at each age: *Your One-Year-Old, Your Two-Year-Old, Your Three-Year-Old, Your Four-Year-Old, Your Five-Year-Old, Your Six-Year-Old, Your Seven-Year-Old* (Ames & Ilg, 1976–1985). The *Gesell Developmental Schedules* (Knobloch & Pasmanick, 1974) can be utilized in assessing the developmental functioning level of children.

Sigmund Freud: Psychosexual Development

Sigmund Freud proposed that children mature through a series of psychosexual stages: oral stage (birth to age one year), anal stage (one to three years), phallic stage (three to five years), latency period (six years to puberty), genital stage (from puberty on) (Mussen et al., 1990). Psychosexual stages according to Freud are developmental stages in which a child's instinctive needs are satisfied through stimulation of different parts of the body and that development ends with the onset of puberty (Peterson, 1991).

Erik Erikson: Psychosocial Development

Erik Erikson built on and drastically changed Freud's theory of development (Peterson, 1991). Erikson believed that social experience, not biology, is responsible for the emergence of significant human qualities (Mussen et al., 1990). He proposed distinct psychosocial developmental stages in life that are marked by a particular conflict or moral dilemma which must be satisfactorily resolved in order for a person to progress through subsequent stages with a positive approach. The stages of concern to most school teachers include the following: Initiative vs. Guilt (4–6 years), Industry vs. Inferiority (6–12 years), Identity vs. Diffusion (13–college years) (Sprinthall et al., 1994).

Jean Piaget: Cognitive Development

Jean Piaget, the most influential of all developmental psychologists, was concerned with the cognitive development of children. Piaget devised a stage theory of cognitive development, proposing that children's thinking developed in an orderly way through four discrete stages:

(1) Sensorimotor period (0–2 years): Cognitive skills of importance during this stage include imitation, object concept, object permanence, and intentionality of purpose.
(2) Preoperational period (2–6 years): Cognitive skills include egocentric thinking, centered irreversible thinking, symbolic mental activity, language development with thought and language dominated by perceptions.
(3) Concrete Operational period (6 or 7 through 11 or 12 years): Cognitive skills include decentered reversible thinking; understanding conservation of mass, volume, length; inductive reasoning, beginning of logic, mental operations on concrete objects and events; immature thought dominated by the present; and thinks about things.
(4) Formal Operational period (12 years through adulthood): Cognitive skills include logical thinking, abstract reasoning, both deductive and inductive

reasoning, hypothetical situations, metacognition, contemplation of effects of actions; mature thought capable of simultaneously dealing with past, present, and future (Bagnato & Neisworth, 1987; Wyne & O'Connor, 1979).

Piaget concluded from his research that the child is not a passive agent in genetic development (Gredler, 1992). He proposed that people reorganized their schemes (organized mental structures) through assimilation (the integration of new data with existing cognitive structures), accommodation (the adjustment of cognitive structures to new situations and information), and equilibration (the continuing readjustment between assimilation and accommodation) (Gredler, 1992).

Research regarding Piaget's theory indicates that about 50 percent of children and youth ages 12 to 18 years of age were functioning within the concrete operational level, and by age 18 years only 19 percent of students were in the formal mature stage (Epstein, 1979) suggesting that Piaget overestimated the abilities of the majority of students. Recent brain research using EEGs indicates that Piaget's sensorimotor stage may extend from birth to three and a half years, and that there is a possibility of a fifth stage beyond the formal operational stage (Sprinthall et al., 1994, 125).

Lawrence Kohlberg: Moral Development

Working at Chicago University and later at Yale University, Kohlberg revolutionized the understanding of moral development by specifying that moral growth occurs in a developmental sequence (Sprinthall et al., 1994). Kohlberg extended and amplified Piaget's work on moral development, thus, moral developmental stages are harmonious with cognitive developmental stages (Mussen et al., 1990). Kohlberg proposed that moral development occurs in a specific sequence of stages regardless of culture or subculture, continent or country (Sprinthall et al., 1994).

Kohlberg identified six stages or judgmental systems of moral growth by asking people from different backgrounds and of different ages to respond to moral dilemmas. The six stages of moral development were divided into three levels—Preconventional Morality, Conventional Morality, and Post-Conventional Morality. Primarily children function at the Preconventional Morality level in which the focus is on judging right and wrong by consequences of actions (Mussen et al., 1990). During Stage 1, obedience and moral decisions are based on the desire to avoid severe physical punishment; while Stage 2 actions are based on satisfying one's own personal needs (Sprinthall et al., 1994). Most adults function on the Conventional Morality level in which judgments are based on reciprocity and interpersonal relationships (Mussen et al., 1990). During Stage III, judgments are based on social conformity, "being good", and empathy; while Stage IV judgments are based on civil and criminal law codes (Sprinthall et al., 1994). Few people function at the Post-Conventional Morality level in which moral judgments are based on abstract principles (Mussen et al., 1990). During Stage V, the principles of justice are based on democratic ideas and processes; while Stage VI involves the application of universal principles of social justice and respect for human life (Sprinthall et al., 1994).

Developmentally Delayed Children

A developmental view of exceptional children is based upon an understanding of normal intellectual, emotional, and physical development and what constitutes deviations in the course of normal development (Wyne & O'Connor, 1979). The developmental view generally holds that deviations from normal development follows a continuum of degree from mild, moderate, and severe to profound (Wyne & O'Connor, 1979).

Though developmental psychologists did not specifically address mental retardation, the Developmental Model has become very influential in explaining mental retardation and in planning educational programs for children with mental retardation. The Developmental Model proposes that there is a normal sequence of skills (cognitive, communication, social/behavioral, fine and gross motor skills) which children accomplish at specific ages. Children with retardation pass through the same developmental skills as normal children, however, they acquire the skills at a slower rate than normal children and they do not reach the later stages. For example, children with mental retardation functioning cognitively at IQ 50 would be expected "developmentally" to function and learn at one-half the rate of his/her same age peers. A six-year-old 1st grade student with an IQ 50 would be expected to function at a level similar to a three-year-old nonhandicapped child.

"Developmentally appropriate" is the current focus of early childhood education programs in which the games and activities are appropriate for the child's chronological age as well as his/her cognitive functioning age. Developmental scales for each age level are utilized as guidelines for age appropriate activities. Thus, educational programs planned for a mildly retarded or developmentally delayed 6-year-old child with IQ 50 include cognitive activities appropriate for a three-year-old. The developmental functioning levels of the child (IQ 50) in cognition, fine and gross motor skills, communication, social and behavioral skills, self-help and adaptive skills would be used to determine the entry level skill in the developmental hierarchy of skills for educational activities.

Implications from Piaget, Erikson, and Kohlberg

Piaget displayed little concern for individual differences among children and published very little explicitly about retarded children (Robinson & Robinson, 1976). Piaget's theory assumes that all children progress through the same stages but at different rates (Sprinthall et al., 1994).

Inhelder (1968), using Piaget's Cognitive Developmental Model, proposed a scheme by which to classify retarded adults according to functioning level or stage. Research indicates that the severely and profoundly retarded adult can be viewed as fixated at the level of sensorimotor intelligence; the moderately retarded adult should be seen as incapable of surpassing the preoperational intellectual stage; the mildly retarded adult can be characterized as unable to progress beyond the level of concrete operations; and the borderline adult is able to use only the simpler forms of formal operations (Inhelder, 1968 as cited in Wyne & O'Connor, 1979). Inhelder's (1968) theory of fixation of thinking implies that retarded individuals are slower in development, and during the latter part of the developmental period when one expects continued cognitive growth, they gradually decelerate, become fixated at a terminal stage and exhibit no further progress (Wyne & O'Connor, 1979).

Erikson's and Kohlberg's theories did not specifically address mental retardation. However, as stage theories, it can be assumed that children and youth with mental retardation pass through the same stages as normal children and youth, but at different rates, and they do not reach the higher functioning levels. Moral and social development are very closely tied to cognitive development. Adolescents with retardation functioning cognitively on the concrete operational level could be expected to be functioning on the Preconventional Morality level and on the Industry vs. Inferiority level of psychosocial development due to their lack of abstract reasoning abilities.

BEHAVIORAL MODEL OF MENTAL RETARDATION

The behavioral perspective assumes that the environment is the primary agent responsible for learning. Behavioral psychologists are not concerned with deriving underlying internal causes for inappropriate behaviors such as repressed desires, minimal brain dysfunction, or low ego strength. Behaviorists pay little attention to internal cognitive structures and even less to genetic predispositions (Sprinthall et al., 1994). Traditional behaviorism generally adhered to three underlying principles: (1) Organisms enter the world as virtual blank slates; (2) There are few important differences in learning and/or conditioning across species; and (3) Learning was seen as occurring in an automatic fashion, and the learner was typically seen as a recipient of environmental stimuli, not a selector of stimuli (Sprinthall et al., 1994).

The basic behavioral learning principles are derived primarily from the work of Thorndike and Skinner. Thorndike's studies of the effects of consequences on behavior led to formulating the law of effect which indicates that responses followed by satisfying consequences are more likely to be repeated (Matson & Andrasic, 1983). Skinner refined Thorndike's law of effect and described behavioral change as a function of response consequences (Gredler, 1992), and introduced the term operant to describe any behavior that a person or animal emits spontaneously (Peterson, 1991). Thus, a basic behavioral learning principle indicates that all learning is a result of reinforcement (Powell, 1971).

An important element of most behavioristic treatment interventions is the manipulation of the student's environment so that undesirable behavior patterns are eliminated and prosocial responses are positively reinforced (Gelfand & Hartman, 1971). Special educators gradually became aware that behavioral principles could be applied to habilitate disabled children in the areas of body management, gross and fine motor coordination, self-care behavior, language skills, appropriate social behavior, and preacademic skills and knowledge (Bijou, 1981).

The treatment of a problem typically involves (1) weakening behavior that is aversive to others and strengthening prosocial (appropriate or desirable) behavior, (2) substituting shy, withdrawn, and phobic behavior with prosocial behavior, (3) extending and elaborating new discriminations and abilities, and (4) bringing inept or inappropriate behavior under appropriate stimulus control (Bijou, 1976). Common features of behavioral teaching to overcome the previously mentioned problems include assessing skills and knowledge (competencies) by means of a developmental chart or a criterion referenced inventory, using schedules of reinforcement to encourage continued use of appropriate behavior, and monitoring a child's performance on instructional objectives and goals (Bijou, 1981).

Behaviorism and Mild Mental Retardation

Among the first researchers to examine Skinner's principles in terms of mentally retarded persons was Sidney Bijou, who after 40 years of work in the field concluded that behavior modification held great promise for preventing mild and moderate degrees of mental or developmental retardation where organic or biomedical involvement was not evident (Scheerenberger, 1983). Behavior modification refers primarily to behavior management based on operant conditioning principles, specifically the manipulation of reinforcers for appropriate behaviors (Gredler, 1992). Behavior modification has long been used with severely mentally retarded students in nonintellectual areas as basic self-care (Scheerenberger, 1983).

Most human behavior at all developmental stages consists of complex interrelationships of respondent and operant behavior (Bijou, 1976). Thus, the principles that govern learning in children with mental retardation are basically the same as for the intellectually unimpaired (Gelfand & Hartman, 1971). However, the anatomy and physiology of the retarded child and the kinds and frequencies of his interactions with physical objects and people may all serve to restrict the opportunities for him/her to develop the essential repertories of behavior at a normal rate (Bijou, 1976).

With young children whose environmental conditions were primarily responsible for their developmental delays, Bijou (1983) recommended using systematic training to modify the behavior of parents and teachers in order to provide children with more and new opportunities and incentives for intellectual and academic achievement. Bijou (1981) hoped that by using behavior modification with preschool children and by using direct teaching and structured modeling for comprehensive educational interventions that by fourth grade these children would function academically, socially, behaviorally, and cognitively within the normal range of development. Though Bijou was unsuccessful in eliminating mental retardation, direct teaching and structured modeling continue to be important teaching strategies used with persons with mild or moderate mental retardation.

COGNITIVE MODEL OF MENTAL RETARDATION

The Cognitive Model of Mental Retardation is based on cognitive psychology, the field of psychology that studies memory and cognition (Peterson, 1991). The cognitive theories assume that the learner's mental processes are the major factor in learning. These theories, therefore, emphasize the ways that processing and application of information changes one's thoughts and internal mental structures (Peterson, 1991).

All cognitive functioning relies on neurological functioning; thus, substances and experiences that improve or impair the efficiency of neurological functioning also improve or impair cognition (Mann & Sabatino, 1985). "Damage to the nervous system's nuclei and ganglia is likely to have devastating effects on specific cognitive functions, e.g., visual, auditory and memory ones" (Mann & Sabatino, 1985, 35). Genetic defects, birth trauma, accidents and injuries that damage specific parts of the nervous system usually cause specific types of cognitive deficits.

Information processing or cognitive processing problems may occur due to an interruption in (1) attention to stimuli, (2) reception of stimuli, (3) storage and processing of information, and (4) expression of cognitive abilities (Fallen & Umansky, 1985). A neurological or sensory impairment may interfere with the child's ability to attend to a stimulus long enough to process it into short-term or long-term memory storage. Persons who have mental retardation seem to have significant difficulty in three major components of attention: attention span (length of time on task), focus (inhibition of distracting stimuli), and selective attention (discrimination of important stimulus characteristics) (Patton & Polloway, 1990, 209).

Children with visual and/or hearing impairments may be unable to receive stimuli appropriately or may receive distorted or garbled information. The child who is unable to use vision to integrate auditory and tactile cues learns much later how to maintain contact with his/her environment (Fallen & Umansky, 1985). If vision is not available, simultaneity of spatial organization may be lost, and if hearing is lost, an appreciation of order or succession may be disturbed (Restak, 1984).

A moderate-to-severe brain damage may disrupt the storage and processing of information and result in various levels of mental retardation.

A general problem of children with retardation is that they seem deficient in cognitive strategies and information acquisition strategies (Brown, 1974). Persons with mental retardation experience difficulty in spontaneously utilizing mediational strategies (e.g., verbal rehearsal and repetition, labeling, classification, association, and imagery) to organize information for later recall (Bray, 1979; Spitz, 1966). Research has shown that learners with retardation have difficulty in the area of short-term memory, but retain information over the long term (Patton & Polloway, 1990). Short-term memory problems have been associated both with deficits in attention and with deficits in spontaneous use of mediational strategies.

Children and youth with mental retardation experience difficulty in generalization, transferring the results of any training to a new situation. They tend to show deficiencies in the ability to apply knowledge or skills to new tasks, problems, or stimulus situations (Stephens, 1972). Students with retardation may fail to use previous experience to formulate rules that will help solve future problems of a similar nature (Patton & Polloway, 1990).

The expression of cognitive abilities may be significantly affected if the disabled child has speech disorders and/or orthopedic impairments that result in poor oral motor control which interfere with articulation and speech production. Orthopedic impairments hinder progress in fine and gross motor development inhibiting early exploratory behaviors and underlying cognitive processes, as a result delaying acquisition of such cognitive skills as object permanence and causality. Thus, cognitive processes may be interrupted due to all four causes in students with mild mental retardation: interruption of attention to stimuli, reception of stimuli, storage and processing of information, and behavioral responses or expression of cognitive abilities.

FUNCTIONAL MODEL OF MENTAL RETARDATION

According to the Functional Model, mental retardation refers to a particular state of impaired functioning involving the ordinary challenges of everyday living in the community, first manifested in childhood, in which limitations in intelligence coexist with related limitations in adaptive skills (Luckasson, 1992). Adaptive behavior is referred to as the effectiveness or degree with which the individual meets the standards of personal independence and social responsibility expected of his age and social group (Grossman, 1973).

Functional activities, in addition to being practical, should be appropriate to a student's chronological age. During infancy and early childhood, adaptive behavior includes sensory-motor skills, communication skills (speech and language), self-help skills, and socialization skills (interacting and getting along with others) (Grossman, 1973). During childhood and early adolescence adaptive behavior includes the application of basic academic skills in daily life situations, the application of appropriate reasoning and judgment in mastery of the environment, and social skills (participation in group activities and interpersonal relationships) (Grossman, 1973). Vocational and social responsibility and performance are the adaptive behaviors of concern during late adolescence and adulthood (Grossman, 1973).

The 1992 AAMR definition of mental retardation indicates that adaptive difficulties derive from limitations in practical and social intelligence (Luckasson et al., 1992). Practical intelligence refers to the ability to maintain and sustain oneself as an independent person in managing the ordinary activities of daily living (Luckasson et al., 1992, 15).

> Practical intelligence is central to such adaptive abilities as sensorimotor skills, self-care (sleeping, bathing, toileting, eating, drinking), and safety skills (avoiding danger and preventing injury). It is also important for other adaptive abilities such as functional academics, work, leisure, self-direction, and use of the community (Luckasson et al., 1992, 15).

According to AAMR (1992), social intelligence refers to the ability to understand social expectations and the behavior of other persons, and to judge appropriately how to conduct oneself in social situations. The principal components of social intelligence are social awareness and social skills; social comprehension, insight, judgment, and communication (Luckasson et al., 1992). In students with mild mental retardation, social intelligence is central to such adaptive abilities as social skills, communication, work, leisure, home living, and use of the community (Luckasson et al., 1992).

A functional or essential living skills program typically is designed for secondary students whose academic skills are below fourth-grade level (Mercer & Mercer, 1993). For many students with intellectual and learning problems, functional living skills must be taught directly and systematically (Mercer & Mercer, 1993). *The Life Centered Career Education* (LCCE) curriculum (Brolin, 1986) identifies 22 major competencies categorized into the three domains of daily living skills, personal/social skills, and occupational skills that are necessary to function effectively in school, family, and community roles (Polloway et al., 1989). Another frequently used functional curriculum, the Adult Outcome Domains from the *Hawaiian Transition Project* (1987) includes the following areas: (1) Vocation/Education, (2) Community Involvement, (3) Home and Family, (4) Recreation and Leisure, (5) Emotional/Physical Health, (6) Personal Development. The functional or living skills curriculum must be taught in the environments in which the student now functions or might function in the future.

SUMMARY

The major perspectives that provide definitions, etiology, treatment, and education of mentally retarded individuals have evolved from several theoretical models—medical, developmental, behavioral, cognitive, and functional. The following table summarizes these theoretical models.

Summary of Theoretical Models of Mental Retardation

Medical	Developmental	Behavioral	Cognitive	Functional
Focus: Physiology	Focus: Stage-Based & Age-Based Views	Focus: Environment	Focus: Information Processing	Focus: Every Day Life Skills
Etiology: MR is caused by underlying disease or medical condition	Etiology: Developmental delay in normal development	Etiology: Unconcerned with internal causes	Etiology: Damaged neurological conditions	Etiology: Deficits in adaptive behaviors
Diagnosis: AAMR Biomedical factors	Diagnosis: Compare skills to hierarchy of normal development	Diagnosis: Criterion-referenced academic tests & task-analyses	Diagnosis: Intelligence Tests	Diagnosis: Adaptive Behavior Assessments

Medical	Developmental	Behavioral	Cognitive	Functional
Treatment: Sensory-Motor Activities, Functional Activities, Medications	Treatment: Developmentally & Age Appropriate Activities	Treatment: Systematic training in deficits, Behavior Modification	Treatment: Focus on attention, perception, & memory. Classification, Generalization	Treatment: *The Life Center Career Educ.* Daily living activities, social skills, work skills
Theorists: Itard, Seguin, Montessori, Doll, Grossman	Theorists: Gesell, Freud, Erikson, Piaget, Hall, Kohlberg	Theorists: Skinner, Bijou	Theorists: Binet & Simon, Inhelder, Piaget	Theorists: Luckasson, Brolin

Chapter 4

LEARNING PERSPECTIVES OF
MILD MENTAL RETARDATION

Individuals with mental retardation, by definition, perform below average on tests of intelligence and are slow and inefficient learners (Thomas & Patton, 1994, 220).

Individuals with mild mental retardation develop at a slower rate in motor, social, and language skills than their peers, however, mild retardation is often not suspected until the children enter school (Thomas & Patton, 1994). Since children with mild mental retardation seldom exhibit any physical characteristics suggestive of mental retardation or any other handicapping condition, they are usually regarded by other members of their family as functioning within broadly defined normal limits (Reschly, 1988). The first indication of mild retardation is often a combination of difficulty with academic subjects and behavioral problems which result in repeated failure in educational settings (Thomas & Patton, 1990).

COGNITIVE LEARNING CHARACTERISTICS

In many ways, the intellectual problems of children with retardation are reflected in reduced capacity for learning and in reduced rate for acquiring new concepts and information (Cartwright et al., 1989). Primary-aged children with mental retardation have significant deficits in their understanding of basic concepts such as size, position, order, and sequence (Nelson, Cummings, & Boltman, 1991). Additionally, students with mild mental retardation appear to have a higher 'forget rate' and do not reach the academic levels of average nonhandicapped peers.

Cognitive Learning Rates/Levels

Most students with mild mental retardation obtain IQ scores between 50 and 75, thus, their learning rate or intellectual progress could be expected to be between one-half to three-fourths the rate of their average intelligence peers. This reduced learning rate, however, begins at birth, so the child with mild mental retardation arrives at the first grade classroom functioning significantly below his same-aged peers.

The general cognitive functioning of a child with a mental age of IQ 100 is the same as his/her chronological age (see Learning Rate Comparisons Table). A child with an IQ of 75 should learn about three-fourths the rate of a child with an average ability of IQ 100, and a child with an IQ of 50 should learn about one-half that rate (see Learning Rate Comparisons Table). Therefore, when a 6-year-old child with an IQ of 100 enters first grade she/he should function cognitively like a 6-year-old child. However, when a child with an IQ of 75 enters first grade, she/he may be functioning like a child of about 4½ years old; at 7th grade she/he may be expected to function like a 9-year-old; and at 12th grade, she/he should function cognitively like a youth about 13½ years old (see Learning Rates Comparisons Table). However, students with mild mental retardation seldom perform up to their cognitive expectations or up to their academic expectations (Hickson et al., 1995).

It is a common assumption that individuals with mild mental retardation will progress through the same Piagetian stages of cognitive development (see Chapter Three) as the nonretarded individual with major differences being in rate and highest level achieved (Thomas & Patton, 1990). Individuals with mild mental retardation will not reach Piaget's

Learning Rate Comparisons

Grade			1	3	5	7	9	11	12	
Age	2	4	6	8	10	12	14	16	18	20
IQ 100	2	4	6	8	10	12	14	16	18	20
IQ 75	1.5	3	4.5	6	7.5	9	10.5	12	13.5	15
IQ 50	1	2	3	4	5	6	7	8	9	10

level of formal thought and, thus, even as adults will be limited to engaging in thought consistent with the stage of concrete operations (Patton & Polloway, 1990). However, longitudinal research (Dudek, Strobel & Thomas, 1987) has indicated that children who are stronger in concrete operations score better in tests of academic achievement in Grades 1–4. More recent research indicated that instruction on the key Piagetian operations of classification and seriation with children with mild retardation increased their cognitive abilities (Slosson Intelligence Test) and their academic abilities (The Peabody Individual Achievement Test) (Markwardt, 1989).

Concrete operational thinkers have limited ability to engage in symbolic and abstract thought. Studies reveal that a critical difference between learners with and without retardation is the ability to reason (plan ahead, exhibit foresight, and understand relations); and that individuals with mental retardation are behind not only their chronological-age nonretarded peers, but also their mental-age nonretarded peers in the ability to reason (Spitz, 1979).

Information Processing Deficits

Research studies indicate that individuals with mental retardation are deficient in most aspects of information processing. This deficit in persons with mild retardation is due partly to sensory input limitations in the visual cortex which processes less visual information and at a slower rate than that of nonhandicapped students (Saccuzzo & Michael, 1984). Research regarding the cognitive functioning of children and youth with mild mental retardation has generally focused on the subprocesses of cognitive functioning including attention, memory, learning efficiency, and generalization.

Attention Deficits

Individuals with mild mental retardation frequently experience attention deficits that interfere with information processing in the following areas: (1) attention span: length of time on task, (2) focus: inhibition of distracting stimuli, and (3) selective attention: discrimination of important stimulus characteristics (Thomas & Patton, 1994). Individuals with mild mental retardation have short attention spans and attend to task for only brief periods before being distracted by extraneous stimuli. They experience difficulty in tuning out noises, movement, and other classroom activities in order to concentrate on their assignment. Frequently, they are unable to determine what should be the focus of their attention—teacher talking to another group, their neighbors whispering, or their partners in a collaboration activity.

Individuals with retardation are deficient in the number of dimensions that can be attended to at any one time (Morrison, 1988). A primary grade child with mild mental retardation may categorize by two dimensions simultaneously—color (red or blue) and shape (blocks), but be unable to categorize by several examples of size, shape, and color simultaneously.

Memory Deficits

Individuals with mild mental retardation experience difficulties in most aspects of memory related to their reduced learning rate and reduced cognitive capacity. "The ability to remember is critical to the cognitive functioning of any individual" (Morrison, 1988, 155).

Short-term memory problems appear to be characteristic of individuals with retardation and arise primarily from their inability to automatically use rehearsal strategies such as verbal rehearsal and image rehearsal (Mercer & Snell, 1977). Individuals with mild mental retardation fail to spontaneously use strategies that facilitate transfer of information through the memory systems (Morrison, 1988). The capacity of the short-term or working memory is smaller among individuals with mild mental retardation than among normal persons (Brown, 1974), thus, the amount of information placed in long-term memory storage is reduced as well.

Long-term memory deficits among individuals with mild mental retardation have been observed in capacity and access to long-term memory. "Differences in knowledge (contained in long-term memory) clearly influence what will be attended to, what will be perceived, and the likelihood of passing new information into long-term memory" (Kramer et al., 1988, 45). Children with mental retardation appear to have less information stored in long-term memory and, therefore, have fewer concepts that can be related to and integrated with new information. Access to long-term storage may be significantly reduced if individuals with mental retardation forget labels for concepts and categories, and thereby, be unable to retrieve information. Most researchers contend that once learned, information is retained over the long term about as well by those with mild retardation as those without (Patton & Polloway, 1990).

Learning Inefficiency

"Mentally retarded individuals are, as a group, inefficient learners. It is this characteristic more than any other that distinguishes them from their nonretarded peers" (Kramer et al., 1988, 43). Learners with retardation are generally characterized as passive learners who do not spontaneously use appropriate strategies (Loper, 1980). "Unfortunately children with mental retardation, when confronted with a problem, tend to do little "up front" intellectual planning. This leads to efforts at problem solving and eventual responses that are often disorganized and off-target" (Hickson et al., 1995).

"Not only are retarded individuals less efficient in formal learning situations, many believe that these individuals are especially deficient in acquiring information; and skills in informal or naturally occurring situations" (Kramer et al., 1988, 43). When deeper levels of cognitive processing are required, learners with mild mental retardation become progressively slower in processing and manipulating information (Schultz, 1983).

Incidental learning is not an effective means of gaining information for children with retardation. "Children who are retarded often do not acquire information that is peripheral or incidental to the main point of attention. They do not seem to be able to handle as many different pieces or kinds of information at one time as normal children can. Consequently, information not directly relevant to the task being performed may not be acquired" (Cartwright et al., 1989, 236).

Generalization Problems

"Students who are retarded tend to show deficiencies in the ability to apply knowledge or skills to new tasks, problems, or stimulus situations" (Patton & Polloway, 1990, 210). "The ability to profit from experiences and to generalize is poor for individuals who are retarded. Therefore, it takes more time for them to form a learning set (a systematic method of solving problems)" (Cartwright et al., 1989, 236). In order to facilitate generalization, students must be expected to perform similar tasks in various settings, using numerous learning materials, and with various teachers.

It has often been found that cognitive strategies trained in a laboratory setting will not generalize to the acquisition of academic skills (Hickson, 1995). Memory strategies, trained successfully in learners with mild retardation, did not generalize spontaneously to the acquisition of reading skills (Blackman et al., 1982).

ACADEMIC LEARNING CHARACTERISTICS

The academic functioning of children and youth with mild mental retardation depends significantly on the student's cognitive ability, his/her socio-economic background and experiences, the presence of other handicapping conditions or health problems, previous developmental and remediation intervention, and the quality and quantity of interactions with parents and caregivers. By virtue of definition, however, children and youth with mild mental retardation will function below age and grade expectations.

General Academic Functioning

Children with mild retardation, whose learning rate is expected to be approximately one-half to three-fourths the rate of nonhandicapped children, exhibit deficits and delays in all academic areas. In general, children with mild mental retardation enrolled in the primary grades (1st–3rd) may be functioning at preschool and readiness levels; intermediate age-grade level students with mild retardation may be functioning at the primary grade level just beginning real academics; and Junior and Senior High School age-grade level students with mild mental retardation will focus on functional academics and prevocational/vocational training.

Preschool-Age Level

The pre-academic functioning of preschool-age children, 3 to 5 years, depends significantly on their cognitive functioning level. Children with mild mental retardation usually demonstrate delays in all developmental areas. Motor skills, speech and language skills, cognitive skills, perceptual-motor skills, and even social and emotional behaviors will be acquired more slowly than by nonhandicapped children. Children with retardation ages 3–5 years with IQs of 75 may be expected to function similar to average nonhandicapped children ages 2¼ to 3¾ years old, while children ages 3–5 years with IQs of 50 may be expected to function in the 1½ to 2½ year range (see Learning Rates Comparisons Table).

A 5-year-old child with mild mental retardation (IQ 75) may function similar to a 3–4 year old nondisabled child. Motorically, she/he may build a tower of 9 blocks, hold crayons with fingers, copy a circle and trace around templates; run around obstacles, balance and hop on one foot, ride a tricycle, walk up and down stairs, throw and catch a bounced ball. She/he may engage in associative group play and imaginative play. Communicatively, the 5-year-old child with mild mental retardation (IQ 75) may use sentences of 3 or more words, talk about the past and use "ed" on verbs to indicate past tense, use "s" on nouns to indicate plurals; understand some time concepts, carry out 2 related directions, and play "Let's Pretend."

Compared to expectations of a nondisabled 5-year-old (IQ 100), the child with mild mental retardation (IQ 75) may not be able to cut simple shapes, copy his/her first name, print numerals 1–5, color within the lines, paste and glue appropriately; skip on alternate feet, gallop and jump and run in rhythm to tunes, jump rope, skate, or ride a small bike without training wheels. Communicatively, the child with mild mental retardation (IQ 75) may not use grammar similar to an adult's, talk casually using "because," nor ask "Why" questions. She/he will not be able to demonstrate preacademic skills.

Primary Grades 1–3 (6–8 years)

Primary age/grade children with mild mental retardation (IQ 75) may be expected to function developmentally within the 4½ to 6 year range. The six-year-old child (IQ 75) functioning similar to a 4½ year old nondisabled child will academically and developmentally work on pre-kindergarten level skills. The eight-year-old child (IQ 75) functioning similar to a 6-year-old nonhandicapped child will be acquiring first grade academic and social skills (see Learning Rate Comparison Table).

Primary age/grade children with mild mental retardation (IQ 50) may function about the 3 to 4 year preschool level. While average children begin formal academics of learning reading, writing, and arithmetic during first grade at six-years-old, the child with mild mental retardation (IQ 75) may not cognitively be ready to begin formal academics until age 8 years or during the 3rd grade year. The child with IQ 50 will not be developmentally ready to begin formal 1st grade level academics until about age 12 years or during the 7th grade year (see Learning Rate Comparisons Table).

Intermediate Grades 4th–6th (9–11 years)

Intermediate age/grade children with mild mental retardation (IQ 75) may function developmentally within the 6 to 8 year range or similar to primary grade students in the 1st to 3rd grade levels. The nine-year-old child (IQ 75) functioning similar to a 6-year 9-month-old nonhandicapped child will academically work on first grade level skills. The eleven-year-old child with mild mental retardation (IQ 75) may function similar to an eight-year-old nonhandicapped child in some third grade level academic skills. Thus, children with mild mental retardation (IQ 75) usually function at primary grade levels during the intermediate grade years when about ages 9–11 years. The 9–11-year-old child with mild mental retardation (IQ 50) may function at the 4½ to 5½ year level similar to preschool and kindergarten levels in academics (see Learning Rate Comparisons Table).

Junior High School Grades 7th–9th (12–14 years)

During Junior High, youth with mild mental retardation (IQ 75) may function cognitively similar to nondisabled youth 9 to 10½ years old on 4th to 5th grade range in some academic areas such as math calculation. Language-based subjects requiring comprehension will be more difficult for youth with mild mental retardation (IQ 75) who generally function on the literal level. Youth with mild mental retardation (IQ 75) seldom progress much above the 3rd to 4th grade levels academically; instead they focus on functional academics, life-skills, and transition skills at junior and senior high school levels. During junior high school years, youth with mild mental retardation (IQ 50) may function at the 6 to 7 year level or cognitively similar to 1st and 2nd grade students in some areas, thus, their academic focus will be on functional skills, community living, and prevocational skills.

Senior High School Grades 10th–12th (15–18 years)

During senior high school years, 15 to 18 year old youth with mild mental retardation (IQ 75) may be expected to function similar to 11–13 year old nondisabled students or 6th grade level in some areas. Though youth with mild mental retardation may reach this level in math calculation and some basic reading skills, they seldom reach this extrapolated level in reading comprehension and math reasoning functioning at the 3rd to 4th grade levels or lower.

Experience and research (Blackman, Burger, Tan & Weiner, 1982) reveal that rather than progressing at the rate of 1/2 to 3/4ths of an academic year for each year in school, in academic subjects students with retardation are more likely to grow at the rate of 2/10 to 3/10 of a year for each full academic year. Much of their academic time in Junior and Senior High School is spent on prevocational or vocational skills, life skills, transition skills, or work/study programs rather than a total academic program.

During senior high school years, youth with mild mental retardation (IQ 50) may function similar to nonhandicapped students ages 7 to 8 years or functioning academically at the 2nd grade literal level in some subject areas. These students will also spend much of their junior and senior high school years learning prevocational skills, life skills, and transition skills rather than focusing on a total academic program.

Specific Academic Learning Problems

Speech and Language Problems

The development of speech and language is closely associated with intellectual development, therefore, it is not surprising that individuals with retardation display more problems in these areas than nondisabled students (Patton & Polloway, 1990). "Where environment appears to play a large role in the etiology of the retardation, as it does for many who are mildly retarded, language deficits may be related to such factors as absence of or limited adequate speech and language models and less encouragement to use language" (Thomas & Patton, 1990, 219). Research indicates that nearly 90 percent of students labeled mildly retarded have speech and language disorders (Epstein et al., 1989). In general, the language of persons with mild mental retardation follows the same developmental stages as that of nonretarded persons, but their language development progresses at a slower rate (Hallahan & Kauffman, 1994).

Speech Problems. Individuals with mental retardation experience a higher prevalence of speech problems especially in articulation areas of substitution and omission of sounds which decrease the intelligibility of speech. Articulation and voice problems are probably a result of marked delays in motor development (Edwards & Edwards, 1970).

Language Problems. Delayed or deviant language development is evident in virtually all persons with mental retardation (Warren & Abbeduto, 1992). These language delays are cognitive, not developmental (Bowerman, 1976) and are similar to the language development found in younger children who are of the equivalent mental age (Morrison, 1988). This delayed language development has been evidenced in a number of language areas including the following: restricted vocabulary development, auditory discrimination, incorrect grammatical structure and usage, and sentence length; pragmatic language; delayed oral language development.

Language difficulties experienced by individuals with mild mental retardation include the following receptive language difficulties: (1) Problems understanding verbal receptive language; (2) Inability to determine main idea of orally presented information; (3) Difficulty in discriminating similar sounding words; (4) Problems repeating a series of words or digits that were orally presented; (5) Problems understanding abstract information and directions; (6) Attention deficits in processing verbal directions (Patton & Polloway, 1990; Wallace et al., 1987).

Expressive language difficulties of children with mild mental retardation include the following: (1) Difficulties with verbal expression; (2) Problems maintaining a conversation (pragmatics); (3) Inappropriately responds to verbal questions (semantics); (4) Problems with verbal tasks that require little listening; (5) Difficulty retelling a story that was previously read aloud; (6) Omits common prefixes and suffixes (morphology); (7) Experiences difficulty understanding pronoun antecedents; (8) Difficulty with grammatical structure (syntax) (Patton & Polloway, 1990; Wallace et al., 1987).

While learners with mental retardation may be proficient in simple settings, they become more challenged in maintaining the topic and other pragmatic skills when the number of speakers, number of utterances, and degree of appropriateness of the speakers' responses change (Koetting & Rice, 1991). "Academic or intellectual tasks that are dependent on language or verbal learning will often be difficult for children who are retarded. . . . Due to the high correlation between cognitive and language abilities, severe language delays may be a sign that a child is not progressing at a satisfactory rate" (Cartwright et al., 1989, 237). Language skills deficits may be one of the greatest obstacles that students with mild mental retardation must overcome if they are to be integrated fully into society (Polloway & Smith, 1982).

Reading Problems

The majority of students who are mildly retarded read at a lower level than would be expected for their mental age, and of the various aspects of reading, comprehension appears to be the most difficult for these students. Since students with retardation appear to have a higher "forget" rate than nonhandicapped students, they may spend years "learning, forgetting, and relearning" the same sight vocabulary words, thus, progress to successively higher levels of academic achievement may proceed very slowly. The child who is mildly mentally retarded may attain some understanding of phonics skills in order to decode unfamiliar words (Snell, 1983).

The difficulties children with retardation have in understanding and using language severely impact reading comprehension. Comprehension of anything but literal level is difficult for these children. Since they will cognitively attain no higher than the concrete operational level, any higher level comprehension skill (e.g., evaluation) will require beginning with the concrete and real-life situations before moving to the abstract.

Mathematics Problems

In mathematics, the majority of students with mild retardation can learn basic computations (Thomas & Patton, 1990). The performance of students with retardation in computation tasks is more consistent with their mental age (Whorton & Algozzine, 1978). However, they must be taught using concrete and practical experiences due to deficits in cognition. Students with mild mental retardation experience significant difficulties in mathematics reasoning and "word" problems. Since generalization is difficult for them, mildly retarded students will need to be taught functional use of mathematics.

Students with mild mental retardation experience difficulty in automatizing basic math skills; they do not reach a level of proficiency in which knowledge of basic math facts is fast, accurate, and consistent (Goldman & Pellegrino, 1987). This lack of automaticity of knowledge of basic facts interferes with calculation accuracy, makes greater demands on attention and memory resources, interferes with performing more complex and higher level tasks including multi-step procedures and word problems, and requires longer periods of time to complete assignments. Recent research indicates that the difficulty which students who are mildly mentally disabled have in developing automaticity relates specifically to lack of speed, rather than to lack of accuracy (Podell et al., 1992).

Written Expression

While students who are retarded may learn functional writing skills, they will probably experience significant difficulty in creative writing or writing a report because they do not possess automaticity in the underlying skills of penmanship, language processing, creative thinking, grammar, punctuation and capitalization, paragraph organization, paragraph transition, and mechanics of paper writing. Programs for students with mild retardation will usually focus on functional writing skills such as letters and job applications.

SOCIAL/EMOTIONAL LEARNING CHARACTERISTICS

One of the major problems of individuals with intellectual deficits is a parallel deficit in social behavior (Kramer et al., 1988). Research clearly indicates that children and adolescents with mild mental retardation display more social and behavioral problems than their nonhandicapped counterparts (Epstein et al., 1989; Polloway et al., 1985).

Social Learning Problems

Individuals with mild mental retardation often develop patterns of behavior that further distinguish them from nonretarded peers because of their experiences in dealing with an environment in which they are less able to cope (Thomas & Patton, 1990). "Children who are retarded may not fully comprehend what is expected of them and may respond inappropriately not so much because they lack the particular response required as because they have misinterpreted the situation" (Cartwright et al., 1989, 239).

"Adaptive behavior deficiencies in school settings are associated with coping behavior, social skills, language development, emotional development, self-care, and applied cognitive and academic skills" (Drew et al., 1995, 252). The remediation of adaptive behavior deficiencies is extremely important in assisting a child to reach "normalization". Appropriate behaviors in adaptive skills areas is frequently the determining factor in not labeling a "high" functioning student as mildly mentally retarded.

For many individuals with mild retardation, it is the lack of social competencies rather than intellectual deficits which bring unwanted attention (Kramer et al., 1988). Students with mild retardation experience difficulties in social sensitivity and insight, social communication, self-concept and self-esteem, and social interactions (Greenspan, 1981; Patton & Polloway, 1990).

Social Sensitivity and Insight

Social and cognitive skills are interrelated in that the development of such skills as role-taking, self-awareness, interpersonal skills, social communication skills reflect both social and cognitive development (Kramer et al., 1988). Research clearly indicates that children with mental retardation display a significant delay in demonstrating the ability to understand another person's point of view or engage in social perspective-taking. Additionally, they do not perceive others in as many ways, view others in more egocentric terms, and demonstrate limited insight into the motives and characteristics of others (Kramer et al., 1988).

During middle childhood intermediate grades, 4th–6th, ages 9–12 years, most nondisabled children make significant growth in the area of social perspective-taking (role-taking). Since youngsters with mild retardation would be cognitively functioning like children of 6–8 years old or 1st–3rd graders, their social development would also reflect delayed development.

Social comprehension and moral judgment are two areas of social ability that depend to a great extent on the cognitive functioning level. "As with other areas of social development, mildly retarded individuals have demonstrated difficulty in developing moral judgment and are perceived to have difficulties dealing with more than one aspect of a moral dilemma" (Kramer et al., 1988, 51).

Social Communication and Problem-Solving

Individuals with mild mental retardation experience deficits in both cognition and language which significantly reduces their functioning level and rate of acquisition of social skills.

> Children who do not have the verbal and communication skills of their age mates may withdraw from interpersonal relationships or seek attention in a variety of inappropriate ways. These children may misbehave because they cannot clearly distinguish between acceptable and unacceptable standards of behavior (Thomas & Patton, 1990, 199).

Children with mild retardation experience significant difficulties in problem-solving due to their reduced cognitive abilities. They appear to have limited, interpersonal problem-solving strategies and fail to see sequential relationships among a series of interactions (Asher & Renshaw, 1981). Individuals with mild retardation experience difficulty in most aspects of social functioning including social sensitivity (role-taking & social inference), social insight (social comparison & moral judgment), and social communication (referential communication & social problem-solving) due to reduced cognitive and language capacities. "Clearly, personal and social characteristics are intertwined. An individual's personal social status is affected by his or her own competencies and by significant others' reactions to those competencies" (Morrison, 1988, 158).

Problem behavior can also result from the frustrations of scholastic failure or as an attempt to gain acceptance from other children, who might encourage deviant behavior. Much inappropriate social behavior that occurs is a result of repeated failures (Thomas & Patton, 1990).

Social Interaction

Individuals who are mildly retarded frequently have poor interpersonal relationships and are more often rejected than accepted by their peers (Polloway et al., 1986). Teachers' and peers' perceptions of academic ability and behavior have been found to be related to social acceptance, and perceptions of aggressive misbehavior have been found to be related to peer rejection (Kaufman et al., 1987). The reasons for this reduced social status seem to reside in a complex interaction of the characteristics exhibited by the children with mild retardation including reduced cognitive competence, lack of social competencies, and inappropriate communication and behavior (MacMillan & Morrison, 1980). Roberts & Zubrick (1992) found that students with mild disabilities were liked significantly less than peers without disabilities, primarily due to disruptive behavior.

"The differences between young children who are retarded and their normal peers seem to be related to behavior; that is, children with mild retardation act like normal children who are younger in chronological age" (Cartwright et al., 1989, 238). Developmentally delayed preschoolers exhibit a general lack of success in initiating social interactions and an absence of individual social behaviors that are closely associated with peer-related social competence such as attempting to influence the behavior of others (Guralnick & Groom, 1987). Young children with mild mental retardation engage in solitary play and limited social interactions.

Social differences among mildly retarded and nonhandicapped children and youth appear to escalate with age as social appropriateness becomes more important. Past mainstreaming efforts failed to achieve increased social interaction, social acceptance, and behavioral modeling by disabled students (Gresham, 1988). Integrative efforts are likely to be more successful after students learn prosocial behaviors and correct inappropriate behaviors; since generalization is so difficult for students with mild mental retardation, it cannot be assumed that exposure to nondisabled peers alone would be sufficient to facilitate social interaction (Kehle & Barclay, 1979).

"Mildly mentally retarded students as adults have serious adjustment problems, often related to the specific domains of behavior that led to the initial referral, classification, and placement. These domains of behavior have to do with abstract thought, application of concepts of time and number, and literacy skills" (Reschly, 1987, 31).

Sense of Personal Control

Metacognitive Deficits

"Efficient problem solvers use metacognitive knowledge to select, monitor, and create problem-solving strategies" (Kramer et al., 1988, 53). The literature has long indicated the failures of individuals with retardation to spontaneously use cognitive strategies such as mnemonics (Ellis, 1970). Additionally, retarded children have difficulty selecting, modifying, and sequencing strategies and they experience problems in the area of self-questioning (Borys, 1979; Campione & Brown, 1977).

"There is solid evidence that educable mentally retarded students can learn and maintain task-specific cognitive strategies" (Kramer et al., 1988, 53). The accumulated evidence from numerous training efforts made it clear that strategies such as verbal elaboration, repetitive rehearsal, visual imagery, and self-instruction could be learned and used to improve performance on specific tasks (Kramer et al., 1988).

However, numerous studies revealed that learners with retardation have failed to generalize the use of trained task-specific cognitive strategies to new situations (Kramer & Engel, 1981). The difficulty that retarded individuals have in generalizing new information is well documented (MacMillan, 1982). Recent studies aimed at improving the intellectual abilities of students with mild retardation have also failed to result in generalization (Kramer et al., 1988, 53). Attempts to train individuals with mild retardation to use cognitive strategies to improve social skills, academic skills, or general problem-solving skills have also revealed failure to generalize.

"Retarded students can be trained to use task-specific cognitive strategies and they will continue to use these strategies when presented with the training task. Attempts to modify more general memory monitoring or problem-solving skills have met with little success" (Kramer et al., 1988, 53). It appears that for generalization to occur, students must demonstrate the effective use of the executive skills (metacognition) such as strategy selection and monitoring (Borkowski and Varnhagen, 1984). The literature clearly indicates, then, that individuals with mild retardation are unable to use metacognitive skills effectively in strategy selection, in monitoring their learning, and in generalizing learning to new situations.

Children with mild retardation do not appear to possess self-monitoring and self-critical faculties (Hickson et al., 1995). Mental retardation might be described as a "self-regulatory disorder" (Whitman, 1990). A manifestation of this self-regulatory disorder in individuals with mental retardation is passivity in finding solutions to learning problems either by withdrawing or relying too heavily on the assistance of the teachers (Hickson et al., 1995).

Attribution Deficits

Attributions involve the reasons children and youth give for their success or failure in academic situations, and the amount of personal control they perceive as having over their successes or failures. "Research has shown that many individuals with retardation do not believe they are in control of their own destinies; they believe they are controlled by external or outside forces. They tend to think that things happen to them by chance and that they can do little to change anything (Hallahan & Kauffman, 1988). External control is considered to be a debilitating orientation, as it keeps the youth from accepting responsibility for his/her own successes and failures and impedes the development of self-reliance (Thomas & Patton, 1990).

"Popular belief indicates that mentally retarded students are more likely to expect to fail because of the belief that they encounter a higher rate of failure in their natural environments and a lower rate of success than normal children of the same age" (Kramer et al., 1988, 49). Individuals with retardation react to failure by decreasing their efforts on tasks following failure experiences (Logan & Rose, 1982). Reschly (1987) called this behavior the "failure set phenomenon." Individuals with mental retardation tend to attribute success or failure to external variables (i.e., luck, difficulty of task) rather than to internal factors (i.e., personal ability or amount of effort expended on the task) (Mehring & Colson, 1993).

When given negative feedback on cognitive tasks they were performing, retarded children stopped looking for effective strategies and many demonstrated learned helplessness (Weiss, 1984). In contrast, successful experiences lead to increases in performance and expectations of success (Ollendick et al., 1971). Thus, it appears that motivation to learn and positive expectancies for success can be enhanced by minimizing the failure experiences of youngsters with retardation and maximizing the successes.

Motivation Deficits

"Given that experiential factors for mentally retarded children differ substantially from that of normal children, it is not surprising that a retarded individual's motivation differs from that of a nonretarded individual of the same mental and chronological age" (Kramer et al., 1988, 49). Little research has been conducted regarding the motivations of youngsters with retardation. However, considering the results of attribution research that with retardation individuals tend to be outer-directed, it is not surprising that tangible reinforcers such as candy, stickers, and toys are more effective in motivating students with retardation than verbal reinforcers or grades.

Self-Concepts of Students with Mild Retardation

General Self-Concepts

Prior to 1960 there were very few research studies pertaining to self-concepts of the mentally retarded. Ringness (1959) was among the first to conduct research regarding the self-concept of students with retardation. His study revealed children with retardation have less well-differentiated and less realistic self-concepts than average or bright children, accompanied by unrealistic levels of aspiration.

The retarded as a group tend to be more anxious than nonretarded children, and their self-concepts more negative and more defensive than those of nonretarded children (Robinson & Robinson, 1976). Cline (1975) reported primary level students with mild retardation had significantly higher self-concept scores than Junior High level students with retardation, but normal children had higher self-concept scores than students with retardation at all levels. Pupils of low ability have lower self-concepts than average pupils, but the low ability pupils generally indicate higher ideal self-concepts than pupils of average ability (Stangvik, 1979).

Students (ages 10–13 years) with mild mental retardation possess significantly more negative conscious and unconscious self-concepts than emotionally disturbed (ED), learning disabled (LD), speech/language impaired (S/L), and nonhandicapped students (NH) (Jones, 1985). The mean performance scores of the EMR students were significantly lower than the nonhandicapped students on five of the six cluster scores and on the total score of the Piers-Harris Scale, indicating high anxiety levels and negative feelings regarding their intelligence and school status, popularity, happiness, and behavior (Jones, 1985).

A number of studies were conducted to determine if placement impacted on the self-concept of students with mild retardation, the "new" EMRs. Luftig (1980) reviewed research on the effects of placement on the self-concept of the "new" EMRs, and concluded that they maintain higher levels of self-concept in special classes than those in the mainstream.

The vast majority of what we know about how mentally retarded students perceive themselves has been derived or inferred from how these children and youth have responded to stimulus situations such as self statements and role-play situations. The limitations in their language and communication skills has made examination of self-awareness particularly difficult. While other individuals can explain their cognitive responses, the mentally retarded people have a more difficult time organizing and expressing their thoughts (Kramer et al., 1988, 48).

The relevant literature on self-concept has generally indicated that students with mild retardation report lower levels of self-efficacy than do their peers who are not retarded (Simeonsson, 1978). It can be concluded that students with mild retardation do not hold strong, positive feelings about their own abilities and potential. However, there is considerable correlation between negative self-concept and chronic failure (Patton & Polloway, 1990). The level of self-esteem remains an important consideration in teaching those with mental retardation, given the vulnerable status of their competencies in relation to others in their environments (Morrison, 1988).

Self-Concept of Academic Achievement

The self-image of the child with retardation is intricately linked to his academic success. Being viewed as academically successful by one's teacher is of utmost importance (Richmond, 1973). In evaluating self-concept differences between low and high achieving adolescents with retardation, Lawrence and Winschel (1973) found a positive relationship between adequate self-concept and high achievement of children with retardation. Children of lower than average ability have more difficulty than other children in gaining feelings of achievement and in developing favorable attitudes (Andrews, 1971).

Research revealed children with retardation tended to be more anxious than nonretarded children (Jones, 1985). Many children with retardation expect failure and learn to defend themselves against it; as a result, their self-concepts are more negative and defensive than those of nonretarded children (Robinson & Robinson, 1976). Low ability pupils are met by more negative attitudes from others both in school and society (Guskin & Jones, 1982). Due to a history of failure and dependency oriented treatment, students with retardation are very sensitive to others' evaluations of them (Stangvik, 1979).

Students with mild mental retardation viewed their intelligence negatively, perceived their school status to be low; experienced high anxiety, low popularity, and low happiness levels (Jones, 1985). The results suggested that students with mild retardation exhibited a negative "school-related self-concept" or negative academic achievement self-concept (Jones, 1985).

SUMMARY

In general, children with mild mental retardation enrolled in the primary grades (1st–3rd) will be functioning at preschool and readiness levels; and intermediate age-grade level students with mild mental retardation will be functioning at the primary grade level just beginning real academics. The majority of students with mild mental retardation read at a lower level than would be expected for their mental age, experiencing deficits in comprehension. They can learn mathematics computations, but experience significant difficulty in math reasoning. Adaptive behavior deficiencies in school settings are associated with coping skills, social skills, language development, emotional development, self-care, and social interaction.

Students with mild mental retardation are unable to use metacognitive skills effectively in strategy selection, in monitoring their learning, and in generalizing learning to new situations. Children with mild mental retardation believe they are controlled by external or outside forces, that things happen to them by chance and they can do little to change anything. Individuals with mild mental retardation react to failure by decreasing their efforts on tasks following failure experiences.

Most of the literature on self-concept of students with mild retardation indicates that they do not hold strong, positive feelings about their abilities and potential. Retarded students appear to have low self-concept of academic achievement including negative feelings about their intelligence, school status, and popularity. They appear to experience significant anxiety about school-related situations and activities.

UNIT 2
STUDENTS WITH BEHAVIOR DISORDERS

Chapter 5

HISTORICAL PERSPECTIVES
OF BEHAVIOR DISORDERS

Historically, responsibility for treating emotionally disturbed children rested with the mental health system (Paul, 1987, 6).

Historical Background of Services
   Early Treatment of the Mentally Ill
   The Psychological Period 1900–1960s
   The Educational Period 1960s to Present
Definitions of Behavior Disorders
   Theoretical Perspectives' Definitions
   Federal Definitions
   Proposed Definitions
Classification Systems
   Psychiatric (DSM IV)
   Quay's Classifications
   Hewett's Levels of Learning Competence
   Degree of Severity
Summary

Children with behavior disorders are referred to by a variety of terms including emotionally disturbed, socially maladjusted, psychologically disordered, emotionally impaired, behaviorally impaired, behavior disordered, and seriously emotionally disturbed to name a few. The term *seriously emotionally disturbed* (utilized in IDEA) communicates a psychodynamic perspective and stresses behavior as a manifestation of disturbed thoughts and feelings (Shea & Bower, 1987). Most educational professionals prefer to use the term *behavior disorders* to reflect a behavioral perspective that views inappropriate behavior more in terms of learned behavior that is problematic (Paul, 1987).

Regardless of the term used to describe these students, there are a significant number of students who display severely inappropriate behaviors in the classroom. *The Sixteenth Annual Report to Congress* indicates that 402,688 children and adolescents with serious emotional disturbance ages 6–21 years, or 8.7 percent of the total special education population, received special education services during the 1992–93 school year (OSEP, 1994). Since the 1976–77 school year, the number of students with severe emotional disturbance served annually has increased by 120,000 (OSEP, 1994).

HISTORICAL BACKGROUND OF SERVICES

The early treatment of persons with emotional disturbance or behavior disorders can be divided into three periods: Early Treatment of the Mentally Ill, The Psychological Period 1900–1960s, and The Educational Period 1960s to Present.

Early Treatment of the Mentally Ill

Generally, the early treatment of mentally ill and insane persons falls into two pre-1900 periods: the Supernatural Period, and the Illness Period. For the most part during these periods, mental illness and mental retardation were not considered two separate conditions with different treatments. Both groups, world-wide, were subjected equally to the brutality and inhumane conditions of people who did not understand their condition nor provide appropriate rehabilitative treatment.

The Supernatural Period

Prior to the late 1700s, the causes of emotional disturbances were attributed to beliefs in magic or possession by a spirit (Peterson, 1991). For primitive people insanity was both terrifying and mysterious. If someone went berserk, spoke in an incomprehensible manner, did strange things, the only explanation was the supernatural (McKown, 1961). The psychiatrists of primitive people were sorcerers, witch doctors, and medicine men who used spells, amulets, talismans, charms, tribal dances, magic wands, or chants to exorcise the invading spirits, and sometimes they cut open the skull of a patient to let the demons escape (McKown, 1961).

Hippocrates, born around 460 B.C. and the father of medicine, who dared to assert that insanity was a disease like any other and not caused by divine origin, observed and described paranoia, mania, and melancholia (McKown, 1961). Soranus of Ephesus, the first clinical observer of the mentally ill, recommended that treatment include comfortable and pleasant surroundings in airy and light rooms of moderate temperature, where undue noise could not disturb them, instead of brutality, chains, and whipping (McKown, 1961).

The Dark Ages began about 200 A.D. and medicine fell into a sharp decline. That part of medicine devoted to mental illness died a long death in Europe stretching for centuries (McKown, 1961). Like the primitives, the early Christians blamed insanity on demons. Relics of saints and bathing in holy waters replaced the charms and talismans of pagan treatment (McKown, 1961). For the most part, the insane and the mental defectives wandered at large, searching for food at night, and hiding in the daytime. The more dangerous might be chained in the public market place or put in stocks. A small percentage found sanctuary in monasteries or religious organizations. Even here they suffered as flogging was considered the most effective means of driving out demons (McKown, 1961).

For hundreds of years, during the Middle Ages, almost everyone believed that mental illness was caused by witchcraft and demons (McKown, 1961).

> In the Middle Ages, when Christians dominated, people equated abnormality with being possessed by the devil. People so "afflicted" were often tortured in order to drive the devil out of their bodies, and failing this, were burned at the stake in order to make their bodies inhospitable for Satan (Peterson, 1991, 494).

In 1488, Pope Innocent VIII issued a manifest calling for the nations of Europe to rescue the Church of Christ from the arts of Satan (McKown, 1961). Almost immediately the deaths of thousands and thousands including mentally ill and mentally retarded occurred to rid Europe of witchcraft (McKown, 1961). During the some 1500 years of the Christian era, the needs of the mentally ill were almost completely neglected (McKown, 1961).

Vincent de Paul, a priest and remarkable church reformer, impacted the treatment of mentally ill, mentally retarded, lepers, the poor, and foundlings during the 17th century (Scheerenberger, 1983). Assisted in his work by the Daughters of Charity, he firmly maintained that mentally ill and mentally retarded persons were not witches (Scheerenberger, 1983). In 1632, Vincent de Paul was given the Parisian priory of Saint Lazure, historically a leprosarium, which gradually became the heart of the religious revival in France and housed missionaries, ecclesiastics, orphans, novices, seminarians, wayward youths, insane persons, mentally retarded individuals, and lepers (Scheerenberger, 1983).

The Illness Period

During most of the 18th century in Europe, the insane were treated like animals, beaten and chained, kept in small cells with no light, and given a ration of bread and gruel daily (McKown, 1961). The dominant theme in treating mentally ill or mentally retarded persons was gaining ascendency over the individual or rendering them subservient and obedient by almost any means (Scheerenberger, 1983). However, the work of four men from different countries (Pinel of France, Tuke of England, Rush of America, and Chiarugi of Italy), who devoted part of their lives to improving institutional care for mentally ill patients, spawned the movement toward more humane treatment and the consideration of insanity as an illness (McKown, 1961).

Philippe Pinel's contributions to the field are many including a book on classification of mental diseases, the development of individual case histories and systematic records, the emphasis on providing vocational and work experience for the insane, and moral management of and treatment at mental hospitals (Scheerenberger, 1983). Moral management involved a treatment oriented approach which emphasized a broad array of medical, psychological, and educational services in a humane living environment (Scheerenberger, 1983). The humane living environment required the elimination of physical abuse and chains to be replaced by a calm retreat for disturbed persons, gentle treatment, and music; and called upon the participation of the patient in the treatment program with a hope for cure and release (Scheerenberger, 1983).

In the late 1700s when Pinel, teacher of Jean Itard, was appointed physician of a hospital for the mentally ill in Paris, he became famous for releasing his patients from their chains (Haring, 1990). Instead of drugs, Pinel recommended work therapy (McKown, 1961). Though Pinel believed that children with insanity were incurable, he was a proponent of more humane treatment (Haring, 1990).

William Tuke, concerned about the treatment of mental illness in England, convinced the Society of Friends to establish a mental hospital for Quakers who may become mentally ill. The establishment of "The Retreat" at York in 1776 provided a milder and more appropriate system of treatment for both mentally ill and mentally retarded which consisted of good food, clean surroundings, no chains, no beatings, warm baths, and dimmed lights for more severe cases (Scheerenberger, 1983). The principle of nonrestraint which William Tuke had inaugurated became the pivot around which the English mental institution reform was to concentrate for the next 50 years (McKown, 1961).

Benjamin Rush, the founder of American psychiatry, recommended and implemented more humane treatment of the mentally ill in America (McKown, 1961). Rush protested the mistreatment of lunatics in the local newspapers until finally the state of Pennsylvania in 1784 constructed a "madhouse" attached to the hospital (McKown, 1961). Rush supervised the hospital section for mentally ill and mentally retarded and instituted a more humane treatment which included work therapy, clean rooms, warm baths, conversational therapy sessions with the physician (Scheerenberger, 1983).

Rush's treatments, however, were a curious mixture of enlightenment and tradition as he practiced substantial bloodletting as a treatment for mental illness (McKown, 1961). Rush designed and utilized several machines as treatment for mental illness including the gyrator (a rotating turntable on which the patient was strapped to increase blood flow to the brain—a cause of mental illness); and the tranquilizer chair for restraining patients (a substitute for the straight jacket), was discontinued due to severe bruising and fractures in patients (Scheerenberger, 1983). Rush's book, *Medical Inquiries and Observations Upon Diseases of the Mind,* published in 1812, was the first book on mental illness in America, the only one for many years, which launched the science of mental care in America (McKown, 1961).

During the Illness Period, abnormality began to be attributed to injury, illness caused by germs, or defects within the body (Peterson, 1991). The first mental disorder to be explained in illness terms was general paresis which involves progressive paralysis and loss of one's intellectual ability (Peterson, 1991). The almshouses, poor houses, and county homes which were erected in the 1820s in America for the destitute, designed to provide humane and moral care for the poor, became catchalls by the 1840s for the retarded, insane, and ill (Henley et al., 1993). State hospitals were built to house and treat the insane, but by the 1830s and 1840s the conditions were little better than the almshouses (Henley et al., 1993). Once again, facilities for mentally ill and mentally retarded became places of abuse, where patients were brutally treated, beaten, and chained.

Jean Etienne Esquirol, a fellow student of Itard under Pinel, reviewed a number of facilities in France serving mentally ill and mentally retarded and found patients naked or in rags, housed in dark and damp cells with no fresh air or light, chained and flogged, and without medical treatment (Scheerenberger, 1983). In 1845, Esquirol published *Mental Maladies: A Treatise on Insanity,* in which he differentiated between mental retardation (amentia) and mental illness (dementia) (Scheerenberger, 1983).

In America, **Dorothea Dix** (1802–1877) campaigned for and got better treatment for the insane in many states as well as federal aid (McKown, 1961). In 1846 she reported to the Massachusetts Legislature of the cruel and inhumane treatment in the state hospitals with nonexistent rehabilitation and education programs (Henley et al., 1993). She strongly advocated that mental hospitals serve mentally ill, epileptic, and mentally retarded persons.

Dorothea Dix was supported in her efforts by Horace Mann, Samuel Howe, and Charles Sumner with positive results that the Lunatic Hospital of Worcester, a reform school in Westborough, MA (first educational facility for socially maladjusted youth), and a residential program for mentally retarded were built (Henley et al., 1993; Scheerenberger, 1983; McKown, 1961). However, overcrowding doubled the clientele of the reform school, so within ten years it became a custodial rather than instructional facility. By 1870, a number of ungraded schools for mischievous and disruptive children were established throughout the United States (Henley et al., 1993). The progress in understanding mental illness and treatment during the 19th century was made mostly by medical doctors who proposed various paradigms to define, determine etiology, and treat the mentally ill.

Biomedical (Biological) Model

The influence of the Illness Period spawned the Biomedical or Biological Model of treatment of mental illness. Psychologists who adopt the Biomedical or Biological Model regard mental illness as having organic causes and may have a genetic predisposition (Peterson, 1991). This model views people as susceptible to injury, breakdown, or malfunction, and that tumors of the nervous system can produce abnormal thoughts, feelings, and actions. Therapy from the Biomedical Model involves physical interventions such as drugs or surgery (Peterson, 1991). The Biomedical Model, although much more sophisticated, continues to be a primary model of analyzing causation and treatment of emotional disturbance today.

Most of the 19th century reform leaders for better treatment for mentally ill were medical doctors, who approached the disease etiology, assessment, and treatment from a medical or illness perspective. These early professionals in the field of mental illness experienced only modest success in their treatment of mentally ill patients (Paul, 1987).

The Psychological Period 1900–1960s

Interpreting abnormality as a psychological phenomenon has dominated the twentieth century (Peterson, 1991). Scientific interest in the psychological treatment of children dates back to the work of Lightner Witmer, one of Wilhelm Wundt's students, who established the first psychological clinic in the United States at the University of Pennsylvania in 1896 to focus on research and therapy with mentally deficient children (Paul, 1987). Psychiatry and the mental hygiene movement as a whole began to examine the occurrence of mental illness among mentally retarded persons with hopes of both clarifying questions of etiology and identifying appropriate resources for treatment (Scheerenberger, 1983).

One of the major problems confronting institutions at the turn of the century and well into the future, involved the appropriate placement of the defective delinquent (Scheerenberger, 1983). Literally, all professionals agreed that defective delinquents should not be institutionalized with the feebleminded. However, prison authorities were equally adamant that the defective delinquent did not belong in the industrial school or penitentiary (Scheerenberger, 1983). The primary recommendation that special treatment facilities be established for both groups was rejected by legislatures due to costs, however, a compromise proposal of setting aside a building or an area within the institutions or reformatory intended to serve only defective delinquents was approved (Scheerenberger, 1983).

In 1908, Clifford Beers wrote *A Mind That Found Itself,* in which he described his recovery from a mental breakdown and the shoddy treatment he received in three institutions (Ysseldyke & Algozzine, 1990). Largely in response to Beers' book the National Committee for Mental Hygiene was formed in 1909, and began to advocate for the humane treatment of emotionally disturbed (mentally ill) individuals (Ysseldyke & Algozzine, 1990). By 1922, this concern and advocacy resulted in the establishment of child guidance clinics, presided by psychiatrists with the collaboration of psychologists and social workers (Kanner, 1964).

In 1943, Leo Kanner, director of the Children's Psychiatry Services at

Johns Hopkins Hospital, reported a new category of mental illness, infantile autism, which often simulated mental retardation (Scheerenberger, 1983). This discovery had a significant impact on the fields of psychiatry and mental retardation as it documented the fact that very young children and infants could become emotionally disturbed (Scheerenberger, 1983).

In 1965, the National Society for Autistic Children, the first major parent interest group devoted to concerns of the emotionally disturbed child, was founded. This organization has sought public school involvement for autistic children, and has opposed their placement in private or residential facilities.

Prior to the 1960s, the mental health system was the primary service provider for children with emotional disturbance, while the medical and/or psychodynamic models provided the primary treatment methods.

Psychodynamic Model

The psychodynamic approach to emotional disturbance is a system of therapy developed by Sigmund Freud that emphasized unconscious motives and conflicts to explain human behavior. A number of psychodynamic schools of thought grew out of Freud's developmental psychoanalytic theory of stages of psychosexual development (Paul, 1991). The common element in these psychodynamic theories is a belief in the existence of a dynamic intrapsychic life (Shea & Bauer, 1987). Children or youth behaving abnormally are believed to suffer unconscious conflicts and inner turmoil that is reflected in their behaviors (Whelan, 1988).

According to psychodynamic theories, impairment in emotional growth during one or more of the stages of ego development results in feelings of inadequacy, distrust of others, hostility or withdrawal in reaction to anxiety (Paul, 1991). Determining the etiology of behavior disorders from this perspective requires an intense examination of the inner turmoil and the defense mechanisms utilized by the disturbed youngsters (Peterson, 1991).

In the 1960s and 1970s, there was tension between the mental health system and the educational system regarding responsibility for identifying, diagnosing, treating, and educating behavior disordered students (Paul, 1987). When the public schools began to assume responsibility for teaching behavior disordered children and youth in the 1960s, there were difficulties translating psychoanalytic theories into educational practices in the classroom (Paul, 1991). A number of alternative paradigms or competing views of etiology and treatment of emotional disturbance in children became significant as psychologists and other professionals attempted to provide models appropriate for implementation in the public schools. The major alternative models included the following: the Behavioral Model, the Humanist Model, and the Ecological Model (Paul, 1991).

Behavioral Model

During the early 1900s, the school of thought known as behaviorism proposed that only overt behavior be the subject matter of psychology and that the inner workings of the mind be ignored (Wallace et al., 1987). By the 1960s, behavioral psychology emerged as a predominant perspective in treating behavior disordered individuals. Traditionally, the behavioral model has focused on B.F. Skinner's Operant Conditioning theories and the use of pleasant and unpleasant consequences to change behavior (Slavin, 1994). Behaviorists, in an effort to make psychology more scientific, focused only on behaviors that were observable and measurable. Behaviorists indicated that the same principles of learning applied to all living things, thus, the results of laboratory research using rats and monkeys could be generalized directly to children. Behaviorism views inappropriate behaviors as learned behavior that can be changed by the use of applied behavior analysis (Paul, 1991).

Current behavioral theories making an important impact in education include Bandura's social learning theory and Meichenbaum's cognitive behavior modification theory. These theorists accepted most of the behavioral principles and integrated the theories with other paradigms. Bandura emphasized the role of observation, modeling, and imitation in learning, while Meichenbaum blended behavioral and cognitive principles in cognitive behavior modification to focus on the use of metacognition in self-regulation (Slavin, 1994). Although behaviorism continues to play an important role in classroom management and behavior modification in the public schools, this approach generally is integrated with other paradigms today.

Humanist Model

The humanist education movement was a dominant force in American education in the 1960s and 1970s, and is making a substantial resurgence in the 1990s (Slavin, 1994). Humanistic theories emphasize the significance of the individual, his or her uniqueness, and the self-concept. Humanist psychologists consider the individual's interpretation of events as most important in the understanding of human behavior (Wallace et al., 1990).

Humanist psychology is a philosophical orientation toward human behavior that does not rely on the scientific method but on understanding the inner life of each person (Wallace et al., 1990). Humanism has led to the development of behavior change techniques that help people feel better about their own individuality and uniqueness and more willing to value their behavior, opinions, and self-worth (Wallace et al., 1990). Carl Rogers' Client-Centered Theory and Maslow's Humanistic Concept of Self-Actualization provided realistic and optimistic views as a basis for treatment, both theories are based on the idea that people potentially have the power to effect changes in themselves and their environment to overcome frustrations and anxieties and to reach their potential (Wallace et al., 1990; Slavin, 1994).

Ecological Model

According to the ecological perspective, the behavioral problems of the child are seen as a result of the reciprocal relationships between the learner and the contexts in which she/he is interacting (Shea & Bauer, 1994). The child is seen as an inseparable part of a small social system, of an ecological unit made up of the child, family, school, neighborhood, and community (Kirk et al., 1993). Thus, behavior problems are a result of destructive interactions between the child and the environment (Kirk et al., 1993).

During treatment, the child or youth is not the sole focus of treatment, but the family, school, neighborhood, and community are changed also in order to improve the interactions (Smith & Luckasson, 1995). Treatment consists of modifying elements in the ecology including the child (through counseling) to allow more constructive interactions between the child and the environment (Kirk et al., 1993). Ecological treatment may involve placing the child in a residential center for counseling, while counselors work with the family, the school, and the neighborhood to provide an environment more accepting of the child when she/he returns home.

The Educational Period 1960s to Present

Until the middle to late 1950s, most professional knowledge about and work with children who were behavior disordered centered in the child mental health field. Children and youth with severe behavior disorders were generally expelled from school and some were placed in residential psychiatric facilities (Paul, 1987). During the social reform movement of the 1960s, a number of factors were responsible for changes in the service delivery options of severely emotionally disturbed or behavior disordered children and youth and their families. Among the factors that provided impetus for reform of the treatment and education of youngsters with behavior disorders were an insufficient number of mental health personnel, dissatisfaction with psychotherapy as a treatment method, and the inability to use the psychodynamic methods in the public schools (Paul, 1987). In 1962, The Council for Children with Behavior Disorders (CCBD), a division of The Council for Exceptional Children, was founded to assist teachers and parents.

Educators and psychologists began to seek other methods of meeting the needs of children with behavior disorders that could be utilized in an educational setting. Hobbs (1978) and Hewett (1968) and others began to focus on systematic issues and the child's social adaptation at home, at school, and in the community rather than on the psychopathology of the mentally ill child (Henley et al., 1993). In the 1960s, Hobbs and colleagues at Peabody College experimented with Project Re-Education, and Hewett at UCLA experimented with the engineered classroom in the public schools in Santa Monica, CA (Henley et al., 1993). During the same period Norris Haring and E. Lakin Phillips combined William Cruickshank's structured environment classroom with Skinner's operant conditioning to develop educational programs for children with behavior disorders (Henley et al., 1993).

Legislation and Litigation

Many of the gains in the education and treatment of children with behavior disorders have been the direct result of legislation and litigation. The legislation and litigation since the 1960s with provisions for children and youth with mental retardation, frequently, also applied to those with behavior disorders. Major legislation that also applied to youngsters with behavior disorders included the Mental Health Centers Facilities and Construction Act (1963); the Elementary and Secondary

Education Act (1965); Handicapped Children's Early Education Program (1968); Vocational Rehabilitation Act and amendments (1973, 1986, 1992); Education for All Handicapped Children's Act (1975); Amendments to EHA including P.L. 98-199 (1983), P.L. 99-457 (1986), and IDEA (1990); and Americans with Disabilities Act (1990) (see Chapter 2).

Much of the litigation involving students with emotional disturbance or behavior disorders concerned the issue of expulsion for inappropriate behavior. In general, the courts today require schools to bear the burden of proof with significant documentation that inclusion in regular education is inappropriate for the student with behavior disorders, that the student with behavior disorders is a threat to the regular class students and teachers, and/or significantly interferes with the educational process, and the student is not benefitting from the regular education placement before authorizing alternative placements. The courts will not support expulsion, but will support placement in a more restrictive environment or short-term suspensions not to exceed 10 days or a cumulative of ten days.

Additional litigation not indicated in Chapter 2 that pertains specifically to children and youth with behavior disorders include the following:

1975	*Lora v. Board of Education of City of New York*
1978	*Stuart v. Nappi*
1979	*"A" Family*
1980	*Benskin v. Taft City School District*
1980	*Gary B. v. Cronin*
1980	*Hines v. Pitt County Board of Education*
1980	*Pratt v. Board of Education of Frederick County*
1980	*Miener v. Missouri*
1981	*Green v. Johnson*
1988	*Honig v. Doe*
1993	*Cornfield v. Consolidated High School District*
1993	*Johnson v. Westmoreland County School District*
1993	*Teague Independent School District v. Todd L.*
1993	*Donnell C. v. Illinois State Board of Education*
1994	*MR v. Lincolnwood Board of Education*
1994	*Ryan K. v. Puyallup School District*

Lora v. Board of Education of City of New York (1975). In this case the courts ruled that children with emotional disturbance must be educated with nonhandicapped children and may not be segregated by race or sex from other children. The court adopted the "mainstreaming principle" (Haring et al., 1994).

Stuart v. Nappi (1978). The court ruled that a school may not expel a disabled child, only change the placement, pursuant to parent notice and IEP conference provisions of P.L. 94-142, if the child's disability is causally related to the behavior for which the school seeks to expel him (Turnbull, 1993).

"A" Family (1979). The court ruled that out-of-state placement in a private residential facility for children with serious emotional disturbance, at which the child will receive psychotherapy, is placement in the "least restrictive alternative" for the child and the tuition and the therapy must be paid by a local school district under P.L. 94-142's provision for "related services" (Turnbull & Turnbull, 1982).

Benskin v. Taft City School District (1980). Parents of children with hyperactivity alleged that the school district pressured them to give Ritalin to their children for behavior control and challenged this practice. The court ruled that the school is precluded from diagnosing hyperactivity or recommending that a child take behavior modification drugs (Turnbull & Turnbull, 1982).

Gary B. v. Cronin (1980). The plaintiff's children with emotional disturbance who alleged that state rule excludes counseling and therapeutic services from special education services. The court issued a preliminary injunction preventing (1) implementation of the rule to deny money from counseling therapy, etc., (2) failure to pay plaintiff for costs of therapy, counseling, etc.; and (3) denial of a free appropriate education to the plaintiffs (Turnbull & Turnbull, 1982).

Hines v. Pitt County Board of Education (1980). The federal court ordered the state to provide a ten-year-old boy with emotional disturbance with residential placement other than the one recommended by county and state officials (Turnbull & Turnbull, 1982).

Pratt v. Board of Education of Frederick County (1980). The court holds that a district policy on IEPs may not prevent youth with emotional disturbance from having an IEP that calls for individualized discipline; the requirement of individualized education prevails over board policy (Turnbull & Turnbull, 1982).

Miener v. Missouri (1980). A federal court in Missouri dismissed the portion of a lawsuit filed by a 17-year-old resident of a state mental hospital that sought compensatory education under P.L. 94-142 and Section 504. The court viewed the compensation as damages, which are barred by the eleventh amendment (Turnbull & Turnbull, 1982).

Green v. Johnson (1981). The court ruled that inmates in prison who are not yet 22 years old have a right to special education under P.L. 94-142 (Turnbull & Turnbull, 1982).

Honig v. Doe (1988). The Supreme Court ruled that the expulsion of dangerous students for more than ten days, when the dangerous behavior is a result of the disability, violates the "stay put" provision and is a "change of placement" (Haring et al., 1994). However, the school may use temporary suspension of up to 10 days if the student poses an immediate threat to the safety of others (Turnbull, 1993). For a change to a more restrictive placement the school district must reconvene the IEP committee, notify parents, reevaluate the child, and prepare a new IEP (Turnbull, 1993).

Cornfield v. Consolidated High School District (1993). When a teacher and school administrator have reasonable cause to believe that a special education student is concealing drugs in his clothing, they may require him to undergo a private strip search and search of his clothing by same-sex adults without violating his constitutional rights to privacy (Turnbull, 1993).

Johnson v. Westmoreland County School Board (1993). When a student's disruptive and violent behavior persists in a day school and in homebound placements, even after the LEA has made efforts to support the student in those placements, the LEA may place the student in a residential program (Turnbull, 1993).

Teague Independent School District v. Todd L. (1993). The 5th Circuit Court ruled that a student with severe emotional and behavioral disabilities should be placed in an LEA's program, not a psychiatric facility, where that placement will yield an academic benefit for the student and the student will have the opportunity to associate with nondisabled peers and participate more fully in the community (Turnbull, 1993).

Donnell C. v. Illinois State Board of Education (1993). Students who qualify for special education or who already have been placed in special education retain their IDEA rights even though they have been adjudicated as juvenile offenders and placed in a state's juvenile correction or criminal justice system (Turnbull, 1993).

M.R. v. Lincolnwood Board of Education (1994). The school district attempted to mainstream a child with emotional disturbance, but the student's behavior became increasingly more disruptive. The court upheld a segregated placement after determining that the attempt at mainstreaming was unsuccessful and that evidence indicated the student was not benefitting from interaction with his peers without disabilities (Osborne & Dimattia, 1994).

Ryan K. v. Puyallup School District (1994). In the case of a 15-year-old boy diagnosed ADHD and Tourette's Syndrome whose behavior problems escalated dramatically to verbally and physically violent aggressive behavior toward peers and teachers, the 9th Circuit Court of Appeals supported the School District's placement in a self-contained classroom (Zirkel, 1995). The court rejected the parents' argument that Ryan's placement in regular classes at the Junior High School with specialized interventions of the resource teacher was the least restrictive environment if the school would also provide him a personal classroom aide. The court indicated that since Ryan's achievement scores had declined during the period of violent behavior, he was no longer receiving academic benefit from regular class placement. The court indicated that Ryan's behavior had become dangerous to other students and teachers and disruptive to the teaching/learning process. The lesson of this case is that "full inclusion" has its limits and that the regular classroom is not always the least restrictive environment for a student (Zirkel, 1995).

DEFINITIONS OF BEHAVIOR DISORDERS

Currently, there is no definition of behavior disorders that is generally agreed on (Heward, 1996). "Lack of a reliable and widely accepted definition has caused difficulties in identifying and estimating the prevalence of children with behavior disorders" (Paul, 1987, 15). The factors that make it particularly difficult to arrive at a good definition of emotional and behavioral disorders include the lack of precise definitions of mental health and normal behavior, differences among the psychological models, difficulties in measuring emotions and behavior, differences in the professions and professionals who categorize and serve children and youth with emotional and behavior disorders (Hallahan & Kauffman, 1994). There is general agreement among professionals that behavior disorders refers to behavior that is significantly or extremely different from usual, the problem is a long standing chronic condition, and the behavior is unacceptable because of social or cultural expectations (Hallahan & Kauffman, 1994).

Theoretical Perspectives' Definitions

Historically, emotional and/or behavior disorders have been defined according to theoretical perspectives or models of behavior disorders (See Chapter 6). The *Biological Model* viewed emotional or behavioral disorders from a medical perspective as resulting from a physical disease, disorder, or dysfunction which could be biogenic or psychogenic in origin (Whelan, 1988). The *Psychodynamic Model* proposed that severe emotional disturbance resulted because the child in conflict had not successfully negotiated the various intrapsychic and external conflicts faced in the process of psychological and physiological maturation (Reinert, 1980). The *Behavioral Model* indicates that severe behavior disorders are inappropriate or abnormal learned behavior that is a result of the child's interactions with his/her environment (Slavin, 1994). The *Humanist Model* views emotional disturbance as inappropriate behavior due to unhappiness and self-defeating behaviors which are due to blocked self-actualization and low self-regard (Shea & Bauer, 1987). The *Ecological Model* views behavior disorders as inappropriate reciprocal relationships between the child and the family, school, neighborhood, community; the child is not considered disturbed (Paul, 1987).

Federal Definitions of Behavior Disorders

The Education for All Handicapped Children Act (P.L. 94-142) definition used the term *seriously emotionally disturbed* as follows:

(i) The term means a condition exhibiting one or more of the following characteristics over a period of time and to a marked degree, which adversely affects educational performance.
　(a) An inability to learn which cannot be explained by intellectual, sensory, and health factors;
　(b) An inability to build or maintain satisfactory relationships with peers and teachers;
　(c) Inappropriate types of behavior or feelings under normal circumstances;
　(d) A general pervasive mood of unhappiness or depression; or
　(e) A tendency to develop physical symptoms or fears associated with personal or school problems.
(ii) The term includes children who are schizophrenic or autistic. The term does not include children who are socially maladjusted unless it is determined that they are seriously emotionally disturbed (Federal Register, 42, (163), August 23, 1977, 42478).

Children classified as autistic were excluded from the federal definition of seriously emotionally disturbed in the 1981 regulations and reclassified as other health impaired (Shea & Bauer, 1994). In 1990, through P.L. 101-476 (Individuals with Disabilities Education Act) known as IDEA, learners with autism were again reclassified, and a separate category of disability was delineated (Shea & Bauer, 1994). Essentially, the P.L. 94-142 definition of seriously emotionally disturbed was maintained in IDEA with the exception of elimination of autism from the category.

Proposed Definitions

In 1985, The Council for Children with Behavior Disorders (CCBD) recommended that the term "seriously emotionally disturbed" be replaced with the term "behaviorally disordered" (Shea & Bauer, 1994). In 1987, CCBD recommended that the federal definition should be revised with a functional educational definition, to include socially maladjusted children and youth, and focus on the sources of data collection necessary to determine if a student is behaviorally disturbed (Shea & Bauer, 1994).

The National Mental Health and Special Education Coalition in 1990 proposed a definitional change and worked to have the following proposed definition and terminology adopted in federal laws and regulations (Forness & Knitzer, 1990, 13):

(i) The term emotional or behavioral disorder means a disability characterized by behavioral or emotional responses in school so different from appropriate age, cultural, or ethnic norms that they adversely affect educational performance. Educational performance includes academic, social, vocational, and personal skills. Such a disability

   (A) is more than a temporary, expected response to stressful events in the environment;

   (B) is consistently exhibited in two different settings, at least one of which is school-related; and

   (C) is unresponsive to direct intervention in general education, or the child's condition is such that general education interventions would be insufficient.

(ii) Emotional and behavioral disorders can co-exist with other disabilities.

(iii) This category may include children or youths with schizophrenic disorders, affective disorders, anxiety disorder, or other sustained disorders of conduct or adjustment when they adversely affect educational performance in accordance with section (i).

CLASSIFICATION SYSTEMS OF BEHAVIOR DISORDERS

Numerous different classification systems of severely emotionally disturbed or behavior disordered have been proposed to provide more specificity in diagnosis, placement, treatment, and educational programming. "The problem of appropriate classification of childhood disorders has been an ongoing one in psychology, psychiatry, and special education" (Rizzo & Zabel, 1988, 7). The classification systems of behavior disorders include the psychiatric system or DSM–IV, Quay Classifications, Hewett's Levels of Learning Competence, and several classifications of Degree of Severity.

Psychiatric (DSM–IV) Classification System

The most widely used classification system for learners identified as behaviorally disordered is the *Diagnostic and Statistical Manual of Mental Disorders* (4th Edition) (American Psychiatric Association, 1994). This manual is used by psychiatrists and psychologists who treat children with behavioral disorders and emotional disturbance (Smith & Luckasson, 1995). The category for infants, children, and adolescents describes ten major groups of disorders, the following eight groups may relate to behavior disorders:

    I. MOTOR SKILL DISORDER
        Developmental Coordination Disorder
   II. COMMUNICATION DISORDERS
        Expressive Language Disorder
        Mixed Receptive-Expressive Language Disorder
        Phonological Disorder
        Stuttering
        Communication Disorder Not Otherwise Specified
  III. PERVASIVE DEVELOPMENTAL DISORDERS
        Autistic Disorder
        Rhett's Disorder
        Childhood Disintegrative Disorder
        Asperger's Disorder
        Pervasive Developmental Disorder Not Otherwise Specified
  IV. ATTENTION–DEFICIT AND DISRUPTIVE BEHAVIOR
      DISORDERS
        Attention-Deficit/Hyperactivity Disorder
           Combined Type
           Predominantly Inattentive Type

Predominantly Hyperactive-Impulsive Type
Attention-Deficit/Hyperactivity Disorder Not Otherwise Specified
Conduct Disorder
Oppositional-Defiant Disorder
Disruptive Behavior Disorder Not Otherwise Specified
VII. FEEDING AND EATING DISORDERS OF INFANCY OR EARLY
CHILDHOOD
Pica
Rumination Disorder
Feeding Disorder of Infancy or Early Childhood
VIII. TIC DISORDERS
Tourette's Disorder
Chronic Motor or Vocal Tic Disorder
Transient Tic Disorder
Tic Disorder Not Otherwise Specified
IX. ELIMINATION DISORDERS
Encopresis
With Constipation and Overflow Incontinence
Without Constipation and Overflow Incontinence
Enuresis (Not Due to a General Medical Condition)
X. OTHER DISORDERS OF INFANCY, CHILDHOOD OR
ADOLESCENCE
Separation Anxiety Disorder
Selective Mutism
Reactive Attachment Disorder of Infancy or Early Childhood
Stereotypic Movement Disorder
Disorder of Infancy, Childhood, or Adolescence Not Otherwise
Specified (APA, 1994, 10–12)

Quay's Classifications

Quay (1986) evaluated large numbers of children and determined that there were four patterns of deviant behavior in children: conduct disorder, anxiety-withdrawal, immaturity, and socialized aggression.

Children who have *conduct disorders* defy authority; are hostile toward authority figures (police officers, teachers, parents); are cruel, malicious, and assaultive; and have few guilt feelings (Quay, 1986). Children who have conduct disorders are disruptive, get into fights, are bossy, and have temper tantrums (Heward, 1996). They are easily distracted, unable to persist at tasks, and often disrupt class, and are a serious problem in school settings (Kirk et al., 1993).

The *anxiety-withdrawal* classification or personality disorder includes children who are shy, timid, seclusive, sensitive, submissive, overdependent, and easily depressed (Quay, 1986). Additionally, these children are identified by social withdrawal, anxiety, feelings of inferiority, guilt, and unhappiness (Heward, 1996). Quay and Werry (1986) indicate that many of these children come from overprotective families in higher socioeconomic levels. Children who are anxious or withdrawn are more often a bigger threat to themselves than to others around them because they usually are not disruptive, they generally do not cause classroom management problems (Kirk et al., 1993). Children who are withdrawn often have limited or ineffectual social relationships (Kirk et al., 1993).

The *immaturity* classification refers to children who are inattentive, sluggish, uninterested in school, lazy, preoccupied, and reticent (Quay, 1986). Additionally, they are characterized by extreme passivity, daydreaming, and clumsiness, and show a preference for younger playmates (Heward, 1996).

Children in the *socialized-aggression* classification share some characteristics with children with conduct disorders (hostility, aggression, few guilt feelings), but are socialized within their peer group, usually a gang (Quay, 1986). Socialized aggression is marked by truancy, theft, and a feeling of pride in belonging to a delinquent subculture (Heward, 1996).

Later, Quay and Peterson (1987) described six dimensions in a classification system rather than four including the following:

- *Conduct disorder:* seeks attention, shows off, is disruptive, annoys others, fights, has temper tantrums
- *Socialized aggression:* steals in company with others, is loyal to delinquent friends, is truant from school with others, has "bad" companions, freely admits disrespect for moral values and laws
- *Attention problems-immaturity:* has short attention span, has poor concentration, is distractible, is easily diverted from task at hand, answers without thinking, is sluggish, is slow-moving, is lethargic
- *Anxiety-withdrawal:* is self-conscious, is easily embarrassed, is hypersensitive, feelings are easily hurt, is generally fearful, is anxious, is depressed, is always sad
- *Psychotic behavior:* expresses far-fetched ideas, has repetitive speech, shows bizarre behavior
- *Motor excess:* is restless, is unable to sit still, is tense, is unable to relax, is overtalkative (Cited in Hallahan & Kauffman, 1994, 211).

Hewett's Levels of Learning Competence

Hewett's (1980) classification system describes six levels of learning competence: (1) Attention: Making contact with the environment, (2) Response: Active motor and verbal participation, (3) Order: Following instructions and routines, (4) Exploratory: Investigating the environment, (5) Social: Interactions with others, and (6) Mastery: Skills related to self-care, academics and vocational interests. The classification scheme views behavior problems along a continuum of too little to too much in respect to the six levels of learning competence (Hewett & Taylor, 1980). For example, in the areas of response the continuum includes the following: too little response: immobilization; less severe too little response: sluggishness, passivity, clumsiness, depression; optimal response; less severe too much response: hyperactivity, restlessness; and too much response: self-stimulation (Hewett & Taylor, 1980). This system classifies behaviors rather than children, and provides links to appropriate curriculum (Hewett and Taylor, 1980).

Degree of Severity

Mild-Moderate/Severe-Profound Disorders

Classifying behavior disorders according to severity generally utilizes two levels of degrees such as mild-moderate and severe-profound in the areas of environmental conflict or personal disturbance (Haring et al., 1994). Environmental conflict includes aggressive-disruptive, hyperactive, and social maladjustment behaviors, while personal disturbance includes anxiety and inferiority, social incompetence, and learning disorders (Haring et al., 1994).

Youngsters experiencing environmental conflict display negativism, destructiveness, and aggression. Those with mild-moderate behavior disorders display these behaviors of aggression (verbal and physical) toward peers and adults, while youngsters with severe-profound behavior disorders engage in self-injury and destructiveness (Haring et al., 1994). Youth with mild-moderate behavior disorders reveal hyperactivity in attention deficits, impulsivity, and over-activity accompanied by aggression toward others, while youth with severe-profound behavior disorders engage in repetitive, bizarre motor and verbal acts and engage in self-stimulation (Haring et al., 1994). Mild-moderate socially maladjusted children and youth engage in group oriented stealing, fighting, substance and sex abuse, and truancy, while severe profound behavior disordered are indifferent to peers and classmates revealing an extreme lack of social interaction (Haring et al., 1994).

Children and youth experiencing personal disturbance in anxiety-inferiority at the mild-moderate level demonstrate low self-confidence, situation specific avoidance, crying, worry and skill disorganization, while severe-profound cases become extremely upset over even very minor changes in familiar routines (Haring et al., 1994). Mild-moderate cases of social incompetence fail to initiate verbal or motor behavior towards peers and are often rejected by peers due to verbal and physical aggression, however, youth experiencing severe profound behavior disorders appear indifferent toward interpersonal activity even with parents and siblings (Haring et al., 1994).

Students with mild-moderate behavior disorders experience learning disorders due to low normal intellectual functioning and reveal substantial deficits in basic academic skills and general educational attainment, while students with severe-profound behavior disorders often function intellectually at moderate to profound mental retardation levels, and experience significant difficulties in language acquisition and self-help skills (Haring et al., 1994).

Most children and youth with behavior disorders in the mild or moderate ranges can be treated in the public schools in regular classrooms, resource rooms, and/or self-contained classrooms with appropriately trained teachers. Children who are severely disturbed (e.g., psychotic, schizophrenic, pervasive developmental disorders) usually require intensive, specially designed programming in residential treatment centers or hospitals.

Externalizing and Internalizing Disorders

Externalizing and Internalizing Disorders is a classification system similar to mild-moderate behavior disorders (externalizing disorders) and severe-profound behavior disorders (internalizing disorders). Externalizing behaviors, especially aggressive behaviors seem to be directed toward others, while internalizing behavior is withdrawn into the individual (Smith & Luckasson, 1995). Externalizing behaviors of hitting other children, cursing at the teacher, hyperactivity, stealing and arson are usually identified more quickly in schools than internalizing behaviors of depression, withdrawal, fears and phobias, anorexia and bulimia, and/or elective mutism (Smith & Luckasson, 1995).

Newcomer's Degrees of Disturbance

Newcomer (1993) has proposed a system of determining the degree of behavioral disturbance over three levels: mild, moderate, severe. He utilized nine criteria for determining the degree of disturbance: precipitating events, destructiveness, maturational appropriateness, personal functioning, social functioning, reality index, insight index, conscious control, and social responsiveness. Each element of behavioral criteria has classification descriptors for mild, moderate, and severe behavior.

SUMMARY

Prior to the late 1700s, the causes of emotional disturbances were attributed to beliefs in magic or possession by a spirit. Insane people were tortured to drive out demons and/or burned at the stake. During most of the 18th century in Europe, the mentally-ill were beaten and chained, and kept in small cells with no light. In the late 18th century, Philippe Pinel' emphasized moral management and treatment at mental hospitals. He became famous for releasing his patients from their chains and providing a humane living environment. Benjamin Rush, using a mixture of tradition and enlightenment, implemented more humane treatment of the mentally ill in America. Rush wrote the first book on mental illness in America.

The Illness Period spawned the Biomedical Model of treatment of mental illness in which abnormality was attributed to injury or disease. During the Psychological Period (1900–1960s) many improvements were made in the treatment of the mentally ill. Clifford Beers' book served as an impetus for humane treatment of the mentally ill. Child guidance clinics were established by the mental health system to serve children and adults. In 1943, Leo Kanner described a condition which he called "infantile autism," a new category of mental illness which mimicked mental retardation. During this period the primary treatment method was the psychodynamic or psychoanalytic approach developed by Freud that emphasized unconscious motives and conflicts to explain human behavior.

In the 1960s and 1970s tension between the mental health system and the educational system regarding identification, diagnosis, and treatment resulted in the development of a number of alternative paradigms—the Behavioral Model, the Humanist Model, and the Ecological Model.

The behaviorists were concerned only with overt behavior. The humanists emphasized the uniqueness of the individual and the self-concept. The ecological perspective considered the child interacting in all of his environments.

The Educational Period (1960s to Present) was concerned with the child with emotional disturbance or behavior disorders in various educational settings. Litigation and legislation resulted in free appropriate public education in the least restrictive environment for behavior disordered children and youth. Behavior disorders was defined and classified from a number of different paradigms.

Chapter 6

THEORETICAL PERSPECTIVES
OF BEHAVIOR DISORDERS

Different theoretical perspectives have different ideological histories and sometimes different views about the nature of scientific inquiry as it applies to the study of human problems (Paul, 1987, 32).

Biological Model of Behavior Disorders
Psychodynamic Model of Behavior Disorders
Behavioral Model of Behavior Disorders
Humanist Model of Behavior Disorders
Ecological Model of Behavior Disorders
Summary

The major psychological perspectives that provide definitions, etiology, treatment, and education of mildly behavior disordered individuals include biological, psychodynamic, behavioral, humanistic, and ecological models (Hallahan & Kauffman, 1994).

BIOLOGICAL MODEL OF BEHAVIOR DISORDERS

The biological model of behavior disorders, also known as biophysical and/or medical model, views emotional disorders as resulting from a physical disease, disorder, or dysfunction (Smith et al., 1987). The biological model is one of the oldest theoretical systems being applied to children in conflict (Reinert, 1980).

Biological Model: Etiology

The etiology of behavior disorders involves the interaction of multiple contributing factors. "It is extremely unusual to find a single cause that has led directly to disturbed behavior" (Hallahan & Kauffman, 1988, 171). The basic theory being espoused in the biological model suggests that a relationship between emotional development and biological growth exists in children (Reinert, 1980). Whelan (1988) indicates the causes of emotional disturbance may be divided into two major categories—biogenic and psychogenic. Biogenic factors focus on four primary etiologies: genetic inheritance, biochemical abnormalities, neurological abnormalities, and/or injury to the central nervous system resulting in the diminished capacity of an individual to cope with environmental demands (Whelan, 1988). Psychogenic factors (psychodynamic model) describe internal conflicts raging within a child and the relationship of these conflicts to external environmental events over time (Whelan, 1988).

Genetic Inheritance

Genetic theories emphasize the role of hereditary endowment on behavior patterns. Congenital theory assumes that a basic defect of genetic structure exists or that damage to the developing central nervous system occurred during gestation (e.g., infections, toxins, and anoxia) (Evans, 1991). Congenital theory implies that the individual at birth possesses an irreversible neurological defect that may have mild to severe consequences upon learning and educational development (Evans, 1991).

Biochemical Abnormalities

The underlying premise is that imbalances in the biochemical system are the source of the problem behavior (Henley et al., 1993). Numerous causes of biochemical abnormalities proposed include an overactive thyroid, poor nutrition, injury, stress that affects diet or sleep patterns, faulty endocrine system, and/or severe allergies (Reinert, 1980). Some evidence exists that suggests that childhood ADD is characterized by an irregular neurotransmitter system (Evans, 1991). For example, in the most severe form of attention deficit disorder (ADD), a child cannot attend in any given situation for a period exceeding several seconds and usually displays associated severe behavior problems (Evans, 1991). Drugs are prescribed to bring abnormal body chemicals into proper balance to change behavior (Henley et al., 1993).

Neurological Impairment

Neurological impairment may be the result of neurological abnormality (i.e., tumors, strokes, sensory-neurological impairment) and/or neurological injury (i.e., traumatic brain injury, minimal brain dysfunction, minor head injury) (Evans, 1991). The majority of brain injuries to young people are the result of accidents (i.e., falls, automobile accidents, sports-related injuries) and child abuse (National Head Injury Foundation, 1986).

Moderate to severe head injuries in children/youth can lead to cognitive and information processing problems in perception, memory, attention, concept learning, and sensorimotor skills (Evans, 1991; Morrison, 1987). Minimal brain damage has been proposed as an explanation for hyperactivity, impulsivity, and emotional instability (Smith et al., 1987). "As with the learning disabled child, head-injured children can exhibit significant and continuing impairment of their learning skills, while at the same time obtaining IQs that fall within normal range, particularly during the first year after the trauma" (Evans, 1991, 108). These children often experience sensory hyperactivity, motor hyperactivity, dissociation (inability to distinguish the whole, Gestalt, relative to the parts) figure-ground reversals, perseveration, and motor immaturity (Shea and Bauer, 1987).

Biological Model: Assessment

Biological assessment focuses on identifying physical abnormalities (i.e., biochemical, neurological, genetic) that adversely affect the child's physical and emotional health. A biological assessment of emotional disorders is conducted by a team of medical specialists including pediatricians, pediatric neurologists, nutritionists, allergists, ophthalmologists and audiologists (Smith et al., 1987). The assessment generally occurs in a hospital or doctor's office and includes a complete physical examination with laboratory studies (i.e., blood tests, urinalysis, glucose tolerance test), vision and hearing tests, a CAT scan, and an EEG (Smith et al., 1987).

The role of the classroom teacher in a biological assessment is limited because of its medical nature. The teacher, however, can provide valuable information by serving as a screening agent identifying symptoms and behavior patterns noted in the classroom. Systematic observations and anecdotal records can provide information regarding the events preceding and following a behavior crisis situation, and the frequency and duration of inappropriate behaviors. Once diagnosed and placed on medication, the classroom teacher can provide valuable information regarding the effectiveness of the medication in producing the desired behavior changes.

Biological Model: Treatment

Medical Treatment

Since the biological model assumes that emotional disturbance results from physical disease, disorder, or dysfunction, the treatment involves altering the presumed internal pathology (Smith et al., 1987). Medical specialists involved in the diagnosis manage the medical interventions.

Treatment for children and youth with biochemical abnormalities considered to be the cause of their behavior problems is taking stimulant medications such as ritalin, dexedrine, and cylert. The therapeutic effect of stimulant medications includes (1) increased goal directedness and attention; (2) decreased impulsivity, disruptions, and negative behavior; (3) improved performance, cognition, and perception; (4) improved motor coordination; (5) improved cooperation and positive behavior (Shea & Bauer, 1987).

Medications are often used in treating cognitive and behavior disorders in children and youth with neurological impairment including psychostimulant compounds (i.e., ritalin, dexedrine, cylert) to improve memory and attention problems and anticonvulsants (i.e., dilantin, phenobarbital) for treating seizure disorders (Evans, 1991). Tranquilizers are prescribed for behavior control (i.e., aggression, assault, self-injury) (Evans, 1991). Psychotropic medications, antianxiety and antipsychotic drugs (i.e., mellaril, thorazine, librium) are administered to increase calmness, and improve behavior and social functioning (Shea & Bauer, 1987). Stabilizer or antidepressant medications (i.e., tofranil, elavil) are administered to elevate mood and reduce depression (Evans, 1991). Medical treatments affiliated with the biological model include allergy control with antihistamines; diet modification to control hyperactive behaviors and the negative factors associated with hypoglycemia (i.e., lethargic and withdrawn or hyperactive and inattentive behaviors) (Shea & Bauer, 1987).

Educational Intervention

A major role of educators within the biological model is to assist in carrying out the medical intervention plan by monitoring medications and assisting the child in diet modifications (Smith et al., 1987). The primary biophysical teaching model involves traditional environmental control (Cruickshank, 1967). The environmental control perspective can be traced to the beginning of modern special education and the techniques of Itard and Seguin. During the 1940s, Strauss and Lehtinen studied brain-injured children who were characterized by hyperactivity, impulsivity, emotional liability, short attention span, and distractibility (Shea & Bauer, 1987). They designed a controlled environment for classroom instruction that focused on the following: (1) Reducing extraneous sights and sounds; (2) Sparsely furnished, spacious classrooms without pictures and bulletin boards; (3) Desks facing the wall with partitions between them; (4) Masked printed matter so that the child could view only the needed portion; (5) Directing motor activity into productive channels; (6) Logical sequencing of learning tasks (Shea & Bauer, 1987; Lovitt, 1989). Cruickshank, Haring, and associates utilized the theories of Strauss and Lehtinen successfully with students of normal or near normal abilities in a public classroom by controlling the educational environment, teaching a highly structured curriculum, and increasing the stimulus value of the teaching materials (Lovitt, 1989).

PSYCHODYNAMIC MODEL OF BEHAVIOR DISORDERS

The psychodynamic model of behavior disorders, also known as psychoanalytical or intrapsychic perspective proposes that the child in conflict has not successfully negotiated the various intrapsychic and external conflicts faced in the process of psychological and physiological maturation (Reinert, 1980). During the 1960s, the psychodynamic perspective dominated educational programs for children and youth with behavior disorders (Shea & Bauer, 1987).

Psychodynamic Model: Etiology

The psychodynamic perspective involves a diversified group of theories which have a common belief in the existence of a dynamic intrapsychic life: Freudian psychoanalysis, Adlerian therapy, Jungian analysis, Rogerian client-centered theory, Ellis' rational emotive system, Glasser's reality therapy, and Erikson's psychosocial theory (Fine, 1973). Understanding the etiology of behavior disorders from this perspective requires an intense examination of the inner turmoil reflected by observable behaviors (Whelan, 1988).

Most psychodynamic schools of thought grew out of psychoanalytic theory and the work of Freud (Neisworth & Bagnato, 1987). Psychoanalysis is an approach to psychology that emphasizes unconscious motives and conflicts (Wade & Travis, 1990). Freud emphasized the evolution of personality through stages of psychosexual development (i.e., oral, anal, phallic, latency) and emphasized the importance of basic biological drives in infancy and childhood development (Rizzo & Zabel, 1988). Behavior was considered to be prompted by needs or motives associated with the person's psychosexual history, and these motives were largely outside one's conscious awareness (Paul, 1987).

According to analytical psychology, the personality of the child is made up of three major systems: the id, ego, and superego. The id, the only system present at birth, aims to avoid pain and achieve pleasure; the ego is the mediating system between the demands of the id and the constraints of the child's life; and, the superego or conscience represents the norms and values of society that are taught to the child by his or her parents (Reinert, 1980). In the mentally healthy child, these three systems work in relative harmony with one another, however, in emotional disturbance there are conflicts between the id, ego, and superego (Neisworth & Bagnato, 1987). A child motivated by the id strives to maximize self gain through aggressive, acting out behaviors, and noncompliance that show little regard for others in the environment (Neisworth & Bagnato, 1987). A child with an overdeveloped superego may be so concerned about societal reactions toward their behavior and their attempt to comply with others' expectations that they withdraw socially (Neisworth & Bagnato, 1987).

More recent proponents have minimized the role of sexual instincts and have become more concerned with interactions between internal personality dynamics and interpersonal relationships (Neisworth & Bagnato, 1987). Erikson emphasized the importance of significant others in the child's environment, thus, diminishing the relative importance of sexual conflicts in the early years of life (Reinert, 1980). Where Freud focused on the importance of internal drives, Erikson emphasized the vital roles of parents, cultural values, and social institutions as influences on development (Rizzo & Zabel, 1988). Erikson indicated that failure to emerge successfully from psychosocial stage crises is associated with emotional disturbance (Reinert, 1980).

Therefore, from a psychodynamic point of view, the child in conflict has not successfully negotiated the various intrapsychic and external conflicts faced in the process of psychological and physiological maturation (Reinert, 1980). "The 'seed' of mental illness might be rejection, hostile criticism, frustration of basic needs, humiliation, neglect, aggression, battering, or abandonment" (Reinert, 1980, 40).

Psychodynamic Model: Assessment

According to the psychodynamic perspective, understanding the etiology of the behavior disturbance requires an intense examination of the inner turmoil reflected by the observable behaviors (Whelan, 1988). The purpose of a psychodynamic assessment is to identify behavior patterns that describe a child's developmental inadequacies, defense mechanisms, inadequate impulse control, inappropriate social behaviors, self-esteem, motivation to learn, and independence (Neisworth & Bagnato, 1987).

The psychodynamic evaluation team is composed of a psychologist, a sociologist, a neurologist, and an educator (Neisworth & Bagnato, 1987). Data are obtained from school records, medical examinations, psychological tests, and interviews with the parents and child. Also, utilized in psychodynamic evaluations are projective techniques based on the assumption that when given a neutral stimulus, the individual will project his/her unique feelings and perceptions (Epanchin, 1987). Examples of projective techniques utilized in psychodynamic assessment include the following: (1) Rorschach test which attempts to predict from the subject's associations to inkblots how she/he will react to others in the environment (Reinert, 1980); (2) Projective drawings which are designed to encourage the individual to project their unique feelings and perceptions within their artwork (Epanchin, 1987); (3) *The Roberts Apperception Test for Children* (1982) composed of pictures to evoke fantasies regarding various problems or experiences of childhood (Reinert, 1980); (4) *Bower-Lambert scales* (1971) are a semiprojective technique which includes the teacher's perception of the child, the child's self-perception, and perceptions of the child by peers (Reinert, 1980). Projective techniques generally have poor reliability and validity, yet often are the only instruments available from a psychodynamic perspective (Epanchin, 1987).

Psychodynamic Model: Treatment

Psychoanalysis

Traditional psychoanalysis used free association "on the couch" to say whatever comes to the client's mind and transference to transfer emotional responses toward the parents to the therapist and over many years work through their emotional problems (Wade & Travis, 1990). Brief psychodynamic therapy is a time limited program of 20 to 25 sessions in which the therapist focuses on the client's self-defeating habits and repetitive problems to change these chronic patterns (Wade & Travis, 1990).

Psychoeducational Interventions

Educators, attempting to apply psychodynamic theories to educational processes for behavior disordered youth developed psychoeducational methods of classroom instruction which includes emphasis on (1) Developing a mentally healthy atmosphere and environment with consistent expectations and consequences, (2) Accepting the child or youth and the pathological condition without reservation, and (3) Providing educational experiences that are developmentally appropriate (Shea & Bauer, 1987).

Milieu Therapy. The development of a total environment with consistent expectations and consequences for students with emotional disturbance and behavior disorders is called milieu therapy and usually occurs in an institutional or hospital setting (Reinert, 1980). Milieu therapy is similar to behavioral manipulation of the environment but without specific behavioral activities such as counting and recording behaviors (Reinert, 1980). The children most frequently receiving total milieu therapy are the schizophrenic and autistic; seriously hyperactive and delinquent; and some organic cases such as severe epileptics, and birth brain-damaged cases (Long, Morse, & Newman, 1965). In cases where the physiological aspects of the children are severely disturbed, the children receive pharmacological or physiological treatment as part of their total milieu therapy along with psychological treatment (Long et al., 1965).

Clinical Teaching. Two teaching models based in psychodynamic theory include the clinical teaching model and the self-concept model which developed into the humanist theoretical model. Clinical teaching procedures are concerned with three major variables: (1) an emotionally disturbed individual, (2) a clinical teacher, and (3) a special education treatment milieu (Shea & Bauer, 1987). Assuming the role of clinical teacher or educational therapist, the teacher accepts, tolerates, and interprets the child's behavior (Walker & Shea, 1984). The primary objective is not the teaching of academic skills, but the resolution of emotional conflicts. The behavior of the child with behavior disturbance must be controlled and limited, thus, she/he is not allowed to engage in behaviors that are self-defeating, self-injurious or harmful to classmates or teacher (Shea & Bauer, 1987). Punishment, if used, is benign and a natural consequence of the child's rule violation (Shea & Bauer, 1987).

Reading, writing, and arithmetic are the core of the child's academic program and as she/he gains skill in these basic subjects others such as science and social studies are added (Shea & Bauer, 1987). The creative arts are strongly emphasized in clinical teaching and are viewed as a basic component of education for personal-social-emotional adjustment.

Life-Space Interviewing (LSI). The concept of life-space interviewing, a school-based counseling technique, was developed by Fritz Redl (1959) to be used with students with emotional disturbance in managing a classroom crisis or a daily problem, to make the students aware of their feelings and motivations, to realize how this has been affecting their lives, and how to break this cycle (Morgan & Rinehart, 1991).

During life-space interviews, an effort is made to determine how the child perceives the problem, discussions are usually private or only with concerned parties, and the focus is on sorting out the issues and preventing future problems rather than on determining punishment (Epanchin, 1991). Since LSI requires utilization of the cognitive skills of modeling, comparison, abstraction, projection, and prediction, it is most useful with older elementary and secondary-aged students (Morgan & Rinehart, 1991).

Reality Therapy. Reality therapy is a school-based counseling technique developed by Glasser (1965) which is used to manage behavior by teaching the child to behave responsibly and to face reality (Mercer & Mercer, 1990). This interview technique, similar to life-space interviewing, attempts to help the student make sound decisions when confronted with a problem (Mercer & Mercer, 1993).

When the student is involved in misbehavior, the teacher helps him/her define the problem by asking "what and where" types of questions (e.g., "What are you doing?"). Then the teacher calls for a value judgment by the student, asking questions such as "Is that helping you or the class?" or "Is that behavior against the rules?" (Charles, 1989). Lastly, the teacher and student develop a plan to help the student behave appropriately and follow the rules. If the student does not adhere to the plan, the teacher assigns "time-out." The "student is not allowed to participate with the group again until making a commitment to the teacher to adhere to the plan. If a student disrupts during time-out, she/he is excluded from the classroom" (Charles, 1989, 124). The principal notifies the parents to pick up the student. "Students who are repeatedly sent home are referred to a special school or class, or to a different community agency" (Charles, 1989, 124).

Interventions for Managing Surface Behaviors. Indirect behavior management interventions or influence techniques can be used appropriately to manage the surface behaviors of children and youth with inappropriate behaviors (Shea & Bauer, 1987). These techniques do not substitute for a well designed classroom management plan, but assist in behavior management. Long et al. (1965) suggested twelve influence techniques including the following: planned ignoring, signal interference, proximity control, interest boosting, tension decontamination through humor, hurdle help, restructuring the classroom program, support from routine, direct appeal, removal of seductive objects, antiseptic bouncing, and physical restraint. For most of these interventions, the title explains the technique. Signal interference techniques are nonverbal gestures used by the teacher to let children know their behavior is inappropriate. Proximity control means interfering with inappropriate behavior by standing near the misbehaving child. Hurdle lessons refer to avoiding problems by providing students extra assistance when they begin to get frustrated. Antiseptic bouncing involves removing the misbehaving child from the classroom by sending him/her somewhere else on an errand, rather than punishing.

Therapies. "Expressive media refer to activities that encourage and permit children and youth with behavior disorders to express feelings and emotions through creative activities with minimal constraints" (Shea & Bauer, 1987, 218). Various expressive media used as behavior management techniques include the following: play therapy and free play; puppetry; role playing and psychodrama; movement, dance, and physical activities; music therapy, art therapy, written communication (journal), storytelling, and bibliotherapy (Long et al., 1965).

BEHAVIORAL MODEL OF BEHAVIOR DISORDERS

The behavioral model is one of the predominant theoretical models taught today for managing students with behavior disorders. Behavioral theories were proposed by psychologists in the early 1900's who argued that the only scientific way to study learning was to base all conclusions on observations of how overt behavior is influenced by forces in the external environment (Biehler & Snowman, 1986). Behaviorists rejected the psychologies that probed the inner workings of the mind to determine the cause of abnormal behavior. Behavioral theory promotes the idea that deviance is a very practical problem with very logical solutions (Reinert, 1980).

Behavioral Model: Etiology

The behavioral perspective is not concerned with why individuals behave the way they do, but with what behaviors the individual exhibits. Behaviorists view inappropriate or abnormal behavior as learned behavior that is observable and is the result of a person's interaction with the environment (Schroeder & Riddle, 1991). The cause of human behavior disorders is viewed as outside of the individual in the environment (Shea & Bauer, 1987).

Behaviorists generally avoid labeling children as behavior disordered, preferring instead to describe the behavior. Behaviorists do not probe the inner lives or motives of violent people "instead they attempt to identify the sorts of situations that promote violence and the benefits to the behavior disordered persons" (Wade & Travis, 1990). In general behaviorists tend to believe that it is a waste of time to search for causation of inappropriate behaviors rather a more efficient system is to determine what reinforcement is maintaining the behavior (Reinert, 1980).

Personality Problems

The causes of personality problems in children from a behavioral perspective take one of three basic departure points: (1) Pavlov's classical or respondent conditioning, (2) Skinner's operant conditioning, and/or (3) Bandura's social learning theory (modeling and imitation) (Rizzo & Zabel, 1988). According to classical conditioning fear is a crucial unconditioned response that can easily become associated with a wide range of subtle and obvious environmental stimuli (Rizzo & Zabel, 1988). Operant conditioning proposes that a youngster learns to avoid any situations in which anxiety occurs because avoidance reduces aversive stimuli and is, therefore, reinforcing (Rizzo & Zabel, 1988). The social learning theory suggests that a youngster may learn to be fearful in particular situations or to use physical illness as a way of avoiding stress simply by observing parents and other family members as they attempt to cope with anxiety (Rizzo & Zabel, 1988).

Research studies have shown that children with personality problems frequently come from homes in which one or both parents also have such problems. "Parents of children with personality problems seem, intentionally or unintentionally, to teach their children that the world at large is to be feared, that spontaneity may bring criticism, and that mistakes are disastrous and will lead to rejection by others" (Rizzo & Zabel, 1988, 96). Behaviorists emphasize the loss of positive reinforcement to explain why depression develops, and the underlying principles are the same for adults and children (Epanchin & Paul, 1987).

Conduct Disorders

Aggressive behavior is probably the most common presenting problem among youngsters classified as emotionally and behaviorally disturbed, and data suggest that the incidence of antisocial, aggressive behavior is rising (Epanchin & Paul, 1987). According to classical conditioning, anger and aggression in response to perceived threat is a response that easily becomes associated with a wide range of events in the environment. From an operant conditioning perspective, anger and aggression are learned behavioral responses that have been reinforced by the child's environment.

According to the social learning perspective, conduct disorders in children and adolescents result either from a failure to learn appropriate social skills, or from learning inappropriate social behaviors, or both (Rizzo & Zabel, 1988). The origin and maintenance of aggressive behavior is learned through such processes as imitation and reinforcement (Epanchin & Paul, 1987). Children learn many aggressive responses through observation of modes in the family, on TV, and among peers.

Children and youth learn aggressive behaviors when they receive no aversive consequences for aggressive behavior or successfully obtain rewards by harming or overcoming their victims (Epanchin & Paul, 1987). Children are more likely to be aggressive when they are aversively stimulated by behaviors such as physical assault, verbal threats or insults from parents and/or peers (Epanchin & Paul, 1987). In these cases the child may learn, imitatively, that one can coerce others into desired responses by force or aggression (Rizzo & Zabel, 1988). In adolescents especially conformity to the norms and behavior of the peer group or deviant subculture groups may bring about social reinforcement in the form of conferred status within the group, associated self-esteem, and often the immediate gratification of material desires as well (Rizzo & Zabel, 1988). In males and in children who have a history of aggression, viewing televised aggression increases aggressive behavior (Epanchin & Paul, 1987).

Behavioral Model: Assessment

Assessment from the behavioral standpoint will focus primarily on operant conditioning and social learning theory procedures and instruments. Behaviorists using operant conditioning focus on the conditions under which the behavior occurs, the consequences of the behavior, and the frequency, duration, and intensity of the behavior (Schroeder & Riddle, 1991). Evaluators utilizing social learning theory procedures focus on information relative to the child (i.e., physical, cognitive, social, emotional, and developmental levels), parent interviews and questionnaires, observation of the child in all settings, observation of parent-child interactions and teacher child-interactions (Schroeder & Riddle, 1991). Unfortunately, many of the instruments and procedures used for assessing behavioral problems have questionable validity.

A multidisciplinary evaluation will include health history, vision, and hearing screening by the school nurse; speech and language screening by the speech pathologist; intellectual assessment by the school psychologist; standardized and criterion-referenced achievement tests by the educational examiner; formal behavioral evaluation by the school psychologist, and/or special education teacher; behavioral ratings from school and family; and a statement of intervention techniques already attempted by the school personnel and parents with or without success. Behavior should be assessed in terms of the social restrictions it places on the child, its interference with development, the suffering it is causing the child, its effect on others in the environment, and the physical state of the child (Schroeder & Riddle, 1991).

Behavior checklists or rating scales, frequently utilized in evaluating children and youth suspected of having behavior disorders include problem behaviors that best discriminate disturbed children from normal (Epanchin, 1987). Most of the rating scales discriminate among aggressive, acting-out children and withdrawn, anxious children. Numerous behavior checklists and rating scales exist including the *Behavior*

Evaluation Scale (McCarney & Leigh, 1983), which has five areas that correspond to the P.L. 94-142 definition of severely emotionally disabled.

In determining whether a behavior is deviant, Rutter (1975) employs nine criteria that take into account specific child and environmental variables: (1) age and sex appropriateness, (2) persistence, (3) life circumstances, (4) sociocultural setting, (5) extent of disturbance, (6) type of behavior, (7) severity and frequency of behavior, (8) change in behavior, and (9) situation specificity of the behavior (Cited in Schroeder & Riddle, 1991). Thus, a diagnosis of behavior disorders requires severely sex, age, and situation inappropriate behavior (aggressive or withdrawn) which occurs in several settings over a period of time, and interferes with the youth demonstrating academic and socially acceptable behaviors.

Behavioral Model: Treatment

Behavior management treatment from the behavioral perspective primarily concerns the use of operant conditioning and social learning theory techniques and procedures to modify behavior (Biehler & Snowman, 1986).

Operant Conditioning

Behavioral programs in schools are based on operant conditioning principles (Schroeder & Riddle, 1991). The commercial and noncommercial programs are typically focused at enhancing the behavior management abilities and skills of teachers in their classrooms. Behavior management programs focus on changing the child's negative or inappropriate behaviors. The most frequently utilized behavior change interventions which incorporate operant conditioning principles include the following: (1) Positive Reinforcement, (2) The Premack Principle, (3) Punishment, (4) Negative Reinforcement, (5) Extinction, (6) Reinforcement of Incompatible Behaviors, (7) Contingency Contracting, (8) Time-Out, and (9) Token Economies (Shea & Bauer, 1994; Schroeder & Riddle, 1991).

Positive Reinforcement, especially immediately applied, strengthens the behavior and increases the chance that the behavior will increase in the future (Schroeder & Riddle, 1991). For example, immediately after the child voluntarily shares toys she/he is given praise or a tangible reward. *The Premack Principle* (Grandma's Rule) indicates that less desired activities can be increased in occurrence by receiving desirable consequences upon their completion (Shea & Bauer, 1994). For example, after the child completes the math assignment she/he may go out to recess.

Punishment or punishers are consequences that are not reinforcing, that weaken the behavior, at least for the present (Reinert, 1980). For example, the young child is spanked for running into the street. Punishment stops inappropriate behavior which is the immediate objective. However, punishment does not eliminate the inappropriate behavior, it merely suppresses it; and punishment does not provide young persons with a model of acceptable behavior (Wood & Lakin, 1978). When punishment must be implemented as a behavior management intervention, two forms are preferred: loss of privileges (negative behavior modification) and reprimands (scolds) which include a statement of an appropriate alternative to the inappropriate behavior (Shea & Bauer, 1987).

Negative Reinforcement involves the escape from an unpleasant task or situation (Shea & Bauer, 1994). For example, if student completes an in-class assignment correctly she/he is excused from doing a regularly scheduled homework assignment. *Extinction* is the removal of a reinforcer that sustains or increases a target behavior, weakening the behavior, so ultimately the behaviors disappear (Schroeder & Riddle, 1991). Teachers often ignore many inappropriate behaviors (withdrawal of attention) in hopes that the behavior will go away. Extinction is an effective means of eliminating annoying and nonproductive behaviors (i.e., whining, tattling, meaningless questions, mild tantrums, inappropriate language) (Shea & Bauer, 1994).

Reinforcement of Incompatible Behaviors involves decreasing the frequency of inappropriate target behaviors by reinforcing a behavior that is in opposition to or incompatible with that behavior (Shea & Bauer, 1994). Since a child cannot be in his/her seat and out-of-seat at the same time, do not mention the out-of-seat behavior, but reward the in-seat behavior.

Contingency Contracting is a behavior change procedure in which a written agreement generally between teacher and student specifying that if the student does certain tasks/lessons/behaviors the teacher will reward with predetermined reinforcers. This procedure has been found to be effective with older children and youth with behavior disorders (Shea & Bauer, 1987). Contingency management has four basic components: (1) contracting for a specific amount of work, (2) making a contract that is fair, (3) rewarding behaviors that approximate desired goals, and (4) rewarding performance only after the behavior occurs (Reinert, 1980).

Time-Out, time away from positive reinforcement, usually involves removing the child or youth from an apparently reinforcing setting to a nonreinforcing setting for a limited amount of time. Some schools/teachers utilize separate time-out rooms, and other teachers use a "quiet corner" in their classroom for the student to "relax and refresh" (Cook, 1986).

Token Economy is a widely used behavioral intervention exchange system that provides immediate reinforcement for appropriate behavior (tokens) that may be saved and exchanged for a desired item (i.e., models, toys, books, privileges). The token economy is frequently combined with a response-cost intervention in which the child earns tokens for appropriate behaviors and is charged tokens for inappropriate behaviors. These operant conditioning interventions are frequently used alone or in combination in the public schools to encourage appropriate behaviors.

Social Learning Theory

The social learning theory emphasizes the role of observational learning (i.e., imitation, vicarious learning) in the acquisition of positive and negative emotional and behavioral responses (Bandura, 1977). Observational learning occurs vicariously when a student observes a model's behavior but makes no overt response nor receives any direct consequences. For example, teacher praises good behavior of student sitting next to target student, hoping that target student will observe the model behavior.

Phases or steps in Observational Learning include the following: (1) Attentional Phase: Paying attention to a model, (2) Retention Phase: Teacher models desired behavior and student(s) imitate, (3) Reproduction: Assessment of student learning, and (4) Motivational Phase: Consists of praise or grades for matching teacher's model behavior (Bandura, 1977). During the intervention the child or youth is systematically reinforced for imitating the model (Bandura, 1977). Observational learning and modeling have been used to desensitize fears, train social skills, and teach new behavior (Schroeder & Riddle, 1991).

Cognitive Behavior Modification

Cognitive behavior modification is a verbal technique utilized in two kinds of interventions: (1) self-instructional training, and (2) problem-solving training (Shea & Bauer, 1994). Meichenbaum (1977) indicated that cognitive techniques for problem-solving assist students to learn how to learn, and to increase their generalization of behaviors and ability to try new strategies.

The major steps in cognitive behavior modification include the following: (1) Cognitive Modeling: Teacher performs task while talking out-loud to describe behaviors; (2) Overt, External Guidance: Child performs task under oral direction of teacher; (3) Overt, Self-Guidance: Child performs task while self-instructing out-loud; (4) Faded, Overt Self-Guidance: Child performs task while whispering instructions to self; (5) Covert Self-Instruction: Child performs task using private speech to self-instruct (Meichenbaum, 1977). This self-instructional model is successful in teaching students the steps or directions the teacher wants them to follow in various classroom procedures such as "Get ready for recess" or "Get ready for Lab." To the students these previously modeled directions may involve the following steps: (1) Clean off your desk, (2) Put completed assignment in the basket, (3) Put incomplete assignment in text, (4) Get out book and clean sheet of paper for next class, and (5) Look at me. If the student uses the same directions or procedures continuously, they become automatic when given the stimulus direction "Get ready for _____."

HUMANIST MODEL OF BEHAVIOR DISORDERS

For decades, behaviorism and psychoanalysis were the major psychologies. In the 1950s, the reaction to both Freudian pessimism and behavioristic "mindlessness" emerged initially in the form of a "third force" in psychology called humanistic psychology or humanism (Wade & Travis, 1990).

Humanistic psychology or phenomenology is an approach to psychology that emphasizes the uniqueness of human beings, personal growth and self-concept, self-actualization, human moral values, and free will (Wallace et al., 1990). Humanists have postulated that human nature or behavior is not completely determined by either the immediate environment or past experiences; and that people are able to make choices and control our own destinies (Wade & Travis, 1990). Psychologists who prefer this perspective consider the individual's interpretations of events as most important in the understanding of human behavior (Wallace et al., 1990).

Humanist Model: Etiology

Humanism is concerned with social, emotional, and self-concept development and is derived from the study of normal individuals (Wallace et al., 1990). From this perspective problems are evident in individuals who demonstrate inappropriate social and emotional behaviors, negative self-concepts, and extreme anxiety. Humanists generally do not delve into past conflicts, but aim to help people feel better about themselves and free themselves from self-imposed limits (Wade & Travis, 1990). They share the belief that the way to do so is by exploring what is going on "here and now," not in the issues of "why and how" (Wade & Travis, 1990).

Negative Self-Concept

Individuals possessing a negative phenomenal self or inadequate personality view themselves in essentially negative ways. They feel unworthy, unacceptable, and unable to deal with the changes in life. Inadequate personalities are unable to achieve need satisfaction, unable to enhance the self, and perceive themselves in constant danger from external events (Combs & Snygg, 1959). The level of self-esteem is very important in determining one's actions and if the self-esteem is inadequate, various forms of maladaptive behavior may be anticipated (Purkey, 1970).

Persons with negative self-concepts lack confidence in their abilities, feel despair because they cannot find a solution for problems, and believe that most attempts will result in failure (LaBenne & Greene, 1969). Inadequate personalities are unable to cope with life because they feel continuously threatened and in constant danger from external events. Threatened people almost always overreact and behave in exaggerated ways that produce the very reactions in others which verify their own already existing beliefs. "The inadequate self may find it necessary to live a life of continuous, aggressive seeking for self-enhancement to protect himself from destruction" (Combs & Snygg, 1959, 267).

Inadequate personalities do not possess strong feelings of identification with others. The inability of a person to accept him/herself is strongly correlated with the inability to accept others. People with little feeling of identification with other people are unlikely to be concerned about them. A low self-opinion is likely to be associated with fear and distrust of others (Combs & Snygg, 1959).

General characteristics of individuals with low self-esteem include the following: (1) Passive and nonassertive in adapting to environmental demands and pressures; (2) Indecisive and tend to vacillate when dealing with problems; (3) Demonstrate feelings of inferiority, timidity, lack of personal acceptance, submissiveness; (4) Exhibit high levels of anxiety, psychosomatic symptoms, and feelings of depression; (5) Experience difficulty forming friendships; (6) Conform more readily to social pressures; (7) Unwilling to express contrary opinions even if correct; (8) React strongly to criticism, (9) Prone to emitting self-defeating responses; (10) Pessimistic in views concerning the future (Coopersmith, 1967; Battle, 1982).

Extreme Anxiety

The self-image serves as a reference point from which to evaluate new experiences. If a person has unclear or negative perceptions of the self, they are prone to be anxious. Anxiety may be defined as a feeling of threat from unknown sources (Hansen & Maynard, 1973). Anxiety and its accompanying tensions are the inseparable partners of inadequacy feelings. Anxiety is the apprehension of not being a worthwhile person (Campbell, 1984).

Anxiety prone individuals have chronically low self-esteem; consider themselves less desirable than their peers; experience more guilt, daydream more, and appear less curious than their peers (Levitt, 1980). "Anxiety is an interpersonal phenomenon that occurs when an individual expects to be or is indeed rejected or demeaned by himself or others" (Coopersmith, 1967, 32). Those who have low self-esteem are very sensitive to criticism (Horney, 1950).

The literature contains a considerable amount of evidence in support of the hypotheses that anxiety interferes with intellectual functioning. Anxiety interferes with accuracy, spontaneity, and expressiveness (Silverstein, 1966). Experimental investigations indicate that anxiety detrimentally affects various cognitive processes such as problem-solving, incidental learning, and verbal communication skills (Levitt, 1980).

The effect of anxiety on intelligence test performance seems to be related to whether the test is timed. Anxiety seems to have a detrimental effect on intelligence measures that are timed, but inconsequential effect on untimed tests (Levitt, 1980). The effects of anxiety appear to be related to the degree or amount of anxiety the student perceives. Moderate anxiety may energize the student and improve performance (Levitt, 1980).

Individuals experiencing extreme anxiety may react in a number of ways to protect the self-concept. Conscious avoidance of the stimuli or situations or circumstances that are anxiety provoking is one of the most common methods of defending against anxiety (Levitt, 1980). The employment of defenses is the most common method used by individuals in their attempts to rid themselves of anxiety, however, defenses tend to deny, falsify, or distort reality, and as a result are basically maladaptive behaviors (Battle, 1982).

Humanist Model: Assessment

Assessment from the Humanist perspective involves assessing the conscious and unconscious self-concept, social and emotional behaviors, and anxiety. Numerous screening and evaluation instruments have been devised to assess the self-concept or self-esteem at various age levels. "Since we have no direct access to a person's self-concept, it must be inferred from stimuli, verbal or nonverbal, which the student emits" (Stangvik, 1979, 91).

With young children most developmental screening and evaluation instruments provide information regarding a child's functioning in all of the major developmental areas and include a section which assesses social and/or emotional behavior. Frequently used developmental criterion-referenced assessments containing a social and emotional subtest include the following: *Portage Guide to Early Education* (Portage Project, 1976) and *Brigance Diagnostic Inventory of Early Development* (Brigance, 1983).

Humanists assume that an individual's verbal statements accurately reflect his/her conscious reality, his/her self-perceptions (Battle, 1982). The conscious self-concept is usually measured by administering self-reporting instruments, such as *The Piers-Harris Children's Self-Concept Scale* (3rd–12th grade) (Piers-Harris, 1984). Adaptive behavior or social competence, a person's ability to cope with the social demands of the environment, is evaluated using adaptive behavior instruments including the following: *Vineland Adaptive Behavior Scales* (birth–18 years) (Sparrow et al., 1984) or *Behavior Rating Scale* (grades 1–12) (Brown & Hammill, 1983).

The unconscious self reveals itself through projective tests and measures which require a trained psychologist or counselor to interpret. Some projective techniques utilized include human figure drawings, sentence completion, pretend situations, and immediate response situations. "When used with clinical skill and sensitivity, the projective techniques are the most effective instruments for penetrating the deeper recesses of the personality. They provide a method of studying personality and conflict through an unstructured medium" (Siegel, 1987, 85).

Humanist Model: Treatment

The humanist perspective assumes that people seek self-actualization and self-fulfillment (Wade & Travis, 1991). Maslow (1954) indicates that in order to become self-actualized a person's basic physiological needs (i.e., food, water), social and interpersonal needs (i.e., companionship and friendship), love and belonging, and self-esteem needs must first be met. For Maslow, normal individuals move through the hierarchy of needs as long as they live in supportive and facilitative family environments (Wallace et al., 1990). Behavior disorders from the humanist standpoint view the inappropriate social and emotional behaviors of students as caused by deficiencies in physiological needs, social and interpersonal relationships, love and belonging needs, self-esteem and self-concept needs accompanied by extreme anxiety and stress. Therefore, the treatment methods must address these areas of basic needs, enhance the self-concept, and reduce extreme anxiety and stress.

Humanistic Therapies

Humanistic therapies administered in the clinic setting include client-centered or nondirective therapy, Gestalt therapy, existential therapy, and invitational education.

Client-Centered or nondirective therapy developed by Carl Rogers (1951) focuses on helping individuals attain self-actualization through listening sympathetically, offering unconditional positive regard, instilling the feeling that she/he is loved and respected in order to build the client's self-esteem. Rogers (1951) espouses humanism in his belief that people are inherently good and motivated toward growth or self-actualization.

Gestalt therapy developed by Frederick Perls (1969) aims at self-actualization through emotional liberation. Since Perls (1969) believed that problems resulted because people think too much and suppress their feelings, he worked in a group setting where people were encouraged to express any feeling without fear of consequences. He utilized direct encounter and role playing during which brutal frankness, ventilation of any and all negative or taboo feelings, and confrontation were encouraged (Wade & Travis, 1991).

Existential therapy helps clients explore the meaning of existence, and face with courage the great questions of life, death, and free will (Wallace et al., 1990). Existential theory recognizes and values each person's individuality and indicates that people's lives are not inevitably determined by their past experiences, but that they have the power to choose their own destinies. Therapists help clients determine what is important to them, what values guide them, and what changes they will have the courage to make (Wade & Travis, 1991).

Invitational education, a self-concept model of teaching, is based on the theory that behavior is a product of how people perceive themselves and the situations in which they are involved (Combs et al., 1978). Since personal perceptions help individuals organize and make sense of their world, the most important perception is self-perception or self-concept, which is the view of who we are and how we fit into the world (Shea & Bauer, 1987).

Purkey & Novak (1984) indicated that invitational education is based on the assumptions that people are able and valuable, teaching is a cooperative activity, and people possess untapped potential that can be realized using this educational approach. The purpose of invitational education is to help the special educator become a beneficial presence in the lives of students (Shea & Bauer, 1987). The child or youth with behavior disorders is treated in a respectful manner and is invited to participate in educational activities.

Educational Approaches

Public School Movement. During the 1960s and 1970s, the humanist movement in the public schools focused on a number of areas including the following: roles of children and teachers, diagnostic evaluation, materials, individualized instruction, multi-age groupings, open space, and team teaching (Slavin, 1994). In humanist schools teachers served in the role of resource person or facilitator, while children were active in guiding their own learning by choosing their materials, the methods they would use to demonstrate competence, and their own learning pace.

The purpose of evaluation in humanist schools is guiding instruction rather than for administering grades or ranking students, so standardized testing was not used. Observation, written histories, and samples of student work were utilized to evaluate progress (Slavin, 1994). The emphasis was on using real-world natural materials rather than textbooks and worksheets. Instruction is given to individuals or small groups based on individual needs and student-set goals. Teachers rarely deliver a lesson to the entire class, but provide guidance to individuals and small groups working on similar projects.

Open schools were composed of classrooms without permanent interior walls to accommodate flexible use of space and furnishings. Open schools readily accommodated team teaching. Learning Centers with individualized projects were scattered about the room with tasks to be accomplished in an order determined by the student. Grade levels were not utilized to categorize students, so students of different ages worked together in the same classroom without age distinction (Slavin, 1994).

Humanistic Schools of the 1990s. The humanist movement of the 1990's appears to be focusing on four major principles: Self-Regulated Learning, Affective Education, Authentic Assessment, and Self-Motivation.

Self-Regulated Learning. Self-regulated learning combines aspects of cognitive constructivist theory to result in self-directed and self-motivated learners. Self-regulated learners take an active role in planning what they will study and when and how they will study it, rather than passively waiting for the teacher to make all of the learning choices (Slavin, 1994). Programs that assist in teaching self-regulation include the following: Cognitive Behavior Modification (Meichenbaum, 1977), Instrumental Enrichment (Feuerstein, 1980), Strategies Intervention Model (Lenz et al., 1988).

Affective Education. Instruction in the areas of social and emotional skills, moral values (consideration, respect, honesty), and self-concept development are considered affective education. Infancy and early childhood self-concept development focuses on activities that encourage a positive body image, a positive social image, a positive cognitive image, and a positive self-concept (Jones, 1992). If a young child is to achieve a healthy self-concept, all parts of his being need to be challenged and developed, and play is one of the easiest, most inexpensive, and most accessible ways to promote a healthy self-concept (Jensen, 1980).

During middle childhood and adolescence, enhancing a negative self-concept is a much more complex process, as the self-concept becomes fairly stable by about ten years of age. The teacher will need to be concerned about cognitive development, behavior control, social/emotional and self-concept development, as well as academic achievement

(Jones, 1992). Cognitive development can be enhanced through the self-regulation programs. Behavior control interventions include preventive discipline, supportive discipline, and corrective discipline strategies, school-based counseling, stress management, and school survival skills (Jones, 1992).

Social and emotional development may be enhanced through formal programs such as *The Metacognitive Approach to Social Skills Training* (Sheinker et al., 1988); *Social Skills for Daily Living* (Schumaker et al., 1984); *Skill Streaming the Elementary School Child* (McGinnis & Goldstein, 1984); *Skill Streaming the Adolescent* (Goldstein et al., 1980). Noncommercial socialization intervention involves enhancing social communication, social problem-solving, social interactions, and social maturity. Some interventions to enhance academic achievement include cooperative learning strategies such as peer tutoring, jigsaw learning, team assisted individualization; whole language and literature-based reading programs; daily journals; literature-based math; writing process approaches; and inquiry science.

Authentic Assessment. Humanist educators avoid the use of A–F letter grades, standardized testing, minimum competency testing, and other formal methods of assessment. Humanists prefer narrative letters to parents rather than report cards, ungraded (pass/fail) versus graded courses, and solving real problems or conducting actual experiments rather than taking tests. The current focus from 1st grade through college is on portfolio assessment to allow the students to decide how she/he will demonstrate competency in various knowledge and skill areas. The portfolio is used developmentally as a means for students to reflect on personal skill progress throughout the semester.

Self-Motivation. Many aspects of the humanist approach stimulate motivation including the academic interventions and authentic assessment methods. Motivation can be enhanced through attribution retraining (effort is related to success), maintaining curiosity, fostering creativity, using a variety of presentation modes, helping students set their own goals, providing frequent feedback, and using effective praise (Slavin, 1994). The primary goal of humanistic approaches to education aim to help students seek self-actualization and self-fulfillment through self-regulated learning, affective education, authentic assessment, and self-motivation.

ECOLOGICAL MODEL OF BEHAVIOR DISORDERS

The ecological perspective of behavior disorders, the newest of the theoretical models first described in the 1960s, by Hobbs (1966) and Rhodes (1967), takes a very different perspective than the other models. From the biological, psychodynamic, behavioral, and humanist perspectives, the behavior problems are within the child and the child is provided treatment: medication (biological model), behavior modification strategies (behavioral model), psychotherapy (psychodynamic model), and/or self-concept enhancement (humanist model). The ecological model rejected these beliefs and practices in mental health and proposed a new way to view and treat emotional disturbance.

Ecological Model: Etiology

According to the ecological model, the child is not disturbed, no one owns the problem or is blamed for it (Swap, 1991). The child's disturbing behavior is a product of the unique interactions between the child's learning style, temperament, developmental phase, and aspects of the setting; that is between his/her particular learning style, temperament, developmental phase, the particular characteristics of the academic setting, the teacher, and the peer group; and his/her ability to adapt to radically different demands in different settings (Swap, 1991; Paul & Epanchin, 1992).

The disturbance, then, is a result of discordance in the reciprocal relationships between the child and his/her neighborhood and community (Shea & Bauer, 1994). The interactions and reactions of others in the child's ecosystem affect the way the child acts, and the child's interactions and reactions, in turn, affect how she/he is treated by others. Behavior disorders from the ecological perspective relate to a mismatch between the child and his or her ecosystem (Neisworth & Bagnato, 1987).

Ecological Model: Assessment

According to the ecological model, assessment of a behavior disordered child or youth is conducted through the cooperative efforts of many professionals using techniques appropriate to their settings (Neisworth & Bagnato, 1987). The child will receive a vision and hearing screening by the school nurse; speech/language screening by the speech pathologist; psychological evaluation (intelligence and self-concept assessments) by the school psychologist; academic assessment by the special education teacher and/or educational diagnostician; environmental analyses by the school psychologist, social worker, and/or teachers.

Most environmental assessments consist of formalized observation techniques and/or checklists that investigate the various environments that affect and are affected by the child including the following: general school climate, nature of the school curriculum, teacher behaviors, peer influences, home influences, neighborhood and community factors. A few formal ecological assessments exist such as the *Ecological Assessment of Child Problem Behavior* (Wahler et al., 1976). After the ecological observations and assessments the school counselor or social worker may complete an ecological map or genogram that charts all the relationships between people who are significant in the child's life (Neisworth & Bagnato, 1987).

Another assessment technique is the heuristic case report in which information is gathered about the family, neighborhood, community, school, and classroom (Cantrell & Cantrell, 1970). Differences between behavior at home, in the neighborhood, and in school are compared and evaluated. After all of the information has been gathered and evaluated the team should be able to identify the disturbing interaction or the exact nature of the problem, identify who is disturbed by the interaction, consider what might be causing the problem (i.e., physical setting, inappropriate contingencies, lack of match between child/s characteristics and the curriculum, peer pressure and expectations, discrepancy between home and school expectations, and the physical or psychological stress factors (Swap, 1991). The team should also document past and present interventions and the success or lack of success experienced with each.

Ecological Model: Treatment

A variety of treatments or interventions based on the ecological model have been successfully implemented. The prime consideration, however, is that the intervention not be designed to change the child only, leaving the contributing factors in the environment unchanged (Swap, 1991). Ecological theory is essentially a holistic approach to children in conflict that emphasizes the importance of the whole and the interdependence of its individual parts (Reinert, 1980). In selecting the teaching strategy, the special education teacher must consider the child, the behavior, the contexts relevant to the misbehavior, the purposes of the intervention, and the characteristics of the intervener (Shea & Bauer, 1994). The major ecological treatments are usually included in four categories: (1) Remedial Interventions, (2) Environmental Interventions, (3) School-Community Interventions, and (4) Family-School Environment Interventions (Wagner, 1972).

Remedial Interventions

Remedial interventions generally focus on assisting the child in developing socially appropriate behaviors by teaching social skills and how to make social adaptations in various environments, helping the child set goals to improve his/her behavior, and by building peer support groups.

Haring and Phillips (1962) indicated that children with behavior disorders need a specialized environment in order to recover and move toward normalization. They recommended modifying the classroom by reducing extraneous auditory and visual stimuli, unnecessary physical activities, and group participation. The control over these areas would be reduced over time as the child adjusts to the program, develops self-control, and prepares for integration into the regular classroom. Additionally, Haring and Phillips (1962) recommend that the subject matter should focus on concrete rather than abstract concepts, the academics and social skills should be at the child's developmental level, immediate feedback should be provided on activities and assignments, and the child/youth should continually be apprised on his/her progress toward goals. Teachers must have clear expectations, follow through on child's efforts, use logical consequences for misbehavior, reduce personal verbalization, and maintain a firm, but kind attitude (Haring & Phillips, 1962).

Developmental Therapy. Developmental therapy was a comprehensive environmental approach to treating behavior disordered children and youth of all ages using the therapeutic classroom setting with small groups of children at Rutland Center at the University of Georgia during the 1970s under the direction of Mary Wood. The developmental curriculum focused on adaptive behavior, communication, socialization, and/or academics or preacademics (Shea & Bauer, 1994). The curriculum focused on encouraging progress through a series of stages from responding to the encouragement, to successful group participation, to applying individual and group skills in new situations (Shea & Bauer, 1994).

Developmental Strategy

Hewett and Taylor (1980) used a developmental strategy with six levels of learning competency (similar to Wood's, 1975) including the following: (1) attention (making contact with the environment), (2) response (interacting within the environment verbally and motorically), (3) order (following set routines), (4) exploratory (exploring the environment), (5) social (understanding approval and disapproval), (6) mastery (academic skills and independent functioning). Assessment materials, educational activities, classroom design, and parental involvement guidelines were developed for each level of competency (Hewett & Taylor, 1980).

School-Community Activities

Both the school and community are concerned with using behavior modification techniques to teach the youth how to function effectively in the school and community environments. Mental health programs of various kinds can be used to assist children to develop appropriate community behaviors in natural settings. Participation in camps and youth organizations is encouraged to develop appropriate socialization skills.

Artificial Community

Sometimes it is necessary to remove a severely behavior disordered youth from the home and school environments in which the maladaptive behaviors are displayed and place them temporarily in residential centers.

Project ReED. The most widely recognized of the artificial community programs was Hobbs' (1978) and Rhodes' (1966) Project Re-Education of the Emotionally Disturbed (ReED) in which a child was removed from the ecosystem in which she/he was experiencing difficulty for about six months, while spending week-ends at home. Wilderness camping was used for highly antisocial adolescents. The focus was on teaching the child how to act appropriately in a range of situations, while at the same time helping teachers and parents to understand their reactions to the child and to respond more adaptively (Swap, 1991), so there is a better fit between the child and his/her environment. Advocates of this model emphasize that removal is necessitated by the need to work with the child and social system independently before the two are reunited (Neisworth & Bagnato, 1987).

Since one of the most common characteristics of children labeled behavior disordered is a lack of school achievement, academic remediation was emphasized at Re-ED centers. The healthy expression of feelings was encouraged, group activities provided a sense of belonging and responsibility, ceremony and ritual give order and stability to chaotic lives, physical activities and sports enhanced the physical and psychological selves (Reinert, 1980). Once the school, child, home and other participants were reeducated, the child was gradually reintegrated.

Family-Oriented Intervention

One of the strengths of the ecological approach is that parents are considered important in the reeducation of the child. Sometimes the architectural and physical character of the child's environment must be adjusted or modified in order to provide privacy and personal space. Social workers and others work with the parents to reeducate them in interacting more positively with the child and to help heal wounds caused by the discordance in relationships.

Liaison teachers may help parents to develop alternative, and more accommodating views of their children and to implement consistent, effective strategies for managing their children's behavior (Rizzo & Zabel, 1988). One of the most important tasks of the liaison teachers is to work with the teachers and administrators of the school, so they can interact more positively with the child. The liaison teacher oversees the planning of the transition back to the home and school environments, and provides ongoing consultation and support following reintegration (Rizzo & Zabel, 1988).

SUMMARY

Five major theoretical perspectives regarding behavior disorders include the following models: biological, psychodynamic, behavioral, humanistic, and ecological. The following table provides a summary of these models with regard to focus, etiology, diagnosis, treatment, and theorists.

Summary of Theoretical Models of Behavior Disorders

Biological	Psychodynamic	Behavioral	Humanist	Ecological
Focus: Medical	Focus: Psychoanalysis	Focus: Operant Conditioning	Focus: Self-Concept	Focus: Environment
Etiology: Physical disease, genetics, biochemical, neurological damage	Etiology: Unconscious motives and conflicts, Interpersonal relationship problems	Etiology: Personality problems, Conduct problems: Aggression, Withdrawal	Etiology: Negative self-concept, extreme anxiety	Etiology: Imbalance in relationships between child & ecosystem
Diagnosis: Medical specialists give physical exams & lab. tests	Diagnosis: Intense examination of inner turmoil, Projective Techniques	Diagnosis: Behavior Checklists & Rating Scales; Frequency, Duration, Intensity of Behaviors	Diagnosis: *The Peers-Harris Children's Self-Concept Scale, Projective Techniques*	Diagnosis: *Ecological Assessment of Child Problem Behavior:* Case report
Treatment: Medication: Ritalin, Diet Modification, Environmental Control Medication: Allergies	Treatment: Psychoanalysis, Milieu Therapy, Clinical Teaching, Life-Space Interviewing, Reality Therapy	Treatment: Social Learning, Operant Conditioning, Contingency Contracting, Time-Out, Token Economy, Cognitive Behavior Modification	Treatment: Client-Centered Therapy, Existential Therapy, Invitational Education, Self-Regulated Learning	Treatment: Therapeutic Classroom, Project ReED, Family-Oriented Intervention
Theorists: Strauss & Lehtinen, Cruickshank	Theorists: Freud, Adler, Rogers, Glasser, Erikson	Theorists: Skinner, Bandura, Thorndike	Theorists: Purkey, Combs, Maslow, Rogers	Theorists: Hobbs, Rhodes, Hewett

Chapter 7

LEARNING PERSPECTIVES
OF BEHAVIOR DISORDERS

*Few experiences are so disturbing to teachers as trying to teach children
who are chronically unhappy or driven to aggressive, antisocial behavior
(Kirk et al., 1993, 410).*

The inappropriate and maladaptive behaviors exhibited by children
and adolescents with behavior disorders are manifested as deficits
in cognitive development, academic functioning, and social interactions.
Due to the significant focus on the inappropriate behaviors engaged in
by children with behavior disorders, discussions of academic and cognitive functioning are frequently omitted from texts on behavior disorders,
and are seldom researched. Obviously, the presenting problem—the
deviant behavior—must be brought under control as a prerequisite to
adequate academic functioning.

Disturbed behaviors frequently are categorized as mild-moderate behavior disorders and severe-profound behavior disorders. Mild-moderate
behavior disorders are described in terms of two major dimensions: (1)
Conduct disorders or aggressive externalizing behavior, and (2) Personality disorders or withdrawn internalizing behavior (Hallahan & Kauffman,
1994). Children with mild to moderate behavior disorders, with intervention, can live at home and attend school during the day (Cartwright

141

et al., 1994). These children usually are educated in self-contained classrooms, and are mainstreamed into regular education classrooms as they learn to control their inappropriate behaviors. Students with mild-moderate behavior disorders often show some degree of learning disorders— cognitive and academic.

COGNITIVE LEARNING CHARACTERISTICS

Cognitively, the average youngster with mild or moderate behavior disorders has an IQ in the dull-normal range around IQ 90; very few behavior disordered children score above the bright-normal range (Hallahan & Kauffman, 1994). Compared to the normal distribution of intelligence, many more children with behavior disorders fall into the slow learner and mildly retarded categories (Hallahan & Kauffman, 1994). The low-normal IQs for children and adolescents with mild-moderate behavior disorders indicate delays in learning to perform academic tasks that nonhandicapped peers can perform successfully, and the failure to gain adequately from their environmental experiences.

Information Processing Deficits

Information processing skills of youngsters with mild-moderate behavior disorders reveal significant deficits in attention, perception, memory, learning efficiency, and automatization.

Attention Deficits

Deficits in attention include sustained attention deficits, selective attention deficits, and selective intention deficits. These attention deficits significantly impact the ability of students with mild to moderate behavior disorders to progress academically in the regular class. *Sustained attention deficits* including coming to attention and sustaining focus are significant problems for behavior disordered students. Their initial problem is paying enough attention to lessons to process information. Since the attention span of students with behavior disorders is so short, they may not pay enough attention to gain all of the salient features required in order to perform lessons correctly. They may read the directions just enough to learn that they are to indicate an answer (or guess and not read the directions at all), thus, they may not have attended well enough to the directions to note that specific items are to be underlined or circled. Due to short attention span, the student with behavior disorders, aggressive or withdrawn, will not be able to attend to task and concentrate long enough to produce a viable report or creative story without intervention.

Children with *selective attention deficits* have erratic focus and concentration, preferring to focus on incidental nonrelevant factors (Levine, 1987). They always know what their classmates are doing, whose class is at recess, what's going on in the hall. They evidence very poor ability to utilize the cues from their teacher that indicates their behavior is inappropriate and that they should modify their behavior. The seriously withdrawn or depressed child or youth with behavior disorders who possesses selective attention deficits experiences overriding anxiety and depression, avoidance of possible failure in academics, daydreaming or "existing in another time and space" which severely impairs their ability to focus attention on classroom tasks at hand. Children and youth with selective attention problems, also, experience *selective intention deficits* such as failure to monitor what they say, poorly planned and inappropriate actions; and inconsistent performance on completed tasks shows sacrifice of accuracy for speed, and failure to learn from experience (Levine, 1987).

Perception

Children with behavior disorders who are also learning disabled may experience perceptual difficulties producing inaccurate information. They may experience visual perception difficulties in the areas of discrimination, figure-ground discrimination, spatial relationships, visual closure, visual sequencing, visual memory, and visual-motor integration. Students may experience auditory perceptual problems in auditory discrimination, auditory memory, auditory sequencing, auditory blending, and/or auditory-motor integration. Deficits or disabilities in one or several of these perceptual skills may negatively impact the student's acquisition of reading, math, and/or written composition skills.

Memory Deficits

Attention deficits reduce the amount of information processed in the short-term memory and stored in the long-term memory. Information that is stored may be composed of only partially accurate information due to lack of attention to detail. Deficits or delays in understanding the complexities of language (i.e., syntax, semantics, pragmatics) may affect the storage and retrieval of information because much information is stored using language as the symbol system. Information may be difficult to retrieve because of lack of labeling and integrating with the long-term memory store. The use of working memory may be very minimal due to lack of metacognitive skills to manage the organization and use of information. Some youngsters with behavior disorders process information appropriately, but experience extreme anxiety about the school setting, the subject, and/or life in general, which may "short circuit" the whole process, and significantly reduce learning.

Learning Efficiency. Learning efficiency among children and youth with behavior disorders may be almost nonexistent. Those youngsters who are also learning disabled may not spontaneously use strategies, such as verbal rehearsal and clustering, to help themselves remember. Since children and youth with behavior disorders, both aggressive and withdrawn, fail to use metacognitive skills to monitor and adjust their behavior, it is unlikely that they will be able to use metacognition to monitor their memory processes and academic functioning.

Automatization Deficits. Automatization is another skill very important to effective and efficient learning. Youth with mild behavior disorders, both aggressive and withdrawn, are so involved with themselves and the deviant behaviors that rule their lives that they may have little time, inclination, or patience and concentration to develop prerequisite academic skills to a level required for automaticity. Children with behavior disorders may lack a fluent automatic reading vocabulary which is a prerequisite to reading comprehension. They may lack automaticity with basic math facts which impairs their ability to perform algorithms (math processes). The frustration of attempting to perform a task for which they do not possess the basic prerequisites may increase the aggressive or withdrawn behaviors of these children, thus, interfering with skill acquisition.

Attention Deficit Hyperactivity Disorder

Aggressive youngsters with mild-moderate behavior disorders frequently demonstrate characteristics of attention deficit hyperactivity disorder (AD/HD) including impulsivity, overactivity, not persisting on tasks, easily distracted, inadequate decision-making skills, interrupting others, and aggression (American Psychiatric Association, 1994). Hyperactive children are frequently at odds with their teachers. Their high energy level often finds them out of their seat and off-task; when at their desk they may be hanging upside down half-way under the desk, reaching to touch or look at their neighbor's paper or book. During classroom discussions they blurt out answers before the teacher finishes the questions. When waiting their turn they may sit on their knees in the seat and wave their arms frantically to be called on—often forgetting what they were going to say when they are called on to provide an answer. During reading group seatwork, while teacher is busy with another group, they will be out of their seat, off-task, engaging in minor mischief, "picking fights", pulling pig-tails, sharpening all of the pencils, continuously talking and cruising the classroom. When teacher verbally reprimands or physically attempts to take students with behavior disorders to their desks, they often become hostile and aggressive. As a result, these students seldom complete assignments, and they interfere with the ability of peers to complete assignments.

CLASSROOM FUNCTIONING AT VARIOUS AGES

Academically, students with mild-moderate behavior disorders are underachievers when considering both chronological age and mental age. Their behavior at school interferes with attending to task and completing the required academic assignments. For some children, the pattern of failure in academic situations is so severe and long-standing that they do not have the skills to handle academic situations (Cartwright et al., 1989).

Preschool "At-Risk" Children

The most severe types of emotional or behavioral disorders often are first observed in the preschool years. Frequently, it is difficult to tell the difference between emotional or behavior disorders in young children and other handicapping conditions such as mental retardation or deafness (Hallahan & Kauffman, 1994). The patterns of behavior that signal problems for the preschool child are those that bring them into frequent conflict or keep them aloof from their parents or caregivers and their siblings and peers (Hallahan & Kauffman, 1994).

Young children with serious social, emotional, or behavioral problems display a wide range of maladjustive behaviors frequently and over a long period of time (Lerner et al., 1987). Common behavior problems of young children include aggression, noncompliance, temper tantrums, social withdrawal, hyperactivity, and phobias (Zirpoli, 1995; Neisworth & Bagnato, 1987). Infants and toddlers who exhibit a very difficult temperament, irritability, intense responses to many stimuli, negative reactions toward new situations accompanied by irregular patterns of sleeping, eating, and eliminating are at risk for developing serious behavior problems (Hallahan & Kauffman, 1994).

"Aggressive behavior is any behavior that occurs without provocation, which is designed to hurt other people or destroy property in the environment" (Lerner et al., 1987, 245). One of the most commonly observed acts of aggression exhibited by preverbal children is biting. Young children with mild-moderate behavior disorders may reveal aggressive behaviors in frequent screaming, cursing, hitting, kicking, temper tantrums, biting, and other forceful and uncontrolled physical aggression toward adults and other children (Zirpoli, 1995). They may observe others at "work" and rush over to kick down the block tower just built or knock over a sand castle, tear up or splash paint on someone else's picture, and in general ruin what others are doing, yet make no attempt to be involved in constructive activity themselves. They may be hyperactive and in constant motion continually involved in aggressive behavior and creating havoc.

"Withdrawal is one of the symptoms of severe social or emotional disability" (Lerner et al., 1987, 246). Withdrawn children move away from others and refuse to interact. They may engage in self-stimulating behaviors such as thumb sucking or body rocking and staring at a light to the exclusion of all constructive behaviors. Withdrawn children may absently wander around the classroom in their "own world". Among the at-risk homeless preschoolers, many show signs of depression including unhappiness, lethargy, crying easily, extreme quietness, no attempts to play, problems with toilet training beyond expected ages.

Children with mild-moderate behavior disorders both aggressive and withdrawn experience developmental delays in cognitive, motor (fine and gross), communication, self-help, and social skills. These children may fail to acquire the language skills to label the objects and activities in their environment. They may be noncommunicative. They may not understand the directions they are expected to follow. Language deficits will significantly negatively impact the acquisition of preacademic skills. Failure to develop appropriate fine motor skills not only interferes with acquisition of prewriting skills, but also, with dressing and eating skills.

The severe noncompliance results in power struggles with adults continuously all day with escalating inappropriate physical and verbal behaviors of the child and the adults in their environment. The child with aggressive behavior disorders continually interferes with the learning of classmates as well as their own learning. The preschool student with behavior disorders progresses to elementary school without the social, cognitive, language, pre-academic, and motor skills required for success in school.

Elementary Students with Behavior Disorders

Students with mild-moderate behavior disorders perform behind nondisabled peers in reading, arithmetic, and spelling (Kauffman et al., 1987). They frequently experience difficulty in written composition due to attention deficits, and the lack of automaticity in prerequisite skills necessary to produce a written assignment. Of significant concern is the fact that academic retardation increases with age or grade level, and increased failure in academics produces even more deviant behavior (Whelan, 1988). Research, however, indicates that students with behavior disorders function at higher academic levels in reading, math, and other academics than do learning disabled peers (Epstein & Cullinan, 1983).

During elementary grades especially during 4th grade when the curriculum transition from "learning to read" to "reading to learn" occurs, the referrals for consideration for placement in programs for children with behavior disorders reaches a peak. At this point, teachers have attempted for several years to control or change the inappropriate behaviors without success. The increased frustration from increased academic demands that the children with behavior disorders can not meet exacerbates the behavior problems.

Conduct Disordered

The elementary-aged aggressive youngster with behavior disorders is not a participant in education. While he (about 75% of the students with behavior disorders are boys) is engaged in off-task aggressive behaviors toward peers, teachers, and school equipment and supplies, he is not only interfering with his own academic progress, but with the progress of his classmates.

Aggressive behavior toward the teacher and other adults may include the following behaviors: disobedience, unmanageable behavior, defiant to instructions or commands, disruptive, arguing, temper tantrums, boasting and bragging that no one can tell him what to do, showing cruelty and attempts to injure the teacher, lying and stealing from the teacher. With peers the aggressive elementary school student purposefully annoys them, is unusually verbally loud, bullies or frightens other children, fights and beats up peers, may use extortion to take peers' lunch money, steals from peers.

Internalizing Disorder

The significantly withdrawn child who retreats into fantasy and depression, refuses to talk in class or complete assignments, experiences "illnesses" and phobic reactions at school, appears extremely anxious and nervous when asked to perform, also, is not an active learner. The child who internalizes may be depressed or chronically unhappy (at least intermittently for a year) experiencing insomnia or hypersomnia, low energy level or chronic tiredness, decreased productivity and accuracy at school, social withdrawal, inability to experience pleasure, brooding, fearfulness, crying, recurring thoughts of death or suicide (Epanchin & Paul, 1987).

Children who are withdrawn or internalizing may experience anxiety, inferiority characterized by low self-confidence, situation-specific avoidance, statements of worry, and skill disorganization (Haring, 1990). Children and youth who internalize may engage in excessive self-blame and excessive suffering including physical and emotional pain (Haring, 1990).

Obviously, children whose lives are dominated by severely aggressive or severely withdrawn behaviors are too self-preoccupied to focus attention, sustain concentration, and utilize academic skills to complete assignments. The aggressive or externalizing student is generally far greater concern to the classroom teacher as this student is often a danger to himself and others, while the withdrawn student is generally only a danger to him/herself.

Secondary Students with Behavior Disorders

Adolescents with behavior disorders may demonstrate severe problem patterns including dropping out of school, conflicts with the justice system, mental illness, depression, and suicide (Shea & Bauer, 1994). These students have high absentee rates, 30 percent drop out of school before completing a diploma or certificate, 20 percent are arrested at least once before they leave school, and 37 percent are arrested within a few years of dropping out of school (OSEP, 1994).

The behaviors of adolescents with behavior disorders continue to be primarily in the areas of conduct disorder (externalizing behaviors) or personality disorders (internalizing behaviors). The problems of adolescents, however, are often magnified compared to similar problems at younger ages due to the physiological and emotional changes experienced by all adolescents.

Conduct Disordered Adolescents

Secondary-aged students with behavior disorders continue to lack social acceptance of peers in part because they lack social experience and possess a limited repertoire of appropriate social skills. The lack of self-control accompanied by inappropriate verbal and physical behaviors continues to make their behavior unpredictable and undesirable. Secondary-aged students with behavior disorders possess very poor decision-making skills, they continue to make the same mistakes repeatedly, persisting in behaviors that have repeatedly brought negative consequences in the past (Rizzo & Zabel, 1988).

Academically, average intelligence adolescents with behavior disorders often function about the fifth grade level in reading and math by the 10th to 11th grade levels, thus, function about 5–6 years behind their same-aged peers. They lack prerequisites and automaticity in the basic skills to function on grade level even if the behavior is under control. This low level functioning and inability to accomplish class assignments results in increased frustration, anger and outbursts, often followed by loud refusals to attempt assignments.

Adolescents with conduct disorders display patterns of aggression, destructiveness, and impulsivity that persist despite most efforts at correction, and they engage in repetitive and persistent violation of the rights of others and of age-appropriate social norms (APA, 1994). Although their problems are often manifested in angry defiance of social conventions or destructive and aggressive behavior, they also experience much of the same internal suffering that characterizes adolescents with personality problems (Rizzo & Zabel, 1988).

Adolescents with conduct disorders do not seem to experience a consistent sense of guilt or guilt of sufficient quantity to prevent recurrences of the inappropriate behaviors (APA, 1994). They demonstrate little capacity to empathize with another person and seem unable to develop genuine affectional bonds, thus, they are insensitive to the feelings and rights of others and to the consequences of their behaviors.

A number of features of secondary schools and adolescence make adolescents with behavior disorders harder to control than elementary-aged students with behavior disorders. The size and organizational structure of secondary schools requiring movement from class to class, adjusting to the behaviors and requirements of several teachers, navigating large schools tends to increase the problems of students with behavior disorders (Silverman et al., 1983). Adolescents, in general, are more mobile and assertive and more difficult to manage than younger students. Adolescents with behavior disorders are physically larger and more threatening to teachers than elementary students with behavior disorders. Behavior control techniques such as physical restraint that are effective with small or younger children are no longer effective and may be dangerous for adults to attempt with behavior disordered adolescents. Additionally, the extreme behavior problems (verbal and physical) of adolescents make it very difficult for teachers to remain emotionally neutral during negative interactions (Shea & Bauer, 1994), which may escalate a power struggle.

Although conduct disorders and substance abuse disorders are distinct sets of problems, the two frequently occur together. Substance use or experimentation among adolescents is extremely common. Due to their lack of self-regulation and lack of ability to predict the consequences of their behavior, conduct disordered adolescents tend to experiment with alcohol and drugs to a greater degree than nondisabled adolescents. Substance use or abuse tends to increase the magnitude of the inappropriate behaviors.

Adolescents with Personality Disorders

Adolescence appears, also, to exacerbate behavior disorders that are internalizing. Anxiety is the single most pervasive characteristic of personality or internalizing problems, and it seems to permeate all aspects of life (Rizzo & Zabel, 1988). Adolescents with personality problems spend large parts of their waking hours worrying about whether they can cope with school work, whether other students will like them, whether teachers will think they are stupid, or whether their parents may die unexpectedly (Rizzo & Zabel, 1988). Wrapped up in worry, self-consciousness, insecurity, physical illness, depression, and low self-esteem, adolescents with personality problems may have little energy left to devote to studies or to common adolescent activities. Adolescents with personality problems suffer in silence and often go unnoticed as they try to avoid attention and notice (Rizzo & Zabel, 1988).

Anxiety disorders are manifested in different ways including phobias, neuroses, school refusal, obsessive-compulsive disorders, physiological disorders that are psychologically based, and eating disturbances (i.e., anorexia nervosa) (Epanchin, 1987). Behaviors associated with these disorders include preoccupation, irritability, fearfulness, overdependence on others, sleep problems, stomachaches, lethargy, unhappiness, frequent crying spells, headaches, nausea, loss of appetite, poor school work, and carelessness in carrying out responsibilities (Epanchin, 1987). Some adolescents experience pervasive and unfounded guilt that increases feelings of worthlessness. Adolescents with anxiety disorders experience neuroses or irrational worries and conflicts that are not responsive to reasoning and reassurance because the adolescent's behavior is beyond the control of reason (Epanchin, 1987).

These adolescents may experience hypersensitivity, self-consciousness, and pessimism in interactions with people (Rizzo & Zabel, 1988). To avoid the possibility of looking foolish or being teased, internalizing adolescents may avoid trying new tasks or going to new places and may be unable to respond spontaneously to a greeting or interaction. Adolescents with personality disorders expect the worst from others and life in general so their own pessimism often results in academic and social failure. One of the most common phobias of school-age children is fear of school or of school-related demands and expectations. Adolescents experiencing personality disorders are too consumed by their own problems to be successful in school work.

An enormous concern among educational, psychological, and medical personnel is the enormous increase in suicide during adolescence among those who experience conduct and personality disorders especially when paired with frequent use of alcohol or drugs. Suicide is one of the leading causes of death among adolescents.

SOCIAL/EMOTIONAL LEARNING CHARACTERISTICS

"Social behavior, which involves interactions with others, is directly observable in the classroom. Emotional behavior is not directly observable but is inferred from more overt behaviors" (Smith et al., 1987, 12). In normal development there is a close relationship among cognitive and social and emotional development. Thus, as a child or youth develops cognitively, she/he acquires more mature ability in social developmental skills such as social perspective-taking, social regulation, moral development, social problem solving, and social relationships. The normal child and youth, also, matures emotionally in terms of self-knowledge (beliefs, commitments, attitudes, values), self-competence, and self-evaluation as she/he develops cognitively. These complex social and emotional skills depend on abstract thinking, the use of logic, and automaticity in self-monitoring.

Social Learning Problems

"The emotionally disturbed child and adolescent (as well as the adult) is likely to differ from peers in terms of greater egocentricity and lack of decentration in cognitive and social tasks" (Monson & Simeonsson, 1987, 67). In other words, the youth with emotional disturbance or behavior disorders is more self-centered, and less able to engage in social perspective-taking, and empathize with others. These weaknesses severely hamper abilities to form satisfying interpersonal relationships, engage in socially appropriate behavior, and understand his/her role in the success or failure of social situations.

Interpersonal Relationships

Peer interaction is a central aspect of child development, providing opportunities for companionship, social status, self-understanding, personal maturing, and adjustment to society (Cullinan & Epstein, 1990). Youngsters exhibiting mild-moderate behavior disorders in interpersonal relationships frequently engage in aggressive behaviors against peers or completely withdraw from them. These children and youth cannot develop normal social interactions and are deprived of normal kinds of approval and satisfaction from others (Lerner et al., 1987).

> Many children with emotional and behavioral disorders are seldom really liked by anyone—their peers, teachers, brothers or sisters, even parents. Sadder still, they often do not even like themselves. The child with behavioral disorders is difficult to be around, and attempts to befriend him—most are boys—may lead only to rejection, verbal abuse, or even physical attack (Heward, 1996, 246).

It is not surprising that aggressive children in regular elementary and secondary classrooms are seldom socially accepted by peers. They are seldom allowed to participate very long in community activities such as Little League ballgames and scouting due to the aggressive and hostile behavior toward other children. "It appears that aggressive behavior patterns have already become a major component of the child's behavioral repertoire by the age of 10 years" (Griffin, 1985, 251).

Withdrawn behavior involves too little social interaction, "children are unusually quiet, having few emotional highs or lows. Preferring to be alone, they will avoid group activities. . . . These children will not spontaneously initiate conversation. Often they will try to avoid verbal contacts" (Lerner et al., 1987, 34). "They are social isolates who have few friends, seldom play with other children their own age, and lack the social skills necessary to have fun. Some retreat into fantasy or day-dreaming; some develop fears that are completely out of proportion to the circumstances" (Hallahan & Kauffman, 1988, 183).

Obviously, neither the youth with mild aggressive behavior disorders, nor the youth with mild withdrawn behavior disorders have appropriate, satisfying interactions with peers. Youth who experience difficulty with peer interactions lack insight into the reciprocal nature of interactions or lack critical social-cognitive developmental skills (Youniss, 1978). Though the youngster with behavior disorders may accept their peers' dislike as unchangeable; they may not see the relationship between their behavior and the social rejection.

Research indicates that children and youth with behavior disorders experience difficulty in decoding voice tone and facial expression (Nowicki & DiGirolamo, 1989). Thus, they experience difficulty in interpreting and understanding the emotions of peers and adults. The nonlinguistic cues interpreted by most individuals provide information regarding the social situation and the need for modification of one's behavior. Children and youth with behavior disorders cannot predict the mood of the teacher and others from facial expressions and vocal intonation. Thus, they interpret conversation literally missing the nuances and inferences provided.

Studies have revealed that children with behavior disorders lack social-evaluation ability (Jurkovic & Selman, 1980). Youth with mild-moderate behavior disorders frequently made errors in interpreting peers' behaviors toward them in that they perceived peers to be hostile whenever the peers' intentions were ambiguous, and they reacted aggressively to perceived hostile behavior (Dodge & Frame, 1982). Youngsters with behavior disorders, also, appear to be less knowledgeable about appropriate ways to be helpful to peers in situations of need.

Inappropriate Behavior

Aggressive Behavior. The most common presenting problem among youth classified as behaviorally disturbed is aggressive behavior (Epanchin, 1987). Aggressive conduct disorders involve repeated episodes of violent confrontation with others including acts of physical assault, robbery or theft with physical confrontation, or sexually assaultive behavior (Rizzo & Zabel, 1988). Within the school setting, aggression involves cruelty, bullying peers, threats, petty extortion, fighting on the playground, screaming, tantrums, hostile resistance; disrespect, disobedience, and threatening teachers (Cullinan & Epstein, 1990). Frequent unpredictable outbursts and threats disrupt the class and interfere with other children's concentration.

Many children with behavior disorders have problems determining when and where certain behaviors are appropriate (Heward, 1996). Aggressive children learn many aggressive responses through observation and imitation of family members. Children are more likely to be aggressive when they are victims of physical assault, verbal threats, taunts, insults; and/or when positive reinforcement decreases or ends (Epanchin, 1987). It is the youth with conduct disorders (hyperaggressive) whose adulthood is most likely to be characterized by socially intolerable behavior (Kazdin, 1987).

Aggressive youth are different in childhood than their nonbehavior disordered peers (Griffin, 1985). As a group, they exhibit a much greater number of conduct-disordered behaviors, developmentally related organic factors, and academic problems prior to age nine than nondisabled students.

Personality Disorders. Personality disorders involving extreme cases of worry, self-consciousness, insecurity, fears, depression, and anxiety often result in inappropriate and deviant behaviors. A major concern regarding adolescents with withdrawn behavior disorders is depression—a condition that may include mood disturbances, inability to think or concentrate, lack of motivation, sadness, apathy, poor self-esteem and pervasive pessimism (Hallahan & Kauffman, 1988). Depression has frequently been linked to suicide among teens. Obviously, these behavior patterns limit the child's chances to take part in and learn from the school and leisure activities that normal children participate in (Heward,

1996). "It seems self-evident that social incompetence reduces the developing individual's opportunities for friendships and other important chances for profiting from classroom and informal learning activities (Cullinan & Epstein, 1990, 169).

Sense of Personal Control

Many children with behavior disorders think they have little control over their lives. Things just happen to them, and being disruptive is their way of reacting to a world that is inconsistent and frustrating (Heward, 1996).

Metacognition Deficits

Children and youth with behavior disorders experience difficulties with the metacognitive aspect that regulates and controls strategic aspects of cognition or their ability to control their cognitions (Mann & Sabatino, 1985). Youth with behavior disorders are deficient in the metacognitive operations to direct the learning process, and to monitor and control their behavior. Major concerns regarding children and youth with behavior disorders include the following: (1) Skill deficits: the absence of a response in the student's repertoire; (2) Motivational deficits: the student's failing to perform a behavior even though the prerequisite skills are present in his repertoire; and (3) Discrimination deficits: result when an individual has the skill and motivation necessary to engage in the desired behavior, but is not aware of appropriate conditions for performing it (Schloss, 1985).

Youngsters with behavior disorders lack functional cognitive strategies to control and direct thinking, learning, and remembering; and lack monitoring skills to determine if their responses (academic and social) are correct or appropriate. Youngsters with mild-moderate behavior disorders experience difficulty with both academic and social problem-solving; and problems with drawing inferences. They frequently lack the automaticity in prerequisite skills to fluently perform academic tasks, and paired with the lack of metacognitive skills relegates them to focusing on the subskills unable to understand the process.

The lack of metacognitive abilities in social areas significantly interferes with the social acceptability of the student with behavior disorders. The lack of social perspective-taking interferes with the youngster's ability to form mutually satisfying social relationships as she/he cannot understand the other person's reasoning, cannot empathize, cannot feel happy at the friend's good fortune, and thus is relegated to immature egocentric behaviors. The lack of self-monitoring and social-evaluation in social situations renders the BD youth unable to determine when his/her behaviors are socially appropriate or inappropriate; thus, she/he can not monitor accuracy or effect and change the behaviors when social responses indicate that the behavior is inappropriate. Since they cannot understand behaviors from the perspective of the other person, they will not understand why they are ignored, not asked to parties, not included in "the group" activities, nor why they are no longer friends. The lack of metacognitive skills means that the youth with behavior disorders will be unable to engage in social problem-solving, will be socially incompetent, and will continue to function at an immature moral development stage.

The lack of metacognitive abilities renders the child unable to control his/her behavior. This deficit means that the hostile, aggressive child continues to rampage until his energy is spent; and the withdrawn, anxiety-inferiority obsessed child will be unable to halt the destructive emotions of depression and fear. This lack of self-control is far more devastating than just academic deficits or just behavioral deficits, for the lack of self-control interferes with independence and appropriateness in all functioning areas: social, emotional, cognitive, and academic.

Motivation/Attribution Deficits

Students with long histories of academic failure and a weak need for achievement typically attribute their success to easy questions or luck and their failures to lack of ability (external locus of control) (Biehler & Snowman, 1986). Research indicates that students with behavior disorders experience an external locus of control (Nowicki & DiGirolamo, 1989). In other words, they do not feel that they have much control over their school successes and/or failures since they are due to luck or ability factors over which they have no control. Depressed children have a more internal locus of control and tend to internalize aggression more than do non-depressed conduct disordered children (King et al., 1986).

> Because low achieving students attribute failure to low ability, future failure is seen as more likely than future success. Consequently, satisfactory achievement and reward may have little effect on the failure avoiding strategies that poor students have developed over the years . . . It may be, then, that rewards will not motivate low-need achievers to work harder so long as they attribute

success to factors that are unstable and beyond their control (Biehler & Snowman, 1986, 482).

Children who are severely anxious and withdrawn often display learned helplessness, a belief that nothing they do can change the bad situations in their lives. Learned helplessness results in severe deterioration in performance after failure because the failure just serves to reinforce in them that there is nothing they can do to change things (Kirk & Gallagher, 1989), which adds to feelings of helplessness and reinforces low self-image and low self-worth.

A typical child or youth with behavior disorders exhibits a profile of unsuccessful academic performance in combination with inadequate social coping behaviors (Whelan, 1988). Thus, all major facets of the lives of children with severe emotional disturbance (internal and external) are chaotic. "The ways that children cope with internal and external chaos are as varied as the children who display them . . . Deficit and excessive behaviors are ways of avoiding circumstances associated with pain and failure, of coping with problems from within and without . . . " (Whelan, 1988, 204). Children and youth with behavior disorders who exhibit learned helplessness may accept an assigned task, but either do not complete it or avoid failure by placidly using up the allotted task time in a nonproductive fashion, or the child may be characterized by the absence of behavior.

Self-Concepts of Students with Behavior Disorders

Much of the early research regarding the self-concepts of children and youth with behavior disorders has concerned children who were severely emotionally disturbed. The behaviors, emotions, motivation, attributions, academic success of youngsters with behavior disorders are frequently compared to those of the average nondisabled child or youth of the same age. A picture of the youngster with behavior disorders or emotional disturbance is in most ways the direct opposite of that of the mentally healthy child.

General Self-Concept

"All human beings have a perspective, or point of view, through which they interpret the world. This personal and unique perspective includes the individual's perception of self and personal actions as well as a perception of others and their actions and places, objects, and events that make up the world" (Shea & Bauer, 1987, 18). Much of the research regarding the general self-concept of youngsters with emotional disturbance indicates an over-evaluated delusional self-concept or a significantly lower self-concept than that of nondisabled youth.

Low Self-Concepts. Research indicates that the self-concept scores for children with behavior disorders were significantly lower than the self-concept scores of normal and able youngsters (Bloom et al., 1979; Politino, 1980). Students with behavior disorders in school settings, mainstreamed for at least part of the day, possessed significantly more negative conscious and unconscious self-concepts than nondisabled students ages 10–13 years old (Jones, 1985). Also, the students with behavior disorders indicated experiencing high anxiety levels (Jones, 1985).

Sweeney & Zionts (1989) examined differences between regular education and emotionally disturbed early adolescents with respect to self-concept, body image, and selected uses of clothing. Their findings revealed that emotionally impaired were less likely to use clothing to influence mood than were regular education students.

Delusional Self-Concepts. A number of researchers found that some children with emotional disturbance tend to over-evaluate their abilities to a delusional degree. In their study of self-concept as related to school phobia, Levanthal and Sills (1964) determined the most severely disturbed of their subjects had self-images that were over-evaluated to a delusional degree. The children were in an almost constant state of anxiety and panic whenever they were forced to go to school because of fear of failure which was incompatible with their over-evaluated self-image. The behavior of emotionally disturbed students was more affected by transferences (interpersonal distortions) and other factors which are irrelevant to, or are misperceptions of, the classroom situation than are normal students (Grossman, 1965).

Anxiety contributes both to the disorganization in a child and to a blurring of his consciousness or reality testing (Levitt, 1967). According to Knoblock (1971) a compartmentalized view of self was characteristic of many children with behavior disorders and approaches to tasks often revealed an inability to conceptualize and look at the total situation.

Self-Concept of Academic Achievement

Although the intelligence quotient is generally agreed to be an excellent predictor of school success and achievement, caution must be used in predicting the achievement level of students with behavior disorders. Achievement is a significant factor in emotional disturbance; however, the cause and effect relationship has not been determined (Shea, 1978).

Generally, the more years a child with emotional disturbance has stayed in school, the further educationally he was behind his nondisabled peers (Stennett, 1966). For many students with behavior disorders being in the classroom was a threatening experience (Grossman, 1965). Many of them had not acquired the educational skills necessary to meet the demands imposed upon them. Their emotional problems interfered with their ability to use even those skills they had developed. Even when their lower-than-normal IQ scores are taken into account, most children with behavior disorders are underachievers, as measured by standardized tests (Hallahan & Kauffman, 1988).

The poor self-concepts of children with behavior disorders manifests itself as a lack of self-confidence, fear of the unfamiliar, feelings of inferiority, hypersensitivity to criticism, resistance to independent functioning, and reluctance to attempt many activities (Shea, 1978). Students with behavior disorders perceived their behavior to be significantly less acceptable to adults and peers than nonhandicapped students; and perceived their intellectual ability, school status, and popularity more negatively than did nonhandicapped students (Jones, 1985).

Children with anxiety-withdrawn behavior disorders have such low self-concepts that failure in a school task or a social setting only confirms for them their worthlessness and helpless in the face of an unfriendly environment (Seligman & Peterson, 1986). Their performance in the classroom may be much worse than they are capable of doing simply because they are so pessimistic about themselves and their ability. "Low self-esteem seems to be at the heart of much of the underachievement of anxious-withdrawn children" (Kirk & Gallagher, 1989, 406).

Hardt (1988) indicated that passive-aggressive behavior in a child with emotional disturbance affects the child's academic progress and affects peer interactions in classroom settings. Passive-aggressive personalities are typically helpless, dependent, impulsive, overly anxious, poorly oriented to reality, and procrastinating (Hardt, 1988). The passive-aggressive child uses numerous tactics to control the classroom environment, such as selective vision, selective hearing, slow-down tactics, losing objects, and the destructive volunteer tactic (Hardt, 1988). Passive-aggressive children fail to develop satisfying interpersonal relationships and possess a negative self-esteem.

Thus, the research indicates that the general self-concepts and academic self-concepts of children with behavior disorders are significantly negative and interfere with their functioning in all aspects of life. Their external locus of control and expectancy for failure perpetuates a severely negative cycle.

SUMMARY

Students with behavior disorders, both aggressive and withdrawn, are a significant concern of the public school system in terms of their social, emotional, cognitive, and academic progress, but also, on the effects they have on other children in the classroom. The inappropriate and maladaptive behaviors exhibited by children and adolescents with behavior disorders are evident in deficits in academic learning, cognitive development, and social interactions. Students with disturbed behaviors are frequently categorized as having mild-moderate or severe-profound behavior disorders.

Children with mild-moderate behavior disorders are usually educated in the public school systems in self-contained classrooms, and gradually mainstreamed to the regular classroom as they learn to control their negative behaviors. Though most students with mild-moderate behavior disorders possess normal-range IQ (around 90), they experience many cognitive delays including metacognitive skills, attention deficits, information processing deficits, inefficiency in learning, and lack automatization. These deficits interact to prevent higher level cognitive functioning and academic success. Students with behavior disorders experience significant deficits in terms of self-concept, external locus of control, and have expectancies for failure.

UNIT 3
STUDENTS WITH
LEARNING DISABILITIES

Chapter 8

HISTORICAL PERSPECTIVES
OF LEARNING DISABILITIES

*The historical development of the field of learning disabilities must be
viewed within the context of society, societal needs, changes, philosophical
convictions, and legislative mandates (Ariel, 1992, 33).*

Historical Antecedents: 1800–1934
- Disorders of Spoken Language
- Disorders of Written Language
- Disorders of Perceptual-Motor Processes

The Brain-Injured Period: 1935–1962
- Disorders of Spoken Language
- Written Language Disorders
- Disorders of Perceptual and Motor Processes

Emergent Field of LD: 1963–1974
- Definitions of Learning Disabilities
- Paradigm Shifts, Changes, Growth

EHA Period: 1975–1989
- Definitions: Federal and NJCLD
- Political Activity, Paradigm Changes, and Theorists

IDEA Period: 1990–Present
- Areas of Concern

Summary

According to the *Sixteenth Annual Report to Congress,* a total of 2,369,385 students with learning disabilities ages 6–21 years or 52.4 percent of all students with disabilities were served during academic year 1992–93 (OSEP, 1994). Learning Disabilities is the largest category of exceptional students comprising about 5.2 percent of all students ages 6–17 years enrolled in school (OSEP, 1994).

As with mental retardation and emotional disturbance, the historical background of services for persons with learning disabilities is frequently traced to European physicians practicing in the 1800s. Although idiocy (mental retardation) and lunacy (emotional disturbances) have long been accepted as human deviancy with definitions, classification systems, and causations, the area of learning disabilities continues to lack agreement as to definition, classifications, and causations among professionals in the fields of education, psychology, and medicine. Several authors (i.e., Wiederholt, 1974; Mercer, 1987; Ariel, 1992; Lerner, 1993) have proposed timelines of the various historical stages or periods in the development of the field of learning disabilities. The historical periods discussed here represent a composite as follows: (1) Historical Antecedents: 1800–1934; (2) The Brain-Injured Period: 1935–1962; (3) Emergent Field of LD: 1963–1974; (4) Education for All Handicapped Children Act (EHA) Period: 1975–1989; and (5) Individuals with Disabilities Education Act (IDEA) Period: 1990–Present.

HISTORICAL ANTECEDENTS: 1800s–1934

Major historical antecedents that influenced the development of the field of learning disabilities include the following: (1) the evolution of the field of special education, (2) early brain research, (3) the influence of 20th century psychology, and (4) the early attempts to remediate learning problems (Ariel, 1992). The development of the field of learning disabilities was significantly affected by the revolutionary teaching methods that Itard, Seguin, and Montessori used with mentally retarded children (see Chapter 2). Their work stressing the importance of sensory-motor training in educational methods became one of the bulwarks of the field of learning disabilities. The brain research of Gall, Broca, Jackson, Wernicke, and Head with adults concerning spoken language disorders; Hinshelwood concerning written language disorders; and Goldstein, Strauss and Werner concerning perceptual-motor disorders provided the research base for the three major dimensions of deficits of learning disabilities. The growth of the new field of physiological psychology through Wundt's research (see Chapter 3), Pavlov's stimulus-response research, and Skinner's research involving stimulus-response-reinforcement studied relationships between brain functions and behavior (see Chapter 5). The efforts of Fernald, Orton, and Monroe to remediate learning problems in reading and written language provided the foundation for remediation of learning disabilities.

Disorders of Spoken Language: 1800–1934

Much of the research conducted during the 1800–1934 period concerned disorders of spoken language. Primary researchers during this period included Franz Gall, Paul Broca, John Jackson, Carl Wernicke, and Sir Henry Head. These early physician scientists studied adults whose behavior and functioning had changed (i.e., lost ability to speak and/or understand language) because of strokes, accidents, war injuries, or illness. These researchers described the behavioral characteristics of their patients; and attempted to localize sensory, perceptual-motor, and language functions to precise parts of the brain (Wiederholt, 1974). They conducted autopsies on the brains of patients who died to determine if the loss of specific functions was related to injury to a specific part of the brain (Lerner, 1993).

"The systematic investigation of learning disabilities began around 1800 with *Franz Gall's* examination of adults who had sustained head injuries and, apparently as a result, had lost the capacity to express their feelings and ideas through speech, while experiencing no intellectual privation" (Myers & Hammill, 1990, 28). Gall, therefore, was one of the first to relate specific localization of brain damage to aphasia (Wiederholt, 1974). Gall's diagnostic evidence demonstrated (1) the presence of intraindividual differences (i.e., patients could not speak but could write thoughts), (2) the problem was a consequence of brain involvement (i.e., damage, disorganization, or dysfunction), and (3) the patient's performance was not caused by mental retardation or deafness (Myers & Hammill, 1990).

In the 1860s, *Paul Broca,* a surgeon and neuroanatomist, discovered during autopsies of adult patients who had lost the ability to speak that certain areas of the brain in the left frontal lobe were damaged (Lerner, 1993). The loss of the ability to speak is often called Broca's aphasia, and the site on the brain related to the ability to speak is called Broca's area (Lerner, 1993). Broca, also, contributed to the hypotheses that the functions of the brain's left and right hemispheres were different, and that language is a left hemisphere function (Restak, 1984).

Another noted contributor to the field was *John Hughlings Jackson,* who from 1864–1893 produced a great number of discussions on speech and language disorders (Wiederholt, 1974). Jackson attempted to locate speech disorders in the cerebral cortex and proceeded to develop an entire classification and definition system for speech components (Mercer, 1987). He did not believe in the localization theory regarding brain functioning, but indicated that the parts of the brain are intimately linked and that damage to one part would reduce general functioning (Lerner, 1993).

In the 1870s, *Carl Wernicke,* a German neurologist, discovered a different type of aphasia in several of his patients who could produce an infinite number of words, but who could not comprehend speech (Restak, 1984; Wiederholt, 1974). Wernicke attributed the understanding of oral language or listening comprehension to the temporal lobe (Wiederholt, 1974). The inability to comprehend oral language is often called Wernicke's aphasia, and the site in the temporal lobe responsible for understanding oral language is called Wernicke's area (Restak, 1984).

Each of the two types of aphasia, Broca's and Wernicke's, correspond to identifiable areas in the left hemisphere of the brain. Based on this anatomical localization, it appeared that language is localized to the left hemisphere (Lerner, 1993). Wernicke referred to Broca's aphasia as conductive aphasia and to Wernicke's aphasia as sensory aphasia; total aphasia was the term used to describe cases in which both understanding and use of oral language was defective (Wiederholt, 1974).

In the mid-1920s, *Sir Henry Head* produced two volumes on aphasia that were the culmination of a lifetime of collecting scientific data from brain-damaged adults, and created a test for aphasia (impairment of the ability to use or understand language) (Lerner, 1993). Head believed that adult patients with aphasia did not suffer generalized impairment of intellectual ability even if they had sustained brain damage evidenced by language difficulties (Lerner, 1993). In 1926, Sir Henry Head consolidated the, then current theory, which led to wide acceptance of several conclusions about disorders in spoken language: (1) Disorders in language could not be dichotomized as sensory or motor, (2) Motor correlates of language disabilities were not necessarily due to a disturbance in higher-level brain processes, (3) Brain localization and hemisphere differentiation were varied concepts, (4) Loss of symbolic speech functions did not necessarily include a concomitant loss in mechanical aptitudes (Mercer, 1987). "Although this period lasted well over a century, there was little agreement regarding the etiology of disorders of spoken language" (Wiederholt, 1974).

Disorders of Written Language: 1800–1934

"During the same period that medical professionals were attempting to discover the etiology of spoken language, other physicians were trying to locate the causes of disorders of written language" (Wiederholt, 1974, 114). Written language disorders include the areas of reading and written expression. The major researchers of written language disorders during the first quarter of the twentieth century were James Hinshelwood, a French physician, and Samuel T. Orton, an American physician and professor of neurology, both of whom originally studied adults with acquired brain damage. During this period several university professors including Grace Fernald and Marion Monroe developed specialized programs to use in teaching disabled students to read (Ariel, 1992).

James Hinshelwood

The first well accepted publication describing etiology and intervention techniques regarding written language deficits was published in 1917 by James Hinshelwood. He described a condition called "word blindness" in adults as the inability to interpret written or printed language despite normal vision, normal speech, and intact intelligence (Lerner, 1993; Wiederholt, 1974). "Congenital word blindness" was the term Hinshelwood used to label school-aged children with reading disorders. He speculated that the problem was due to a defect in the angular gyrus, a specific area of the brain which stored visual memories for words and letters (Wiederholt, 1974). Hinshelwood proposed an educational intervention technique that was designed to improve the visual memory part of the brain, to teach reading by spelling words aloud, and using auditory memory for retrieval of the whole word (Wiederholt, 1974).

Samuel T. Orton

Samuel Orton disputed many of Hinshelwood's positions and formulated his own theories regarding the causes for and the remediation of specific reading problems that he called "strephosymbolia" or twisted symbols (Myers & Hammill, 1990). Orton speculated that one side of the brain dominated language processes (Bender, 1995), and that language disabled children who had no demonstrable brain injury had failed to establish hemispheric (cerebral) dominance (Mercer, 1987). Such deficits led Orton to advocate an educational approach that included phonics and kinesthetic (touch and movement) teaching aids (Wiederholt, 1974).

Though little empirical evidence supports Orton's theories concerning brain dominance, the teaching concepts are still in use today because they are effective with some children who display written language difficulties (Mercer, 1987). In 1937, Orton published *Reading, Writing, and Speech Problems in Children* which described a number of remediation programs that utilized a systematic phonics program reinforced with kinesthetic aids that followed the instructions in his 1925 publication (Lovitt, 1989). Among the investigators who developed techniques based on Orton's recommendations and put them into practice were Marion Monroe, Anna Gillingham, Bessie Stillman, Grace Fernald, and Romalda Spalding (Lovitt, 1989).

Grace Fernald

In 1909, Grace Fernald and William Healy established the Juvenile Psychopathic Institute in Chicago, which would become the model for child guidance centers. In the 1920s, while working at the Clinic School at the University of California, Grace Fernald developed a multisensory teaching approach (VAKT) to remediate reading and writing deficits that has become known as the Fernald Method (Mercer, 1987). The teaching approach focused on providing stimuli in a multisensory basis using visual, auditory, tactile, and kinesthetic means with students of normal and superior intelligence who displayed extreme deficits in reading and writing (Fernald, 1943). The method incorporated both language experience and tracing techniques in a multisensory procedure (Kirk et al., 1978). The program took approximately eight months of attending the Fernald School from 9:00 A.M. to 3:00 P.M. and was laborious and slow. In 1943, Grace Fernald published *Remedial Techniques in Basic School Subjects* detailing the Fernald Method of remediation which continues to be used today in modified form with some disabled students.

Marion Monroe

Marion Monroe, Orton's research assistant at the Iowa State Psychopathic Hospital, helped test the efficacy of his theories for education (Mercer, 1987). In 1932, Monroe published *Children Who Cannot Read* in which she described assessment tests and a teaching strategy called the "synthetic phonetic approach" (phonics skills taught in isolation) (Ariel, 1992). Her method used drills and the kinesthetic approach (tracing words) and was called a phonic-tracing method. Monroe tutored Samuel Kirk in the diagnosis and remediation of severe cases of reading disabilities before he became affiliated with the Wayne County Training School (Mercer, 1987).

Disorders of Perceptual and Motor Processes: 1800–1934

The perceptual-motor theorists can be traced back to Kurt Goldstein, a physician and student of Gestalt psychology interested in perception (Bender, 1995). Goldstein studied World War I brain-injured soldiers and noted that they experienced perceptual impairment characterized by figure-ground difficulties, distractibility to external stimuli, perseveration (uncontrollably repeating an action) (Lerner, 1993). Goldstein's work led to the use of the term *brain injured* to identify children having these problems (Bender, 1995).

Alfred Strauss, a psychiatrist, and Heinz Werner, a psychologist, continued Goldstein's work, expanding the study from brain-injured soldiers to brain-injured children (Lerner, 1993). In 1937, Strauss immigrated to the United States from Germany where he served as research psychiatrist, and later as director of child care at the Wayne County Training School in Michigan (Scheerenberger, 1983).

THE BRAIN-INJURED PERIOD: 1935–1962

During this period researchers continued to study brain-injured patients and the manifestations as deficits in spoken and written language, and deficits in perceptual-motor skills. Scientific studies of the brain were applied to the clinical study of children and translated into ways of teaching; and numerous instruments were developed for assessment and remediation. Several name changes occurred during this period to describe the condition of children with otherwise normal intelligence who had difficulties acquiring academic skills including brain-injured children, Strauss syndrome, and minimal brain dysfunction (Lerner, 1993). The brain-injured period was noted for the distinguished work of Charles Osgood, Joseph Wepman, Helmer Myklebust, Mildred McGinnis, Samuel Kirk, and Jon Eisenson with spoken language disorders; Samuel Kirk, Anna Gillingham, Romalda Spalding with written language disorders; and Alfred Strauss and Heinz Werner, Laura Lehtinen, William Cruickshank, Newell Kephart, and Marianne Frostig in perceptual and motor disorders.

Disorders of Spoken Language: 1935–1962

During this period widespread attention was given to diagram makers or model builders including Osgood, Wepman, and Myklebust who attempted to use graphic representations to explain the communication process and the problems experienced by those with spoken and written language disorders (Wiederholt, 1974).

Charles Osgood

Charles Osgood postulated a model of the communication process that attempted to demonstrate the information processing that transpired between the presentation of an external stimulus and the individual's overt response (Mercer, 1987). Osgood's diagram is a mediation-integration model which represents an extension of Skinner's single-stage conception of behavior in that it includes the stimulus-response (S–R) paradigm (Wiederholt, 1974). It also attempts to account for the symbolic processing that takes place between the stimulus and the response (Wiederholt, 1974). Osgood's communication model was later utilized in the development of the *Illinois Test of Psycholinguistic Abilities* (ITPA) (Kirk & McCarthy, 1961).

Joseph Wepman

Joseph Wepman and colleagues developed a communication model that was somewhat similar to Osgood's but included memory, internal and external feedback, and modalities of transmission (Wiederholt, 1974). Wepman translated his model into tests of aphasia and word discrimination. Wepman (1958) developed an auditory discrimination test (that continues to be used today) designed to ascertain a child's ability to recognize fine differences between phonemes of the English language. Children who experience difficulty with auditory discrimination frequently experience difficulty with speech articulation and with decoding words using a phonetic approach. *The Language Modalities Test for Aphasia* (Wepman & Jones, 1961) classified items in terms of learning modalities (auditory, visual, graphic, gestural) (Wiederholt, 1974).

Helmer Myklebust

During this period Helmer Myklebust, who conducted research at Northwestern University, was the primary researcher on studies focusing on neurological impairment and language development (Lovitt,

1989). Myklebust attributed learning problems to some neurological impairment, coining the term "psychoneurological learning disabilities" to describe such problems (Wiederholt, 1974). In other words, Myklebust maintained that neurological dysfunction was the basis for disabilities in learning. He proposed that a number of types of learning disorders could result from central nervous system impairment including problems with perception, symbolization, imagery, and conceptualization (Mercer, 1987).

Myklebust maintained that an unimpaired peripheral and central nervous system was prerequisite to the development of language (defined as symbolic behavior) (Mercer, 1987). He became interested in aphasic children as a direct result of his experience with a number of children believed to be deaf who, in fact, had auditory and language disorders due to other causes (Wiederholt, 1974). In collaboration with Doris Johnson at Northwestern University, Myklebust identified five specific areas in which disorders might be noticed in classrooms including auditory language, reading, written language, arithmetic, and nonverbal disorders of learning; and began focusing on remediation of both spoken and written language disorders (Johnson & Myklebust, 1967).

Mildred McGinnis

Mildred McGinnis, the Director of the Speech and Corrections Division of the Central Institute for the Deaf in St. Louis, proposed two types of language disorders in children: receptive and expressive. She designed the associative method of teaching aphasics that systematically developed skills in understanding and in utilizing spoken language based upon the principles of phonetics, expression, precise articulation, sound-symbol association, and sensorimotor association (Wiederholt, 1974).

Jon Eisenson

Jon Eisenson believed that children with aphasic disorders had difficulty in symbolic abilities, experienced intellectual changes, and suffered from problems in symbolism (Wiederholt, 1974). He co-authored with Beery in 1942 a textbook, *The Defective Speech* (Wiederholt, 1974). Eisenson authored a test in 1954 for adolescents and adults who developed aphasia, *Examining for Alphasia,* that was constructed to assess the degree of symbol dysfunction, and the areas of symbol dysfunction such as reading, writing, spelling, and arithmetic (Wiederholt, 1974).

Written Language Disorders: 1935–1962

A concerted effort was made during this period to translate the theoretical postulates derived previously into remedial practice (Myers & Hammill, 1990). The focus of research and the theories that had been developed from the study of adults were transferred to the study of children with developmental disorders in spoken and written language and perceptual motor processing. During this period many tests and training programs were developed that first were used in isolated clinics, institutions, and private schools, and later in public schools as well. Remediation of written language disorders was impacted by Samuel Kirk, Anna Gillingham and Bessie Stillman, and Romalda Spalding. Many researchers during this period including Orton, Monroe, Kirk, Fernald, Gillingham and Stillman, used a multisensory approach to remediate language problems and improve perceptual processing and perceptual integration skills.

Samuel Kirk

Samuel Kirk's work spanned the later years of the Historical Antecedents Period, the Brain-Injured Period, the Emergent Field of Learning Disabilities Period, the EHA Period, and the IDEA Period. Kirk's work enormously impacted the field of special education. In 1936, while at the Wayne County Training School for mentally retarded children, Hegge, Kirk, and Kirk developed and published the *Remedial Reading Drills*. The reading drills were systematically developed according to programmed instruction principles of minimal change; overlapping; prompting and confirmation; one response for each symbol; and social reinforcement (Kirk et al., 1978). This approach is a programmed phonic system which emphasizes sound blending and kinesthetic experiences or a phonic-graphic-vocal method of teaching (Wiederholt, 1974). Kirk specified that this method of remedial training was applicable only to retarded readers in 1st, 2nd, and 3rd grades (not higher grades), who have failed to learn to read after a number of years in school (Kirk et al., 1978).

In 1940, Kirk published, *Teaching Reading to Slow Learning Children*, which revealed that his approach to reading disabilities had been influenced by Orton, Fernald, and Monroe (Wiederholt, 1974). He used the phonic method by Monroe to instruct regular or phonetic words, and Fernald's kinesthetic method to teach irregular or nonphonetic words (Lovitt, 1989). Kirk co-authored the *Illinois Test of Psycholinguistic Abilities*

(ITPA), which was designed to identify visual-and auditory-based deficits and linguistic problems that affect achievement in various academic subjects (Kirk & McCarthy, 1961; Lovitt, 1989). For a number of years, the ITPA was the major diagnostic instrument in determining a diagnosis of learning disabilities.

During the 1950s and 1960s, Kirk served in several governmental capacities including the first director of the Division of Handicapped Children in the U.S. Office of Education, influencing the formative years of federal policy, and becoming a major force in the development of the field of learning disabilities (Bender, 1995).

Gillingham and Stillman

In the 1930s, Anna Gillingham and Beth Stillman developed a program to instruct the kinds of children diagnosed by Orton as language-disordered (Mercer, 1987). The Gillingham method is an alphabetic approach to reading, writing, and spelling by teaching units of sounds or letters of the alphabet one at a time in a multisensory approach (Kirk et al., 1978).

According to Orton's theory, reading problems occurred because of an incomplete cerebral hemispheric dominance which could be improved by developing language-pattern associations between the visual, auditory, and kinesthetic mechanisms and using the modalities simultaneously (Mercer, 1987). During instruction the learner sees the letter, hears the sound of the letter, traces the letter, then writes the letter (Kirk et al., 1978). The Gillingham method was designed for children identified as dyslexic with normal or superior intelligence. This approach has been criticized because it's extremely difficult for children with auditory processing problems, uninteresting, and it takes two years to be effective (Kirk et al., 1978).

Romalda Spalding

In 1957, Romalda Spalding also developed a multisensory approach based on Orton's research which she called "Unified Phonics Method" that used teaching 70 common phonograms as the basis for teaching speaking, spelling, writing, and reading as one integrated subject (Wiederholt, 1974). Reading from a book was delayed until the child had a fund of sight words great enough to read and comprehend.

Disorders of Perceptual and Motor Processes: 1935–1962

The research and remediation strategies of the perceptual motor theorists, many of whom were students of Strauss and Associates at the Wayne County Training School for Mentally Retarded Children, a clinical setting for children whose retardation resulted from nongenetic factors, provided a dominant influence during the 1960s (Bender, 1995). Foremost among those students during this period were Laura Lehtinen, Newell Kephart, and William Cruickshank, who tested and expanded the theories of Strauss and Werner (Mercer, 1987). Thus, Strauss and his co-workers laid the foundation for the field of learning disabilities by (1) perceiving similar characteristics in a diverse group of children who had been misdiagnosed by specialists, misunderstood by parents, and often discarded by society; (2) planning and implementing educational settings and procedures for teaching these children successfully; and (3) alerting many professions to the existence of a new category of disabilities (Lerner, 1993).

Strauss and Associates

Strauss and Werner's research and direct influence began during the Brain-Injured Period and played a critical role in the 1960s during the emergence of the field of learning disabilities. Strauss and Werner's research findings (1939–1942) with brain-injured mentally retarded children led to the identification of two subgroups: endogenous (familial and environmental causation) and exogenous retardation (due to nongenetic factors such as brain injury) (Mercer, 1987). Children with exogenous retardation were described as hyperactive, impulsive, emotionally labile, perceptually disordered, destructible, and perseverative (Ariel, 1992). Strauss and Werner focused their study on a subtype that eventually became known as the "Strauss syndrome", the brain-injured child who had perceptual problems, distractibility, disinhibition, and perseveration (Myers & Hammill, 1990).

In 1946, Strauss resigned his position as director of child care at the Wayne County Training School. He established his own school in Racine, Wisconsin called Cove School for Brain-Injured Children, in 1947 where his research concerned brain-injured children with normal intelligence who demonstrated the same characteristics as exogenous retarded children (Wiederholt, 1974). Laura Lehtinen, the educational director of the

Cove School, worked with Strauss to develop teaching procedures (Mercer, 1987).

Strauss and Lehtinen published a book in 1947 entitled *Psychopathology and Education of the Brain-Injured Child, Vol. I,* which introduced brain-injured children to the educational profession (Mercer, 1987). They discussed two categories of characteristics that were required for a diagnosis of brain-injured: biological and behavioral. The biological characteristics included (1) soft neurological signs, (2) a history of having had a brain injury, and (3) no familial history of mental retardation (Lerner, 1993). Behavioral characteristics included perceptual disorders, perseveration problems, conceptual disorders, and behavioral disorders (i.e., explosive and erratic) (Lerner, 1993).

Strauss and Lehtinen used a number of revolutionary teaching techniques in attempting to reduce distractability and enhance learning including painting the classroom windows black, removing visually stimulating decorations from the classroom, establishing routines and organization, placing students in partitioned cubicles, and having teachers dress in plain clothes (Mercer, 1987; Lerner, 1993). Underlying all of their practices were recommendations that children must develop visual, auditory, and kinesthetic perceptions before they can progress to basic skills (Lovitt, 1987).

Soon after the publication of the book, professionals expressed doubts about the usefulness of the term "brain-injured", thus, the term "Strauss syndrome" became the popular term used to describe these children (Mercer, 1987). The term "Strauss syndrome" was used to describe a child who exhibited several of the composite characteristics of exogenous retardation and brain-injured children: (1) erratic and inappropriate behavior, (2) increased motor activity, (3) poor organization of behavior, (4) excessive distractability, (5) persistent faulty perceptions, (6) persistent hyperactivity, and (7) awkwardness and poor motor performance (Lerner, 1993).

Newell Kephart was greatly influenced by Werner and Strauss while he was a psychologist at the Wayne County School. In 1955, Strauss and Kephart co-authored a revision of the Strauss and Lehtinen text, *Psychopathology and Education of the Brain-Injured Child, Volume II,* (Mercer, 1987). In this book, Kephart postulated that all learning was based on perceptual-motor development and thus expanded the concerns of this group of theorists to include various aspects of motor learning (Bender, 1995).

Focusing on practical applications, Kephart developed an assessment scale, *Perceptual Survey Rating Scale,* and specified remedial strategies for children with perceptual-motor problems (Mercer, 1987). Wiederholt (1974) noted that there are similarities between Kephart's remedial activities and those suggested by Seguin as activities that utilize the physiological method.

Kephart's (1960) most significant accomplishment to the field was publishing, *The Slow Learner in the Classroom,* in which he discussed numerous remedial and educational techniques for children with perceptual-motor difficulties (Lovitt, 1989). Kephart's principal hypothesis on educating these children was that a perceptual-motor match must be made and that the child be educated in his/her primary modality (Lovitt, 1989). Additionally, Kephart taught for many years at the University of Northern Colorado.

William Cruickshank

Cruickshank, who was also greatly influenced by Werner and Strauss, played a significant role in the development of the field of learning disabilities. His career spanned the Brain-Injured Period: 1935–1962, the Emergent Field of LD: 1963–1974, the EHA Period: 1975–1989, and into the IDEA Period: 1990 to Present. He taught for many years at the University of Syracuse and at the University of Michigan. While Cruickshank was associated with perceptual-motor disabilities, he was also noted for his adaptation and refinement of the educational methods employed by Strauss and Lehtinen (Weiderholt, 1974).

Cruickshank was involved in the demonstration-pilot project in Syracuse, New York to establish a public school program for children with "Strauss Syndrome." This project adapted and refined the educational methods proposed by Strauss and Lehtinen in their book about teaching nonretarded brain-injured students. The specific elements of the special classroom required the following modifications in the teaching environment: (1) reducing unessential visual and auditory environmental stimuli, (2) reducing the space in which the student works, (3) providing a highly structured daily schedule, and (4) increasing the stimulus value of the teaching methods (Lerner, 1993).

In the late 1950s, Cruickshank and colleagues designed the Montgomery County Project to further study reduced environmental stimuli and highly structured educational programs with children ranging in ability from mildly retarded to normal intelligence (Ariel, 1992). In 1961,

Cruickshank, Bentzen, Ratzburg, and Tannhauser published a book concerning the education of brain-injured children, *A Teaching Method for Brain-Injured and Hyperactive Children* (Bender, 1995).

Cruickshank maintained that learning disabilities were the result of neurological impairment and perceptual deficits (Lovitt, 1989). He utilized the general techniques of reduction of stimuli, reduction of space, structure in programming, and increased instructional stimulus with a multisensory approach to teaching. Cruickshank recommended using concrete materials such as peg boards, puzzles, form boards, stencils, and blocks in teaching readiness and perceptual tasks before teaching academics (Lovitt, 1989).

Marianne Frostig

During the 1950s, Frostig tested delinquents in Los Angeles and noticed indications of perceptual deficits, especially disturbances in body image and spatial orientation (Mercer, 1987). After years of clinical observation and reading the research of Goldstein, Strauss and Werner, Frostig concluded that many children might be suffering from neurological dysfunction (Mercer, 1987). She determined that a number of areas of visual perception could be delineated for testing and teaching including eye-hand coordination, figure-ground, form consistency, position in space, and spatial relations (Wiederholt, 1974). Frostig constructed the *Developmental Test of Visual Perception* (Frostig et al., 1961) and developed training materials for remediating visual perceptual difficulties, *Frostig Program for the Development of Visual Perception* (Frostig & Horne, 1964), which continue to be used today.

EMERGENT FIELD OF LD: 1963–1974

This emergent period in the field of learning disabilities began in 1963 with the use of the term "learning disabilities" to describe children with learning problems who were not retarded and ended just before the passage of PL94-142 in 1975. By the early 1960s, many professionals recognized that the common element among these children with perceptual and language problems seemed to be an inability to learn, not caused by low intelligence or environmental factors, but by a dysfunction in the central nervous system that affected the way a child processed information (Bender, 1995).

Definitions of Learning Disabilities

On April 6, 1963 as keynote speaker at a conference in Chicago sponsored by the Fund for Perceptually Handicapped Children, Dr. Samuel Kirk, the director of the new Division for Handicapped Children in the U.S. Office of Education, indicated that he had used the term "learning disabilities" to describe these children and youth (Myers & Hammill, 1990; Bender, 1995). During this meeting Kirk (1962) indicated that he had used the following definition of learning disabilities:

> A learning disability refers to a retardation, disorder, or delayed development in one or more of the processes of speech, language, reading, spelling, writing, or arithmetic resulting from a possible cerebral dysfunction and/or emotional or behavioral disturbance and not from mental retardation, sensory deprivation, or cultural or instructional factors (263).

This meeting, also, resulted in the creation of the Association for Children with Learning Disabilities (ACLD) now, the Learning Disabilities Association.

The learning disabilities movement was encouraged by a concern for civil rights for minorities, the organization of strong parent advocacy groups that sought funding for research on children's problems, and by professional educators concerned about learning disabled children (Bender, 1995). The focus on three strands of characteristics and research— oral language, written language, and perceptual-motor areas—dissipated as theorists shifted their energies to providing an adequate definition and characteristics of LD.

Barbara Bateman (1964, 220) made a significant contribution with her definition that learning disabled children must:

> Manifest an educationally significant discrepancy between their estimated intellectual potential and actual level of performance related to basic disorders in the learning processes, which may or may not be accompanied by demonstrable central nervous system dysfunction, and which are not secondary to generalized mental retardation, educational or cultural deprivation, severe emotional disturbance, or sensory loss.

In 1966, the National Society for Crippled Children and Adults and the National Institutes of Neurological Diseases and Blindness, and National Institutes of Health sponsored a task force known as Task Force I charged with providing an adequate definition of learning disabilities. Clements (1966) found over thirty-eight different terms that were suggested to identify these children. This group, however, decided to use the term "minimal brain dysfunction" instead of learning disabilities. Clements (1966) the director of Task Force I proposed the following definition based on the earlier definitions of Strauss and Kirk:

> The term "minimal brain dysfunction syndrome" refers to children of near average, average, or above average general intelligence with certain learning or behavioral disabilities ranging from mild to severe, which are associated with deviations of function of the central nervous system. These deviations may manifest themselves by various combinations of impairments in perception, conceptualization, language, memory, and control of attention, impulse, or motor function (9–10).

In 1969, the Elementary and Secondary Education Act (ESEA) of 1965 was amended to facilitate the development of learning disabilities as a field within special education. This legislation provided for a five-year program of teacher training, research, and the establishment of model education centers for learning disabled children (Mercer, 1987). In this amendment, The Children with Specific Learning Disabilities Act of 1969 (PL91-230), learning disabilities was defined as follows:

> Children with special learning disabilities exhibit a disorder in one or more of the basic psychological processes involved in understanding or using spoken or written languages. These may be manifested in disorders of listening, thinking, talking, reading, writing, spelling or arithmetic. They include conditions which have been referred to as perceptual handicaps, brain injury, minimal brain dysfunction, dyslexia, development aphasia. They do not include learning problems which are due primarily to visual, hearing, or motor handicaps, to mental retardation, emotional disturbance, or to environmental disadvantage (USOE, 1969, 34).

This definition served as the basis for the definition of learning disabilities incorporated into PL94-142 in 1975. "For the first time, the field of learning disabilities was acknowledged in federal law, with funding provided for teacher training. This law laid the foundation for the inclusion of learning disabilities in subsequent federal and state laws" (Lerner, 1993, 42).

Paradigm Shifts, Changes, Growth

In the late 1960s to early 1970s serious conflicts, which continue today, erupted over paradigms, definitions, diagnostic procedures, and instructional interventions among advocates of the process approach and advocates of the behavioral approach. Historically, almost all of the pioneers (i.e., Strauss, Lehtinen, Kirk, Orton, Cruickshank, Myklebust, Frostig, Kephart, etc.) were advocates of the process approach to diagnosis and intervention (Myers & Hammill, 1990). The process approach has been incorporated into the cognitive processing or information processing approach.

The 1960s to early 1970s saw the development of behavioral techniques in the field of learning disabilities. Norris Haring and E. Lakin Phillips combined Cruickshank's structured environment and Skinner's work in operant conditioning to develop educational programs for emotionally disturbed children (Mercer, 1987). Haring hired Ogden Lindsley to develop measurements for classroom behavior, and Lindsley developed a set of measurement procedures which he called Precision Teaching, later used with learning disabled, which included counting and charting performance, and making instructional decisions based on performance data (Mercer, 1987).

By 1972, research by Hammill and associates indicated that process abilities as measured by existing tests did not particularly relate to cognitive or academic performance and that presently available methods for training process had failed to produce desired gains in cognitive, academic, or even process abilities (Myers & Hammill, 1990). In 1974, Hammill and colleagues' attention was shifted to the study of the processing approach represented by the ITPA and its related training programs (Myers & Hammill, 1990). The controversy polarized the field, and most professionals identified with one approach or the other.

During this emergent phase of the field of learning disabilities, public school programs were rapidly being established throughout the nation. Many of the early programs were for students at the elementary level, and they followed the traditional delivery system in special education at that time: self-contained classrooms (Lerner, 1993). Federal funding of Child Service Demonstration Centers in the 1970s supported the development of learning disabilities model programs throughout the country which provided opportunities for innovation and experimentation (Lerner, 1993). Parent interest was continued and encouraged through the growth of ACLD affiliates throughout the United States. In 1968, the Council for Learning Disabilities, a division of the Council for Exceptional Children, an organization for professional educators was founded, and growth spread rapidly as professionals with diverse backgrounds joined the learning disabilities movement. During this period an enormous interest was shown in developing models, materials and resources, professional publications, and in establishing learning disabilities as a professional entity (Ariel, 1992).

In 1970, the Task Force of Children Out of School studied the Boston public school system. The Task Force report found over ten thousand children and youth excluded from public school classrooms because they did not match school standards for the normal student (Bender, 1995). In 1974, Congress estimated that over a million school-aged youngsters were denied a proper education in America's schools because they were different in some way (Henley et al., 1993). Thus, the emergent period came to a close with great strides having been made in the education of handicapped children, however, nation-wide estimates indicated that many children and youth could not attend public schools.

EHA PERIOD: 1975–1989

The period of 1975 to 1985 was characterized by turmoil, confusion, criticism of the practices of the 1950s and 1960s, and uncertainty about the nature of learning disabilities, the various treatment approaches, and the theoretical construct of learning disabilities (Ariel, 1992). The major special education event of 1975 was the passage of PL94-142, the Education for All Handicapped Children Act, in which learning disabilities was included as one of the handicapping conditions. "The 1975–77 period was highlighted by much debate and controversy over the learning disabilities definition and identification practices. On December 29, 1977, The Federal Register was released with regulations for defining and identifying learning disabilities" (Mercer, 1990, 111).

Definitions and Paradigm Changes

Federal Definition

The most widely used definition of learning disabilities is the definition in Public Law 94-142, the Education for All Handicapped Children Act (1975), which continued in the Reauthorization of the Education of the Handicapped Act (1986), and was incorporated into Public Law 101-476, the Individuals with Disabilities Education Act or IDEA (1990) (Lerner, 1993). This definition, as follows, is the basis for most state definitions:

Specific learning disability" means a disorder in one or more of the basic psychological processes involved in understanding or in using language, spoken or written, which may manifest itself in an imperfect ability to listen, think, speak, read, write, spell, or to do mathematical calculations. The terms includes such conditions as perceptual handicaps, brain injury, minimal brain dysfunction, dyslexia, and developmental aphasia. The term does not include children who have learning problems which are primarily the result of visual, hearing, or motor handicaps, of mental retardation, or emotional disturbance, or of environmental, cultural, or economic disadvantage (USOE, 1977, 65083).

The operational portion of the definition of learning disabilities appeared in the Federal Register (USOE, Dec. 29, 1977). It stated that a student has a specific learning disability if (1) the student does not achieve at the proper age and ability levels in one or more of several specific areas when provided with appropriate learning experiences, and (2) the student has a severe discrepancy between achievement and intellectual ability in one or more of these seven areas: (a) oral expression, (b) listening comprehension, (c) written expression, (d) basic reading skills, (e) reading comprehension, (f) mathematics calculation, and (g) mathematics reasoning (USOE, 1977).

In summary, the federal definition of learning disabilities as contained in the law IDEA (1990) includes the following major concepts: (1) *Academic Component:* The individual has difficulty learning, specifically, in speaking, listening, writing, reading, and mathematics. (2) *Psychological Processing Component:* The individual has a disorder in one or more of the basic psychological processes including perceptual processing, attention, and memory. (3) *Language Component:* There is an underlying language processing problem in which the child may have difficulty "in understanding or in using language, spoken or written, which may manifest itself in an imperfect ability to listen, think, speak, read, write, spell, or do mathematical calculations. (4) *Exclusionary Component:* The problem is not primarily due to other handicaps, such as visual or hearing impairments, motor handicaps, mental retardation, emotional disturbance, or economic, environmental, or cultural disadvantage. (5) *Severe Discrepancy Component:* A severe discrepancy exists between the student's apparent potential for learning and low level of academic achievement (Lerner, 1993; Mercer, 1987; USOE, 1977).

NJCLD Definition

The National Joint Committee on Learning Disabilities (NJCLD) is an organization of representatives from several professional organizations and disciplines involved with learning disabilities. Due to controversies regarding PL94-142 definition including issues of basic psychological processes, the inclusion of various conditions such as minimal brain dysfunction, and whether learning disabilities can occur concomitantly with other handicapping conditions, the NJCLD proposed a definition which was revised in 1990:

> *Learning disabilities* is a general term that refers to a heterogeneous group of disorders manifested by significant difficulties in the acquisition and use of listening, speaking, reading, writing, reasoning, or mathematical abilities. These disorders are intrinsic to the individual, presumed to be due to central nervous system dysfunction, and may occur across the life span. Problems in self-regulatory behaviors, social perception, and social interaction may exist with learning disabilities, but do not by themselves constitute a learning disability. Although learning disabilities may occur concomitantly with other handicapping conditions (for example, sensory impairment, mental retardation, serious emotional disturbance) or with extrinsic influences (such as cultural differences, insufficient or inappropriate instruction), they are not the result of those conditions or influences.

Although the NJCLD has proposed this definitional change and other organizations have proposed definitional changes, there have not been changes made in the federal definition of learning disabilities to this date.

Political Activity, Paradigm Changes, and Theorists

The primary legislation and litigation relevant to individuals with mild mental retardation (see Chapter 2) and individuals with behavior disorders (see Chapter 5), also, applied to and/or affected students with learning disabilities. In 1978, the Office of Education established five Learning Disabilities Research Institutes to conduct research on basic issues related to the field of learning disabilities. A different area of learning disabilities was targeted for investigation at each of these five institutes: (1) University of Kansas: Learning disabled adolescents and the Learning Strategies Curriculum, (2) University of Illinois at Chicago: Social competence and communication, (3) University of Virginia: Cognitive theory and controlling attention, (4) Columbia University: Improving basic skills, and (5) University of Minnesota: Assessment and evaluation (Lerner, 1993).

Litigation: 1975–1989

Much of the litigation during this period attempted to interpret the letter of the law. The litigation previously discussed in Chapters 2 and 5 apply, also, to students with learning disabilities. Litigation not previously discussed and specific to learning disabilities includes the following:

1976   Frederich L. v. Thomas
1980   Riley v. Ambach
1985   Hall v. Vance County Board of Education

Frederich L. v. Thomas (1976). The case was a class action suit that reaffirmed the right of students with learning disabilities to have appropriate education programs. Children with learning disabilities are not educated appropriately, as is their right, when they are not taught by qualified specially trained teachers (Henley et al., 1993, 5).

Riley v. Ambach (1980). New York's Commissioner of Education was enjoined from defining a child with learning disabilities as one who exhibits a discrepancy of 50% or more in achievement based on intellectual ability and actual academic achievement. The court criticized the state's regulation for determining a learning disability on grounds that the standard is too inflexible, tends to under-identify children with learning disabilities, and is not sufficiently individualized (Turnbull, 1993, 98).

Hall v. Vance County Board of Education (1985). The court ruled that when a student has made no improvement in performance on standardized tests over a three-year period and continues to receive failing grades over the same period, the student has not been provided an appropriate education, even though he or she has been in a mainstreamed program, and should, therefore, be transferred to a special education (learning disabilities) program (Turnbull, 1993, 98).

Paradigm Changes

During this period (1975–1985) the behavioral approach with its focus on direct instruction of the skills model received the primary support of the field. The processing approach with its focus on correcting perceptual and perceptual-motor abilities lost support when the effectiveness of this model was questioned (Mercer, 1987). The cognitive approach saw limited activity during the 1960s and 1970s except for Piaget's work (Mercer, 1987). However, the latter part of this period was characterized by the emergence of cognitive and cognitive constructivist theories and the application of information processing theories, strategy intervention models, and metacognitive theory to the diagnosis and treatment of learning disabled students (Ariel, 1992).

Major Theorists: 1975–1989

During the early years of the PL94-142 Period, many professionals who influenced the emergence of the field of learning disabilities continued to impact the field. The professionals who impacted the field during this period are too numerous to mention. Some professionals and their accomplishments are as follows:

Beth Slingerland	A Multisensory Program for Language Arts for Specific Language Disability Children (1976).
B.S. Bloom	Taxonomies of Educational, Affective, and Psychomotor Objectives
J.P. Guilford	Structure-of-Intellect Model
D. Deshler and Associates	Strategies Intervention Model
R. Feuerstein	Instrumental Enrichment
J.K. Torgesen	Psychological Processing
C. Thornton & M. Toohey	Multisensory Mathematics
J.H. Flavell	Metacognition
D. Hammill & S. Larsen	Assessment, Pro-ed
L. Idol	Collaborative Consultation
D. Meichenbaum	Cognitive Behavior Modification
J. Lerner and C. Mercer	Academic Remediation
J. Salvia & J. Ysseldyke	Assessment
G. Senf	Information Processing
E. Wiig & E. Semel	Language Assessment & Intervention
K. Reid	Cognitive Developmental Approach
J. McKinney	Learning Disabilities Subtypes

During this period, the field of learning disabilities mushroomed with LD teacher training programs, LD professors at most colleges and universities, and LD public school teachers at most elementary and secondary schools in the United States. As this period came to a close, many professionals were still concerned about a theoretical construct of learning disabilities, a taxonomy of learning disabilities, discrimination among learning disabled and other low achieving students, referral and placement procedures, and learning disabilities subtypes. With the elimination of proving a processing problem as a diagnostic characteristic of learning disabilities and merely using the deficit academic criteria, the number of students labeled learning disabled escalated from the original

2 percent cap to over 2 million students, about 4 percent of the school population and 40 percent of the total handicapped population served in the public schools.

IDEA PERIOD: 1990–PRESENT

The IDEA Period continues to be filled with inconsistencies, lack of cohesiveness in the field, concerns over definitions, disagreements over service delivery models (i.e., Inclusion), differences among the major theoretical instructional models, and education of at-risk students including minority students. Two pieces of significant legislation (ADA and IDEA) were both passed in 1990 (see Chapter 2). Funding, a continuing concern for special education students, has become a critical issue during this period. A major focus during this period has been on transition programs for secondary special education students. Parent groups of ADD/ADHD children have lobbied unsuccessfully for ADD/ADHD as a separate category of special education.

Congressional legislation passed in 1991 not previously discussed is PL102-119, the Early Childhood Amendment. This amendment to PL99-457 and to IDEA affects handicapped and at-risk preschoolers ages 3-to-5 years and infants birth to 2 years with established risk (medical diagnosis), biological risk (premature, low birth weight), and environmental risk (poverty and correlates) (Lerner, 1993).

Important litigation during the IDEA Period includes the following:

1991   Carter v. Florence County School District #4
1992   John & Kathryn G. v. Board of Education of Mt. Vernon, NY.

Carter v. Florence County School District #4 (1991). The court held that a student classified as learning disabled is entitled to a placement at a private school (although the school is not state-approved) where the facts indicate she will make educational progress there and benefit from its program to a greater degree than from the public school program. The Court of Appeals affirmed and noted that reimbursement of tuition for placement in an unapproved school was permissible (Turnbull, 1993, 140–141).

John & Kathryn G. v. Board of Education of Mt. Vernon, NY (1992). Parents of a child with learning disabilities sued the school district claiming that they are entitled to monitary damages because the district failed for four years to identify the student's disabilities and then failed to provide an appropriate education under IDEA. The court ruled that the parents may hold the school liable under Section 504 only if they can show that the school acted in bad faith in not diagnosing the student (Turnbull, 1993, 141).

Areas of Concern

Definitions of Learning Disabilities

Debates over the definition of learning disabilities continue. The PL94-142 and NJCLD definitions continue to be the most popular definitions of LD. The psychological processing portion of the LD definition has been subsumed under the theory of information processing. With the advent of computerized tomography (CT), magnetic resonance imaging (MRI), neurometrics, PET scans, CAT scans, physicians now have the ability to actually determine how a specific student processes information. Though still too expensive to be used on a routine basis, the Menninger Foundation School frequently uses neurometrics to help determine cognitive processing or information processing of students. These capabilities suggest that professionals could once again use the psychological processing deficits component of the LD definition to help diagnose LD students.

Severe discrepancy continues to be a much debated issue. Current practice generally involves the use of discrepancy formulas to determine standard score differences between aptitude and achievement (i.e., the difference between the IQ score and standard scores for math and reading). Discrepancy formulas generally set a specific number of standard score points as a critical discrepancy (e.g., 15–30 points). Many states have begun to use regression analysis for determining the potential-achievement discrepancy because it includes a correction for many of the statistical flaws of standard scores. Regression analysis requires the use of Regression Standard Score Tables.

The exclusionary component continues to be a significant concern. Frequently, minority students and students from low socioeconomic environments are diagnosed learning disabled without consideration for the impact of these factors on the student's academic functioning. This may be one reason for the steady increase in the number of LD students. Since many minority students also come from low socioeconomic environments, the effect of both factors on a student of average potential may be devastating, however, the students may not be "true LD."

Full Inclusion Movement

The Inclusion movement began with the Regular Education Initiative (REI), a philosophy that maintains that general education, rather than special education, should be primarily responsible for the education of students with disabilities (Hallahan & Kauffman, 1994). Full Inclusion specifies that all students regardless of severity of disabilities should be educated in regular classrooms in their neighborhood schools (Hallahan & Kauffman, 1994). The advocates of full inclusion recommend the elimination of a continuum of special education services including resource rooms and self-contained classrooms, and placing all students in the regular education classrooms. The proponents of Full Inclusion recommend that teachers utilize cooperative learning and peer instructional methods, and that special education services be provided within the regular education classrooms.

Full Inclusion has met with considerable resistance from regular education teachers, special education teachers, and parents. Recent surveys have indicated that 77 percent of parents of students with disabilities were satisfied with the current special education system, the current level of integration of mainstreaming, and the current continuum of services (Hallahan & Kauffman, 1994). In practice, attempts to implement full inclusion in the regular education classrooms have frequently been disastrous for all students. In the regular education classroom, special education students do not receive intensive individualized instruction in prerequisites to skills studied in the regular classrooms, all students often receive the same textbook whether or not they can read at that level, often there are expectations that regular education students should help teach the disabled students, and special education teachers have often been placed in the role of teacher-aide to the regular education teacher in subject areas in which they are not certified to teach (especially at middle and high school levels).

The Council for Exceptional Children (1993), Division of Learning Disabilities has issued a policy regarding inclusion as follows: "The Council SUPPORTS the education of students with LD in general education classrooms when deemed appropriate by the IEP team. The Council CANNOT SUPPORT indiscriminate full-time placement of all students with LD in the regular education classroom or full inclusion. The Council CANNOT SUPPORT any policy which minimizes or eliminates service options designed to enhance the education of students with LD and guaranteed by IDEA."

Subtypes of Learning Disabilities

At present, learning disabilities is one of the few recognized disability conditions that does not have empirically identified subgroups (Bender, 1995, 374). However, over one hundred classification studies of learning disabilities have been conducted since 1963 (Lerner, 1993, 21). Early subtype studies indicated three subgroups: (1) Deficits in visual learning tasks, (2) Deficits in auditory learning tasks, and (3) Deficits in both visual and auditory tasks (Bender, 1995).

A practical, though not empirical, classification scheme was suggested by Kirk and Chalfant (1984): Developmental Learning Disabilities and Academic Learning Disabilities. "Developmental learning disabilities include the prerequisite skills (attention, memory, perceptual skills, thinking skills, and oral language skills) that a student needs to achieve in academic subjects. Academic learning disabilities refer to school-acquired learning (reading, arithmetic, handwriting, spelling, and written expression" (Lerner, 1993, 21).

SUMMARY

Five historical periods in the development of the field of learning disabilities were discussed. During these periods the primary researchers seemed polarized into three major areas—disorders of spoken language, disorders of written language, and disorders of perceptual-motor processes. The research of Strauss and students at the Wayne County Training School provided the theoretical background and the primary theorists in the development of the field of learning disabilities. Strauss and Lehtinen proposed educational interventions (reducing distractability, reducing student work space, and establishing routines and organization) for students with learning disabilities which have stood the tests of time.

The emergent period in the field of learning disabilities began in 1963 when Sam Kirk described these children as having "learning disabilities." During this period professionals sought a definition that would be agreed upon by major professions involved with LD children. Historically, almost all of the pioneers in the field (i.e., Strauss, Lehtinen, Kirk, Orton, Cruickshank, Myklebust, Frostig, Kephart, etc.) were advocates of the process approach to diagnosis and remediation. The 1960s and 1970s saw the development of the behavioral model as a primary force in the field of learning disabilities.

The PL94-142 definition of learning disabilities continues to be the major definition of LD with the following components: (1) Academic deficits; (2) Psychological Processing problems in perception, attention, and memory; (3) Language processing deficits; (4) Exclusion of other handicapping conditions and low socio-economic conditions as the primary cause; (5) Severe discrepancy between intelligence and actual academic functioning.

The primary concerns today, the IDEA Period, continue to include definition debates, disagreements over service delivery (i.e., Inclusion), differences among the major theoretical instructional models, education of at-risk preschoolers, transition programs for secondary special education students, and learning disability subtypes.

Chapter 9

THEORETICAL PERSPECTIVES OF LEARNING DISABILITIES

Contemporary treatment practices in learning disabilities stem from four major theoretical models: the medical model, the psychological process model, the behavioral model, and the cognitive/learning strategies model (Poplin, 1989).

The major theoretical perspectives that provide definitions, etiology, diagnosis, treatment, and education of specific learning disabled individuals include the medical model, the psychological process model, the behavioral model, and the cognitive model.

MEDICAL MODEL OF LEARNING DISABILITIES

The field of learning disabilities traces its history to the 1800s and the early brain research of physicians and surgeons. These professionals provided a description of learning disabilities as minimal brain dysfunction and investigated etiology and diagnostic procedures, and proposed treatments. The concept of minimal central nervous system dysfunction is primary to the medical perspective of learning disabilities (Mercer, 1987).

Medical Model: Etiology

Most professionals in the field maintain that "true" learning disabilities are the consequences of subtle central nervous system (CNS) dysfunction, damage, or structural anomaly (Myers & Hammill, 1990). The perspective that subtle neurological impairment results in learning problems in specific academic areas has a strong historical legacy beginning with Strauss and continuing with others such as Clements and Cruickshank (Mercer, 1987). Genetic or developmental variations in CNS structure, biochemical irregularities, and cerebral trauma can cause the brain to function abnormally and produce disorders in listening, speaking, reading, writing, math, and thinking (Myers & Hammill, 1990). Additionally, environmental influences and/or teratogenic insult increases the likelihood of malformations of the brain and central nervous system (Bender, 1995).

Normal CNS Structure and Function

The central nervous system (CNS) is composed of the brain and spinal cord and serves as a processor of information by regulating the incoming impulses and outgoing responses and the interconnecting neural associations (Myers & Hammill, 1990). The brain is composed of three major regions: the brain stem which controls the life-sustaining functions of the body; the cerebellum which receives sensory input and controls most of the motor nervous system; and the cerebrum which controls most of the higher thought functions (Bender, 1995).

The cerebrum is divided into two hemispheres which are "cross-wired", in other words, the left hemisphere is related to motor nerve control of the right side of the body, and the right hemisphere controls the left side of the body (lateralization) (Mercer, 1987). The two hemispheres seem to relate to different types of learning and brain activity with the left hemisphere processing language and linguistic thought and the right hemisphere controlling spatial orientation, time sequences, visual imagery, and creative expression in music and art (Bender, 1995). People with left hemispheric dominance are normally right-handed, and those with right hemispheric dominance are usually left-handed. The left hemisphere controls language functions in 99 percent of right handed people and in 60 to 70 percent of left-handed people (Lovitt, 1989). However, the learning process depends on both hemispheres and their interrelated functioning, in other words, the brain operates as a holistic structure combining all of its skills (Restak, 1984).

Etiologies of Learning Disabilities

The search for the etiologies of learning disabilities has led medical researchers in the areas of developmental pediatrics, neurology, genetics, anatomy, physiology, radiology, pathology, pharmacology and ophthalmology; and researchers in allied health fields including psychology, audiology, physical and occupational therapy, and speech pathology to study the structure and functioning of the human brain during prenatal, perinatal, and postnatal periods (Swanson & Bray, 1991). Recent studies of central nervous system (CNS) structure to determine the presence of CNS irregularities in learning disabled individuals have involved both traditional approaches (i.e., autopsy) and diagnostic imaging approaches including electroencephalography (EEG), computerized tomography (CT), magnetic resonance imaging (MRI) (Myers & Hammill, 1990), and brain electrical activity mapping (BEAM) (Swanson & Bray, 1991). Although numerous potential medical insults to the child's body or to the mother's body during pregnancy may cause learning problems, there is no evidence that a particular type of insult results in the particular problem — learning disabilities (Bender, 1995, 37). The numerous etiological factors which negatively impact CNS development and functioning and potentially cause learning disabilities can be categorized as follows: (1) Genetic and/or Developmental Factors, (2) Biochemical Irregularities, (3) Acquired Trauma, and (4) Environmental and Teratogenic Influences.

Genetic Factors. Genetic and developmental conditions known to cause brain dysfunction may result in mild to severe variations in CNS structure and function with minimal (mild) brain dysfunction associated with learning disabilities. Although genetic research concerning learning disabilities is in its formative stages, researchers have documented (e.g., adoption studies, twin studies, gene mapping, pedigree analysis) an increased incidence of learning disabilities, hyperactivity, and minor neurological disorders in the biological relatives of children with learning disabilities (Swanson & Bray, 1991).

There are two types of genetic-related causes of central nervous system variations including chromosomal abnormalities caused by damage to genetic material (e.g., Down syndrome) and hereditary transmission

(Hallahan & Kauffman, 1994). Though genetic causes are more frequently associated with mental retardation, those children who are
functioning at the mild end of the continuum may be labeled learning
disabled. Fragile X syndrome, the most common hereditary cause of
mental retardation, and PKU which results in abnormal brain development are the result of hereditary transmission (Hallahan & Kauffman,
1994). Smith and Pennington (1987, 57) have indicated 14 different genetic
syndromes related to learning disabilities including neurofibromatosis,
Noonan syndrome, Tourette syndrome, Lesch-Nyhan syndrome, and
Turner syndrome.

Developmental Factors. Developmental learning disabilities appear in
young children as developmental delays or deficit patterns in prerequisite skills including motor, attention, perception, language, memory,
and thinking skills (Lerner, 1993). In many ways, the behavior and
performance of children with learning disabilities resembles that of
much younger individuals (Reid, 1988). Learning disabled children and
youth often exhibit maturational delays such as slower development in
language skills, delays in fine and gross motor skills, delays in social
development as well as academic delays. Maturational delay of the
neurological system, however, is not likely a causative factor in all types
of learning disabilities, but it has received considerable support as one of
many (Hardman et al., 1996). Neurological abnormalities associated
with learning disabilities are described as neurological soft signs which
include mild coordination difficulties, minimal tremors, motor awkwardness, visual-motor disturbances, deficiencies or abnormal delay in language development, hyperactivity, and attention problems (Lerner, 1993;
Levine, 1987).

One early theory of the field of learning disabilities proposed by
Orton indicated that children suffered from learning disabilities because
of some lag or incomplete development of normal cerebral dominance
patterns (Bender, 1995). Orton's theory indicated the left hemisphere
should be the dominant or controlling hemisphere, and the interference
of the right hemisphere during language activities caused language
confusion (Lerner, 1993).

Recent postmortem anatomical studies of learning disabled (dyslexic)
individuals' brains by Galburda and neurological associates at Harvard
Medical School revealed an absence of standard brain symmetry, abnormalities in the language-related areas of the brain (Lovitt, 1989; Lerner,
1993). The researchers indicated that the abnormalities were develop-

mental and not the result of lesions or trauma (Lovitt, 1989). This on-going brain research provides strong evidence that dyslexia does have a neurological basis that is related to brain structure (Lerner, 1993).

Biochemical Irregularities. The most promising recent advances in scientific knowledge about learning disorders have resulted from more detailed anatomical studies of brain metabolic activity; more sophisticated studies of brain electrical activity; and indirect measures of neurotransmitter activity (Swanson & Bray, 1991). It has been postulated that metabolic deficiencies or basal metabolism imbalance may be a contributing factor in learning disabilities, for example, too much thyroxin results in hyperactivity and attention problems while too little thyroxin results in hypoactivity (Mercer, 1987). Many youngsters with learning disabilities are administered psychoactive drugs (i.e., stimulant medication) because the positive effects indicate a chemical imbalance which is corrected through the administration of drugs (Mercer, 1987).

Studies of the electrical activity of the brain have generally supported the theory that neurological sites of learning disorders are in the language areas of the temporal and parietal lobes (Lovitt, 1989). The research suggestion that the difficulties of poor readers may be related to a reversal in the brain's normal asymmetry for language has been substantiated by studies comparing the electrical activity of normal brains and those of learning disabled children (Lovitt, 1989). This research has consistently shown different electrical activities in the language-related areas of the brains of students with and those without reading disorders during reading and listening activities (Lovitt, 1989).

Researchers have postulated that deficits in neurotransmitter (the biological substances that allow individual neurons to connect with each other) function and quantity may be a cause of attention deficit disorders (Swanson & Bray, 1991). Imbalances in neurotransmitters (e.g., serotonin, dopamine, norepinephrine) are assumed to cause difficulties in neural impulse transmission and consequent learning and behavior problems (Mercer, 1987). Numerous sophisticated techniques including magnetic resonance imaging, positron emission tomography, and brain electrical activity mapping have been used to study reading disabled subjects (Swanson & Bray, 1991).

Acquired Trauma. Cerebral or acquired trauma involves injury to the central nervous system during prenatal, perinatal, and/or postnatal periods that originates outside the individual and results in learning disorders (Mercer, 1987). Prenatal period exposure to teratogenic substances such as alcohol, tobacco, caffeine, legal prescription drugs, and illegal street drugs increases the likelihood of malformations of the brain and CNS damage (see Chapter 1). Additionally, effects of maternal accidents, diseases (e.g., rubella), autoimmune disorders, and chronic illnesses frequently cause injury to the CNS and have been directly linked to learning disorders (Swanson & Bray, 1991). Perinatal period problems affecting the central nervous system include prematurity and birth complications. Postnatal causes of acquired trauma include accidents with head trauma (e.g., severe concussion) and diseases with high fever and convulsions (e.g., encephalitis, bacterial meningitis) (Bender, 1995). Other postnatal causes of acquired trauma include child abuse, immune deficiencies, chemotherapeutic treatment of leukemia and cancer, and chronic malnutrition (Swanson & Bray, 1991).

Environmental Influences. Numerous environmental factors can impact negatively on the development of the child at the prenatal, perinatal, and postnatal periods. Chapter 1 discusses many of these factors that render children at-risk for academic failure including environmental chemicals, lead poisoning, accidents and injuries, the effects of child abuse and neglect, and allergies. Among the greatest environmental problems are the correlates of low socio-economic environments such as inadequate nutrition, inadequate shelter and appropriate clothing, inadequate safety, inadequate medical care including preventive medicine, harsh child rearing methods, and the emotional effects of these environmental inadequacies.

Medical Model: Diagnosis

The medical perspective views learning disabilities as a function of neurological, neurobiological, genetic, or hormonal dysfunction related to the biological functioning of the brain (Hresko & Parmar, 1991). Physicians define specific learning disabilities as problems with processing information, memory, attention, perception, language, organization, and motor skills. These problems are manifested as difficulties in learning academics.

A medical diagnosis usually begins with a complete physical examination with laboratory tests provided by the child's primary care physician. The comprehensive evaluation involves sensory-perceptual examinations by an audiologist and ophthalmologist; motor evaluations by physical and/or occupational therapists; language evaluation by a speech/

language pathologist; attention, cognitive potential, and memory evaluations by a psychologist. A medical evaluation may also include a neurological assessment (formal or informal) which would include tests of auditory and visual discrimination, ability to benefit from feedback, novel problem solving to determine the functional integrity of the cerebral hemispheres, psychological "set" to determine cognitive flexibility, power and speed tests, timed and untimed tests (Lovitt, 1989). Neurological test batteries used with children include Halstead-Reitan Neuropsychological Test Batteries for Children (Selz, 1981) and The Luria-Nebraska Children's Battery (Golden, 1981).

Primary care physicians are frequently involved with the evaluation of attention problems. Although attention-deficit hyperactivity disorder (ADHD) is not synonymous with learning disabilities, up to 40 percent of children with learning disabilities display symptoms of the disorder (Silver, 1989). Attention problems are not disability category specific, they may be associated with any disability. Additionally, the majority of students diagnosed ADHD are not also diagnosed as learning disabled.

The Diagnostic and Statistical Manual of Mental Disorders, Fourth Edition (DSM–IV) (American Psychiatric Association, 1994) is the primary medically based diagnostic system in diagnosing attention problems (Bender, 1995). There are four subtypes of attention-deficit hyperactivity disorder (DSM–IV, 1994): (1) ADHD/Inattentive Type, (2) ADHD/Hyperactive-Impulsive Type, (3) ADHD/Combined Subtype, and (4) ADHD/Unspecified Type.

Although the etiological research uses diagnostic imaging approaches including electroencephalography (EEG), computerized tomography (CT), magnetic resonance imaging (MRI), these sophisticated computerized techniques are seldom used in the diagnosis of learning disabilities. Students attending The Menninger Foundation Psychiatric Hospital inpatient school in Topeka, Kansas are frequently evaluated using neurometrics as one aspect of a multidisciplinary evaluation. Neurometrics is a method of evaluating brain activity through the use of sophisticated computer techniques to detect the presence of brain dysfunction that could affect behavior or learning skills. Activities performed during a session include assembling blocks from patterns, silent and oral reading at easy and difficult levels, listening to tapes of stories, and telling about favorite TV shows (Lovitt, 1989). Neurometrics statistical analysis reveals which areas of the brain are functioning abnormally, so strengths and weaknesses in processing information can be identified.

It should be clear, however, that the physician has limited ability to diagnose specific learning disabilities through physical examination because specific learning disability is an educational diagnosis requiring a complete academic evaluation. The role of the physician is usually to determine a differential diagnosis for poor school achievement by ruling out conditions that do not seem to impede the learning process, while ascertaining the factors that may be contributing to low school achievement (Swanson & Bray, 1991).

Medical Model: Treatment

Medical treatments prescribed for individuals with learning disabilities have typically been divided into four categories of treatments: Developmental or Neuromotor Treatment, Biochemical Treatments, Acquired Trauma Treatment, and Environmental or Teratogenic Treatment. Treatments with a medical basis are among the most vigorously debated issues in the field of learning disabilities (Lerner, 1993).

Neuromotor Treatments

Orton's Theory. A primary neuromotor treatment evolved from Orton's theory that learning disabilities were caused by a lack of cerebral dominance. Orton postulated that learning disabilities were caused by the interference of the right hemisphere during language activities. Thus, the language center in the left hemisphere could be strengthened and made dominant by strongly establishing the right-sided motor responses of the body (Mercer, 1987). The Gillingham-Stillman Method based on Orton's work was devised to help establish cerebral dominance.

Patterning. Patterning has been advocated as a method to remediate learning disabilities by promoting neurological reorganization and cerebral dominance through retracing or retraining basic motor sequences in a systematic way (Swanson & Bray, 1991). This program was sponsored by Doman (a physical therapist), Delacato (an educational psychologist), and Fay (a neurosurgeon) who proposed that the student must relearn and properly perform the motor exercises in creeping, crawling and walking to establish hemispheric dominance (Mercer, 1987; Lerner, 1993). If the person was unable to make the movements him/herself, other persons moved the limbs through the prescribed motions (Mercer, 1987). This approach is based on the largely unsubstantiated view that a lack of cerebral dominance is a prominent feature of learning disabilities (Swanson & Bray, 1991).

Sensory-Integrative Therapy. The major purpose of sensory-integrative (SI) therapy is to improve fine motor skill functioning by stimulating vestibular (balance in the inner ear) and somatosensory (sense of body position) systems (Swanson & Bray, 1991). Treatment was designed to enhance sensory integration, thereby improving the ability of the brain to function (Mercer, 1987). Ayres (1969) developed a test battery that sampled behavior in motor accuracy, perceptual-motor skills, figure-ground skills, visual-perception, kinesthesia, tactile perception, and space perception. A recent study indicates that there is no relationship between academic achievement and vestibular dysfunction (Polatajko, 1985).

Pharmacological Treatment

Medication treatment for students with learning disabilities consists primarily of administering stimulant drugs to improve cognitive and attentional deficits as well as to manage hyperactive behaviors (Mercer, 1987). Stimulant drugs fall within the category of psychotropic drugs, which are drugs that influence moods, behavior, and cognition (Mercer, 1987). Research has consistently shown that the majority of children on stimulant medication, both with and without attention deficit disorders, will show more consistent on-task behaviors (Swanson & Bray, 1991).

The most commonly used stimulant drugs with children with learning disabilities include Ritalin (methylphenidate) used with 90% of children; and Dexedrine (dextroamphetamine) and Cylert (Pamoline) (Swanson & Bray, 1991). Ritalin is a short-acting drug (3–5 hours), takes effect within 30 minutes, has short-lived side-effects, and can be used in children over six years old (Mercer, 1987). Dexedrine is a short-acting drug (3–5 hours), takes effect within 30 minutes, and can be used in children over three years old (Swanson & Bray, 1991). Cylert is a long-acting drug used with children over six years old and may take 2–4 or 5 weeks before effects are noticed (Swanson & Bray, 1991). The negative side-effects may include weight loss, stomach ache, abdominal pain, diarrhea or constipation, dizziness, etc. (Mercer, 1987).

> Medication treatment by itself is seldom a sufficient remedy for the total set of symptoms of maladaptive behavior. Educational and psychological treatments are also needed. The medications by themselves do not teach anything. The student still needs continued attention to educational instruction (Lerner, 1993, 232).

Biochemical Treatment

The major biochemical treatments concern the relationship between diet and brain function or development. Nutrition deficiency in early life may impair the growth of both the body and the central nervous system (Lerner, 1993). There are several diet-related theories concerning the cause and treatment of hyperactivity and learning disabilities including theories of food additives, megavitamin therapy, and hypoglycemia (Lerner, 1993).

One of the most controversial diet-related theories was proposed by Feingold who indicated that food additives such as artificial flavors, colors, and preservatives in a child's diet induce hyperactivity, therefore, treatment is a restrictive additive-free diet (Swanson & Bray, 1991). Although numerous studies have been conducted on the Feingold diet, most have found that the method is not effective in controlling hyperactivity (Silver, 1992).

Megavitamin therapy is based on the hypothesis that vitamin deficits cause hyperactivity and learning problems, therefore, children need large vitamin doses, especially B vitamins (Mercer, 1987). There is no convincing evidence that mild vitamin deficiencies play a role in any type of brain dysfunction (Swanson & Bray, 1991). The idea that deficiencies of certain minerals (e.g., copper, zinc, magnesium, etc.) are associated with learning difficulties still persists despite the lack of credible evidence to support it (Swanson & Bray, 1991).

The hypothesis that children with learning disabilities may be suffering from hypoglycemia (low blood sugar) has not been substantiated by research, nor is there objective evidence of deterioration of behavior or learning with children with ADD when they ingest large amounts of sugar (Swanson & Bray, 1991). However, the notion that the degree of hyperactivity in children intensifies with eating sweets is commonly believed by the general public.

Acquired Trauma/Environmental Treatment

For the most part, the best treatment for learning disabilities due to acquired trauma or environmental influences is prevention during prenatal, perinatal, and postnatal periods through good preventive maternal and child health, immunizations, good medical care during illnesses, adequate maternal and child diet, avoidance of teratogens, and improvement in the negative factors involved in low socioeconomic environments.

However, once the CNS damage has occurred, each child's conditions will need to be considered individually depending on current functioning and presenting conditions.

PSYCHOLOGICAL PROCESS MODEL OF LEARNING DISABILITIES

The psychological process model is one of the theoretical foundation models of learning disabilities. This model, also called the perceptual model, the perceptual-motor model, the psycholinguistic process model, and the specific abilities model is associated with the work of outstanding figures in the development of the field of learning disabilities including Strauss and Werner, Lehtinen, Cruickshank, Frostig, Kirk, Kephart, Wepman and Myklebust (Henley et al., 1993; Mercer, 1987).

Psychological Process Model: Etiology

The early researchers discovered that individuals with normal intelligence who had learning problems exhibited performances and characteristics similar to those of brain-damaged mentally retarded individuals (Hresko & Parmar, 1991). The learning disabilities, then, were due to minimal brain dysfunction manifested as an inability of the brain to process information accurately (Poplin, 1989; Hresko & Parmar, 1991). In other words, learning disabled individuals experienced deficits in the basic psychological processes of perception, attention, memory, and linguistic functions which severely interfered with their ability to learn because they lacked underlying or prerequisite abilities to process and use information. However, the early proponents of psychological processing focused primarily on perceptual and perceptual-motor processing. Attention and language problems of learning disabled students are discussed in Chapter 10.

Perceptual and Motor Problems

"Specialists in learning disabilities have traditionally given much attention to perceptual problems that affect learning, especially to visual and auditory disabilities" (Haring & McCormick, 1990, 122). Perception is the recognition and interpretation of sensory information including visual, auditory, tactile-kinesthetic perceptions, and perceptual-motor integration.

Visual Perception. Visual perception is the ability to make visual sensory stimuli meaningful. The major visual perceptual skills include spatial relationships, visual discrimination, figure-ground discrimination, visual closure, visual memory, and visual-motor integration. **Spatial relationships** refers to the spatial relation of an object or symbol to others surrounding it and to the empty space between letters and words (Lerner, 1993). "Children with spatial-relationship difficulty will often skip words or lose their place while reading" (Cheek et al., 1989). In math, children with visual spatial relationship difficulties may experience difficulty writing on lined paper, noticing size differences in shapes, noting equal-sized fractional parts, and aligning numbers for computation (Bley & Thornton, 1981).

Visual discrimination refers to the ability to perceive dominant features in different objects and thus discriminate one object from another (Mercer, 1987). The skill of matching identical pictures, designs, shapes, letters, and words is a visual discrimination task. Objects are discriminated by color, shape, pattern, size, position, or brightness. The ability to discriminate letters and words visually becomes essential in learning to read (Lerner, 1993). In mathematics, children with visual discrimination difficulties may have difficulty differentiating coins, discriminating numbers (3 for 8; 2 for 5), and discriminating operation symbols (+ - × -) (Bley & Thornton, 1981).

"**Figure-ground discrimination** refers to the ability to distinguish an object from its surrounding background. The student with a deficit in this area cannot focus on the item in question apart from the visual background" (Lerner, 1993, 325). Students with figure-ground discrimination deficits may experience difficulty on a page of text determining where one word ends and another begins. On a page of mathematics problems, they may have difficulty discriminating the separate problems, may not finish all problems on a page, frequently lose their place, have difficulty seeing subtraction in a division problem (Bley & Thornton, 1981).

Visual closure involves identifying an object although the total stimulus is not presented (Lerner, 1993). This skill helps a child when reading to predict words based on the first several letters increasing reading speed and assists a child during spelling to complete the word based on a few clues or letters. "Students with visual-closure problems have difficulty doing dot-to-dot activities and completing word puzzles" (Cheek et al., 1989, 80). In math they may have difficulty completing problems with missing addends and experience difficulty reading a multidigit number (Bley & Thornton, 1981).

"**Visual memory** is the ability to recollect the dominant features of a stimulus item or to recall the sequence of a number of items presented visually" (Mercer, 1987, 230). "Students with visual-memory difficulty could have problems naming letters of the alphabet and learning sight words" (Cheek et al., 1989, 81). In mathematics, they may experience difficulty with regrouping, retaining basic facts, and solving multioperation computations (Bley & Thornton, 1981). Visual sequential memory disorders may manifest themselves as difficulty telling time, difficulty following through on multiplication or long division problems, and difficulty solving column addition problems (Bley & Thornton, 1981).

Auditory Perception. Auditory perception is the ability to make auditory sensory stimuli meaningful. The primary auditory perception skills include the following: (1) phonological awareness, (2) auditory discrimination, (3) auditory memory, (4) auditory sequencing, and (5) auditory blending (Lerner, 1993). Learning disabled children frequently experience difficulty with all areas of auditory processing. Deficits are frequently related to histories of ear infections and allergy problems.

Phonological awareness is the realization that language is segmented into words, syllables, and phonemes (letter sounds) and is an essential precursor to learning to read (Lerner, 1993). Children experiencing difficulty in learning to read often cannot recognize or isolate the separate sounds in words nor the number of sounds in a word. Consequently, these children cannot understand or use the alphabetic principle needed for learning phonics and decoding words (Lerner, 1993).

"**Auditory discrimination** refers to the ability to recognize differences between sounds and to identify similarities and differences between words" (Mercer, 1987, 231). "Children with auditory discrimination problems may have difficulty learning phonic generalizations and principles and may have difficulty with some rhyming activities" (Cheek et al., 1989, 82). Children with auditory discrimination problems frequently experience difficulty with spelling words that are phonetic, especially those with short vowels. In mathematics, they may experience difficulty distinguishing between 30 and 13, and with decimal numbers (Bley & Thornton, 1981).

"**Auditory memory** is the ability to recognize and/or recall previously presented auditory stimuli. The recall may feature a sequential order (e.g., phone number or letters in a word) or simply remembering information presented through the auditory channel" (Mercer, 1987, 231). Students use their auditory memory skill to recall facts and ideas during oral reading, to follow verbal reading directions, and to remember reading verbal information. Children with auditory memory problems may have difficulty learning the alphabet, identifying important vocabulary presented, learning nursery rhymes and poems, and reading and answering comprehension questions (Cheek et al., 1989). Students with auditory memory problems experience difficulty in spelling. In mathematics, students with auditory memory problems may experience difficulty with oral drills, dictated assignments, and retaining a story problem that is dictated (Bley & Thornton, 1981).

"**Auditory sequencing** is the ability to remember the order of items in a sequential list" (Lerner, 1993, 323). Auditory sequencing is a very important skill in learning to spell words to get the sounds and symbols in the correct order. It is an important skill in following directions and being able to carry out more than one direction at a time. Auditory sequencing is an important skill in remembering the letters of the alphabet in order and in remembering the sequence of numbers in counting.

"**Auditory blending** is the ability to blend single phonic elements or phonemes into a complete word" (Lerner, 1989, 286). "For example, a child with a deficit in auditory blending may be unable to blend the phonemes /c/, /a/, /r/ to complete the word *car,* even though he can differentiate the individual letter sounds in isolation" (Mercer, 1989, 231).

Tactile-Kinesthetic Perception. Tactile and kinesthetic sensory systems are two near sensory perceptual systems as compared to vision and hearing which are distance sensory perceptual systems. Tactile perception is the sense of touch with fingers and skin surfaces the primary information receptors. Kinesthetic perception concerns body movement in space, muscular tension, contraction, and relaxation; and is very important in motor development. In most everyday and school tasks, the information gained from the tactile-kinesthetic perceptual systems is integrated with information from the distance senses. Students with learning disabilities frequently experience difficulty in motor skills, spatial relationships, and in integration of all sensory perceptual information.

Perceptual-Motor and Motor Deficits. "LD students manifest disorders in coordinating visual or auditory behaviors with motor responses" (Cheek et al., 1989, 408). Visual-motor integration involves the ability to integrate perceived visual stimuli with movements of body parts (Mercer,

1987). Young children with visual-motor deficits may have difficulty in buttoning, cutting, copying from the chalkboard, and handwriting. With older children one of the most significant visual-motor integration deficits involves lack of automaticity in handwriting which interferes with progress in all academic areas requiring paper-pencil responses, especially writing an essay, a term paper, and/or answering essay questions on a test.

Visual-motor integration difficulties also interfere with progress in mathematics in terms of copying problems and computing them on a separate sheet of paper. "For many children, the actual process of writing numbers may be so difficult that the ability to succeed in mathematics is greatly affected" (Bley & Thornton, 1981, 10). Any activity involving eye-hand coordination and eye-foot coordination require good visual-motor integration skills.

Students with learning disabilities often have difficulty in physical activities involving the use of gross and/or fine motor skills. They may have difficulty balancing, walking, running, jumping, skipping, throwing, and catching (Hallahan & Kauffman, 1988). Children with learning disabilities are often observed to have "awkward motor functions, unstable balance causing frequent falls, or a lack of manual dexterity. Parents may report a delay in acquiring motor skills, such as riding a bicycle, buttoning a coat, catching a ball, or using eating utensils" (Lerner, 1989, 273). "A general description frequently used to describe the coordination of LD students is 'clumsy' " (Cheek et al., 1989, 409). "For many learning disabled students, motor incoordination is a serious impediment. They may exhibit motor behaviors that are typical of much younger children" (Lerner, 1989, 274).

"LD students with auditory-motor problems have difficulty following verbal directions, repeating oral commands, and verbalizing their motor activities" (Cheek et al., 1989, 408). They, also, experience difficulty during spelling dictation tests, in taking notes during class from lectures or films, during listening comprehension activities or tests where they are expected to listen and write responses, especially exact responses.

Psychological Process Model: Diagnosis

The major focus of diagnosis according to the psychological process model is to identify the student's strengths and weaknesses in receiving and processing information, primarily visual and auditory, in other words, identifying the student's learning modality strengths and weaknesses or learning style. Historically, during the 1960s and 1970s, the primary test administered to determine the presence of a learning disability was the *Illinois Test of Psycholinguistic Abilities* (ITPA) (Kirk & McCarthy, 1961). Another frequently administered test was the *Developmental Test of Visual Perception* (Frostig et al., 1964). The ITPA was designed to measure differences in learning style and psychological processing abilities within the individual child being tested or intraindividual differences in the auditory and visual learning channels.

> What makes the ITPA unique is that it seeks to tap selected psychological and linguistic abilities that are assumed to underlie, relate to, or contribute to academic achievement. In format and subtest content it bears considerable similarity to the Wechsler Scales, the major difference being that the latter is interpreted within a cognitive-intellectual rather than in a psycholinguistic frame of reference (Myers & Hammill, 1990, 353).

Skills assessed by the ITPA (Kirk & McCarthy, 1961) included the following: reception (auditory, visual), association (auditory, visual), expression (verbal, manual), sequential memory (auditory, visual), closure (grammatical, visual, auditory), and sound blending. Thus, the ITPA focused more on the perceptual processing factors than on the language factors. Since the major psychological processing assessment instrument focused primarily on perceptual processing, this became the primary focus of the psychological processing model.

Psychological Process Model: Treatment

The proponents of the psychological process model were diagnostic-prescriptive in orientation as they developed many materials for teaching the deficits identified by the ITPA and other processing tests. Kirk and Kirk (1971) published their recommendations for remediation in *Psycholinguistic Learning Disabilities: Diagnosis and Remediation.* Basically, they suggest that teachers train the deficit perceptual areas by pairing with areas of strength, using multisensory approaches to remediate prerequisite deficits first, and developing functional perceptual-motor abilities (Kirk and Kirk, 1971). Bush and Giles (1977) published *Aids to Psycholinguistic Teaching,* organized into chapters that correspond to the subtests of the ITPA with training activities sequenced for kindergarten through eighth grades. Another remedial program tied directly to the ITPA was *The MWM Program for Developing Language Activities* (Minskoff, Wiseman

& Minskoff, 1972) which proposed remediation for each of the 12 processing areas tested. A number of other professionals prepared programs to remediate perception and perceptual processing deficits including *Slow Learner in the Classroom* (Kephart, 1971), and the *Frostig-Horne Program in Visual Perception* (Frostig & Horne, 1964).

The psychological process model began to receive considerable criticism during the 1970s for several reasons. Some professionals adhering to the psychological process model believed that process training should take precedence over teaching academics directly. As a result, many learning disabilities specialists did process training while regular education teachers did direct remediation in reading, writing, listening, and math (Myers & Hammill, 1990). Another major source of criticism came from researchers including Hammill, Larson, Wiederholt, Salvia, Ysseldyke who attacked the reliability and validity of the ITPA, its usefulness, and the relationship between the constructs and academics.

By the early 1980s, the perceptual process model had almost died out. "The consensus of numerous researchers is that visual perception training alone does not have a significant effect on reading achievement" (Mercer, 1987, 231). Thus, perceptual training in isolation appeared to be ineffective in remediating children's learning problems.

> Perceptual and perceptual-motor training seems to be ineffective in increasing academic achievement. The teacher of children with perceptual difficulties must directly teach curriculum skills to foster academic gains, and when perceptual-motor activities are used, they should be incorporated within academic content (Mercer, 1987, 234).

BEHAVIORAL MODEL OF LEARNING DISABILITIES

The behavioral model theory, etiology, diagnosis, and treatment, previously discussed (see Chapters 3 and 6), remains the same regardless of disability. The behavioral model is relatively unconcerned about determining the etiology of learning disabilities. However, teaching failure is considered a major factor in students' learning disabilities (Mercer, 1987). Behavioral model academic diagnosis utilizes criterion-referenced or informal measures to determine student entry level in a task analyzed hierarchy of skills in various academic subjects. Proponents of the behavioral model proposed direct instruction of academic and social skills. Prerequisite processing abilities were minimized in delivery of special education services.

Behavioral Model: Treatment

Three behaviorists active in the 1960s, 1970s, and into the 1980s in the use of behavioral techniques with students with learning disabilities included Norris Haring, Ogden Lindsley, and Thomas Lovitt, all of whom worked with students with learning disabilities at the Children's Rehabilitation Center at the University of Kansas Medical Center in Kansas City (Mercer, 1987). Earlier, Haring was a doctoral student of William Cruickshank, who implemented the structured program of Strauss and Lehtinen in the public schools (Lovitt, 1989). Ogden Lindsley, a doctoral student of B.F. Skinner, and Thomas Lovitt were highly skilled in the use of operant conditioning (Henley et al., 1993).

Haring championed the use of behavior modification which focused on immediate reinforcement for appropriate or desired behaviors. Lindsley focused on precision teaching, a type of instruction that directly measures and charts student performance daily (Mercer, 1987), and contingency management which is similar to behavior modification (Henley et al., 1983). Lovitt operationalized Applied Behavior Analysis, an instructional methodology utilizing direct and daily measurement, replicatable teaching procedures, individual analysis, and experimental control (Henley et al., 1993). Thus, major behavioral academic instructional processes that transferred from the laboratory into the public school classrooms included behavior modification, contingency management, precision teaching, and applied behavior analysis (Mercer, 1987). Programmed texts, short-term objectives, task analysis, and criterion-referenced tests were developed as educational materials during this decade to provide classroom teachers with a functional, sequenced approach to academics (Poplin, 1989).

The behavioral approach for teaching students with specific learning disabilities has been criticized because the approach is teacher-directed and student passive, thus, inadequately preparing students for self-sufficiency (Henley et al., 1993). The behavioral approach has been seen by many as too segmented due to the heavy use of task analysis and hierarchies of skills in planning instructional objectives (Mercer, 1987). The critics of the behavioral model were the new wave of professionals adhering to the cognitive approaches of treating learning disabled students.

COGNITIVE MODEL OF LEARNING DISABILITIES

The cognitive model is currently dominating the field of learning disabilities as the major approach to education. The cognitive approach takes into account the active participation of the learner, views learning disabilities from a cognitive psychology perspective, and uses information processing and other cognitive theories to answer the question of how children with learning disabilities learn (Hresko & Parmar, 1991, 21).

Cognition can be considered from three major perspectives: as a process, as a capacity, and as a product (Mann & Sabatino, 1985). The cognitive process, frequently referred to as information processing, is concerned with receiving, interpreting, and managing information. Cognitive capacities include structures, skills, and abilities that make cognitive processing possible (Mann & Sabatino, 1985). Among the cognitive capacities are the perceptual and perceptual-motor skills, memory structures, metacognition, cognitive strategies, control processes, cognitive control styles, and other cognitive skills (Mann & Sabatino, 1985). Cognitive products include the cognitive perceptions, images, concepts, decisions that may be expressed behaviorally in oral or written language or drawing (Mann & Sabatino, 1985). These three hypothetical perspectives of cognition—process, capacity, product—are interwoven and interdependent concepts.

Cognitive Model: Etiology

All cognitive functioning relies on neurological functioning. Thus, damage to the nervous system's nuclei and ganglia is likely to have devastating effects on specific cognitive functions (Mann & Sabatino, 1985). Genetic defects, birth trauma, accidents and injuries that damage specific parts of the nervous system usually cause specific types of cognitive deficits (Jones, 1985).

Information Processing

Information processing is the process by which the brain receives information from sensory perceptions, interprets and mediates the information using thinking and memory strategies, and acts upon the information by means of a verbal (vocal), fine motor, or gross motor response. Information processing or cognitive processing problems may occur due to an interruption in (1) attention, (2) reception of stimuli, (3) storage and processing of information, and (4) expression of cognitive abilities (Fallen & Umansky, 1985). A neurological or sensory impairment may interfere with the child's ability to attend to a stimulus long enough to process it into short-term or long-term memory storage. Acquisition of information first requires attention to relevant stimuli. Attention problems of learning disabled students are discussed in Chapter 10.

The information processing model subsumed the psychological process model, therefore, deficits in basic psychological processes of attention, perception, perceptual-motor skills (previously discussed), and memory are seen as underlying learning problems. The information processing model is also concerned with the storage of information in memory systems, and the retrieval of that information for use.

Memory Problems. "Memory pertains to sensations and data already received and perceived. The ability to store and retrieve previously experienced sensations and perceptions when the stimulus that originally evoked them is no longer present is called memory...." (Lerner, 1989, 181). There are at least three stages of memory in which the child with learning disabilities could have difficulty: (1) reception (perceptual difficulties), (2) storage or consolidation of data (short-term, long-term, working memory), and (3) retrieval (metacognition and strategy deficits) (Levine, 1987).

Children and youth with learning disabilities may experience difficulty with short-term memory and/or working memory, which are temporary storage facilities. They may experience difficulty holding onto information while they are attempting to solve problems or read words. "Children with active working memory dysfunction may become seriously frustrated. They may study hard for examinations but find when they take tests that the material fails to cohere. They appear to do particularly poorly under timed conditions" (Levine, 1987, 115). Deficits in sustained attention, language, and high levels of anxiety often make it difficult to hold information in short-term memory long enough to process it to long-term memory.

Long-term memory is a permanent memory storage (Lerner, 1993). Many students with learning disabilities experience "difficulty consolidating data in long-term memory. Consolidation weaknesses are often seen in students who overrely on rote learning and fail to engage in elaboration. They are less prone to relate new information to their prior knowledge, nor are they apt to extrapolate, reason, or speculate upon their new knowledge" (Levine, 1987, 116). "Learning disabled children often have trouble integrating what they learn. There is some interference that prevents them from pulling information together to draw conclusions, to make associations or simply to use building blocks of information to learn material adequately" (Bley & Thornton, 1981, 13).

There are several types of long-term memory: episodic memory (personal history episodes), semantic memory (general knowledge, concepts, school-type learning), and procedural memory (the tasks that have been repeated until they are automatic) (Slavin, 1994). "The problem people face in long-term memory is not storage but retrieval, that is, how to recall (or remember) information stored in long-term memory" (Lerner, 1993, 199).

Retrieval Problems. "Retrieval dysfunctions become particularly problematic in late elementary and junior high school, when there is an enormous stress on retrieval abilities. Much of what has been learned during the earlier grades must be recalled with speed, ease, and precision" (Levine, 1987, 118). "When asked a question, an affected child's response time may be prolonged due either to slowness of retrieval of the information sought or difficulty finding the right words with which to encode a response" (Levine, 1987, 117). Retrieval problems in students with learning disabilities may be related to their deficits in metacognition.

Metacognition Problems. Metacognition refers to both one's knowledge about cognition and the regulation of their own cognition (Reid, 1988). The first aspect of metacognition refers to the awareness of one's systematic thinking strategies that are needed for learning (Lerner, 1993). The second aspect of metacognition involves one's self-regulation, higher-order conceptualization skills (Mann & Sabatino, 1985).

Students with learning disabilities do not spontaneously use strategies that nondisabled students readily use, thus, they experience strategy deficits (Mercer, 1987). For example, verbal rehearsal and clustering are strategies that efficient learners automatically use to help themselves remember information" (Robinson & Deshler, 1988, 125). It is "especially difficult for some children to use strategic maneuvers to aid registration, consolidation, and retrieval. Subvocalizing, imaging, verbal mediation, and other such techniques may feel alien to certain children, who consequently exhibit deficient memory" (Levine, 1987, 121). Some students develop very little insight into the workings of their own memories, thus, fail to develop good memory strategies (Levine, 1989).

"Failure to use effective strategies may exist with or without accompanying signs of attention deficit" (Levine, 1987, 121). "It is difficult to determine whether the superficiality in processing, the failure to use mnemonic strategies, and the ineffective registration of data result from cognitive impulsiveness . . . or are separate characteristics of children with attention deficits" (Levine, 1987, 121).

For efficient learning, an individual's memory in many areas of performance must become an automatic, habitual response to stimuli (e.g., remembering words when speaking, remembering a word by sight) (Lerner, 1993). "The concept of automatization is related to retrieval memory. Automatization is rapid and unconscious (or nearly unconscious) retrieval memory" (Levine, 1987, 119). For children with learning disabilities, the flow of information is hampered because they have difficulty acquiring the automatization needed for successful learning (Stanovich, 1986). Children with learning disabilities are slower and more gradual in their acquisition of automatization abilities than normal learners. They must exert too much effort on tasks that should be automatic, having little left with which to attack other areas of the learning process (Lerner, 1993).

Cognitive Model: Diagnosis

Psychometric Approach

According to the cognitive approach to assessment, the three aspects of cognition—process, capacity, product—must be assessed to determine the student's functioning levels. This assessment process generally utilizes standardized instruments to identify a student's strengths and weaknesses. Most assessment instruments to be discussed include subtests that assess some aspect of cognitive process, capacity, and product. The process aspect or information processing is concerned with receiving, interpreting, and managing information. Cognitive capacities include perceptual and perceptual-motor processing skills, cognitive strategies, cognitive control processes, cognitive control styles, thinking strategies, memory strategies, expressive and receptive language, and attention. Cognitive products include the cognitive perceptions, images, concepts, decisions that may be expressed vocally, verbally and motorically.

Examples of assessment instruments frequently utilized to assess cognitive functioning (process, capacity, products) of students with learning disabilities include the following tests and some of the skills assessed:

(1) *Wechsler Intelligence Scale for Children — Third Edition* (WISC–III) (Wechsler, 1991): Estimate of overall cognitive capacity, receptive and expressive language, short-term and long-term memory, abstract reasoning, perceptual and perceptual-motor skills and nonverbal conceptualization.

(2) *Developmental Test of Visual-Motor Integration (VMI)* (Beery, 1989): Visual-Motor functioning

(3) *Woodcock-Johnson Psycho-Educational Battery — Revised: Tests of Cognitive Ability* (Woodcock & Mather, 1989): Subtests assess perception, perceptual-motor skills, memory skills, and linguistic skills.

(4) *Detroit Tests of Learning Aptitude — 3* (Hammill, 1991): Subtests are grouped into four domains: Linguistic Domain, Cognitive Domain, Attentional Domain, and Motoric Domain.

(5) *Peabody Picture Vocabulary Test — Revised* (PPVT–R) (Dunn & Dunn, 1981): Receptive Language

(6) *Test of Language Development — 2: Primary* (TOLD–P:2) and *Test of Language Development — 2: Intermediate* (TOLD–I:2) (Newcomer & Hammill, 1988): Phonology, Syntax, Semantics, Morphology, Receptive and Expressive Language

(7) *Test of Pragmatic Language* (Phelps-Teraski & Phelps-Gunn, 1992): Pragmatics — ages 5–13

(8) *Woodcock-Johnson Psycho-Educational Battery — Revised: Tests of Achievement* (Woodcock & Johnson, 1989): Academic achievement in Reading, Mathematics, and Written Language.

This is a small sample of norm-referenced standardized tests which may be utilized to assess students to determine functioning levels, strengths and weaknesses in cognitive processing, cognitive capacities, and cognitive content areas.

Multidirectional Approach

Swanson (1991, 253) has proposed a multidirectional cognitive assessment model to assess student functioning across five cognitive planes: (1) Executive function — ability to order, prioritize, and coordinate strategies; (2) Knowledge base — assessing long-term memory of academics; (3) Metacognition — self-knowledge about learning; (4) Strategy — skills in explanation, prediction, integration and classification; (5) Strategy Abstraction — zone of potential, generalization, transformation. In addition to the "thinking aloud" protocols, Swanson's (1991) proposed assessment would include the following: academic intelligence, responses to strategy instruction, Piagetian measures, rule learning, recall of prose material, WISC–III subtest Similarities and Block Design, probe questions on child's self knowledge of learning and self-diagnosis of success, child's ability to benefit from instruction on failed tasks (290–291). "The apparent difficulty in applying this assessment has been lessened to a certain extent with the development of sample problem questions across and within planes" (Swanson, 1991, 289).

Cognitive Model: Treatment

From the cognitive perspective, educational goals for individuals with learning disabilities include several dimensions: (1) Developing strategies for encoding and elaborating new information, (2) Developing the abilities needed to retrieve information from long-term memory, (3) Developing the ability to engage in planning approaches to information acquisition and learning, and (4) Developing the ability to access and use prior-learned information and engage in new learning activities independently and successfully (Hresko & Parmar, 1991, 25). In order to reach these goals, cognitive strategists emphasize self-monitoring or metacognitive approaches to learning which include self-planning, self-organizing, self-questioning, self-evaluation, self-monitoring, and self-reinforcement. "In the cognitive curriculum, transfer and generalization become the criteria for judging instructional effectiveness, because they are signs that the knowledge accrued is likely to be used independently in appropriate situations" (Reid, 1991, 305).

Major cognitive approaches currently utilized to enhance information processing, metacognition, and acquisition and application of learning strategies include Cognitive Behavior Modification, Instrumental Enrichment, the Strategies Intervention Model (SIM), and Reciprocal Teaching.

Cognitive Behavior Modification

Cognitive behavior modification is a cognitive intervention which analyzes the thinking processes involved in performing a task, and combines behavior modification techniques with self-treatment methods (Mercer, 1989). Meichenbaum (1975), the pioneer of cognitive behavior modification, utilized a four-step process in the self-instructional program including the following: (1) Cognitive Modeling: Adult performs a task while describing the task orally, (2) Overt Self-Guidance: Student performs the same task under the direction of the adult model, (3) Faded-Out Guidance: Student whispers instructions to self as she/he performs task, (4) Covert Self-Instruction: Student performs task using his/her inner speech to guide performance. The basic tenet of this approach is to use inner speech to modify cognition and behavior.

Instrumental Enrichment

Feuerstein's (1980) *Instrumental Enrichment* is a "content-free process" to remediating deficient cognitive functions that occur during information processing (input, elaboration, output) which negatively affect learning. The instructional approach focuses on the training and development of cognitive skills and the development of metacognitive skills that lead to self-regulation and the independent use of cognitive strategies (Taylor, 1988). *Instrumental Enrichment* (IE) consists of fifteen instruments (groups of lessons) that require from 3 to 5 one-hour sessions over the course of two to three years to complete. In addition to the carefully structured materials, the most critical element of the program is the specially trained teacher, who provides mediated learning experiences (Lerner, 1993).

Strategies Intervention Model

The Strategies Intervention Model (SIM) was designed and tested at the University of Kansas Institute for Research in Learning Disabilities under the direction of Donald Deshler, as an instructional alternative for low achieving (e.g., 4th to 5th grade reading level) mainstreamed adolescents to provide them with strategies for learning. A major objective of SIM is to provide direct instruction to strategy deficient adolescents in metacognitive processes involved in monitoring a task, planning and implementing problem-solving strategies, and evaluating the performance success.

The Learning Strategies Curriculum is organized into three strands — Acquisition, Storage, and Expression and Demonstration of Competence. The Acquisition strand includes strategies that help students acquire information from written materials: The Word Identification Strategy, The Paraphrasing Strategy, The Self-Questioning Strategy, etc. The Storage strand includes strategies that enable students to identify and store important information: The First Letter Mnemonic Strategy, The Paired Associates Strategy, and The Listening and Notetaking Strategy. The Demonstration of Competence strand includes strategies that have been designed to enable students to cope with the written expression demands in secondary schools: The Sentence Writing Strategy, The Paragraph Writing Strategy, The Theme Writing Strategy, etc. Teachers need very specialized training in order to implement the Strategies Intervention Model.

Reciprocal Teaching

Reciprocal Teaching, developed by Palinscar and Brown (1984), is a technique for teaching cognitive strategies through using a social dialogue between the teacher and students. During this technique, the teacher and students take turns leading the discussion about their reading assignment. The students are trained in four strategies: (1) Summarizing the content of the passage, (2) Asking questions about a central point, (3) Clarifying the difficult parts of the materials, and (4) Predicting what would happen next. This technique can be utilized with any content area materials. Research with reciprocal teaching suggests that it is an effective teaching approach (Lerner, 1993).

SUMMARY

The following table provides a summary of the etiology, diagnosis, treatment, and some theorists of the primary theoretical models of learning disabilities: Medical Model, Psychological Process Model, Behavioral Model, and Cognitive Model.

Summary of Theoretical Models of Learning Disabilities

Medical 1950s	Psychological Process 1960s	Behavioral 1970s	Cognitive 1980s–1990s
Focus: Brain Damage	Focus: Perceptual Processing	Focus: Operant Conditioning	Focus: Information Processing
Etiology: Brain Damage caused by genetic, biochemical, cerebral trauma, environmental influences.	Etiology: Minimal Brain Dysfunction with deficits in attention, perception, memory, linguistic functions.	Etiology: Unconcerned about etiology.	Etiology: Neurological problems which cause problems in information processing and metacognition.

Diagnosis: Medical—EEG, CT, MRI, BEAM, physical exam. DSM–IV.	Diagnosis: Illinois Test of Psycholinguistic Abilities	Diagnosis: Criterion-Referenced Tests, Task Analyzed Skills	Diagnosis: WISC–III, DTLA-3, Woodcock-Johnson cognitive and academic tests. PPVT–R, TOLD–I:2
Treatment/ Instruction: Medication-Ritalin, Patterning, Sensory-Integrative Therapy	Treatment/ Instruction: ITPA programs MWM Program for Language Activities, Perceptual training	Treatment/ Instruction: Direct Instruction, Social Learning, Precision Teaching, Behavior Modification	Treatment/ Instruction: CBM, Learning Strategies: SIM, Instrumental Enrichment, Reciprocal Teaching
Theorists: Strauss, Lehtinen, Orton, Cruickshank	Theorists: Kirk, Kephart, Myklebust, Frostig	Theorists: Haring, Lovitt, Bandura, Lindsley, Hammill	Theorists: Deshler, Levine, Swanson, Piaget, Meichenbaum, Feuerstein

Chapter 10

LEARNING PERSPECTIVES OF
LEARNING DISABILITIES

Individuals with learning disabilities represent a diverse group with multiple characteristics. (Ariel, 1992).

The major characteristics of children and youth with learning disabilities can generally be categorized as cognitive learning problems, academic learning problems, and social and emotional learning problems.

COGNITIVE LEARNING PROBLEMS

"The definition of learning disabilities stipulates that these children have average or above-average intelligence" (Bender, 1995, 112). Research suggests the mean IQ levels of students currently labeled learning disabled range from low 80s to middle 90s (Keogh, 1987); thus, many students with learning disabilities are functioning within the lower average range of cognitive functioning. Students with learning disabilities, also, experience numerous information processing and language processing problems.

Information Processing Problems

The legal definition of learning disabilities specifies that students with learning disabilities have a disorder in one or more of the basic psychological processes, currently referred to as information processing problems. The information processing problems of students with learning disabilities are usually in the areas of (1) attention problems, (2) perception deficits (see Chapter 9), and/or (3) memory problems (see Chapter 9).

Attention Problems

Students with learning disabilities frequently experience difficulties focusing attention on academic tasks, maintaining attention and thought on relevant classroom tasks, and shifting attention to new tasks. Students who display attention problems may experience difficulties not only with information processing, but also, with productivity (Levine, 1987). The primary areas of attention difficulties that students with learning disabilities display at school include selective attention and selective intention problems.

Selective Attention Problems. Selective attention is the ability to attend to relevant (central) information in the face of irrelevant (incidental) information (Lerner, 1993). Often, students with learning disabilities are attending, but they are attending to the wrong stimuli. Students with selective attention problems cannot screen out extraneous stimuli, and irrelevant stimuli attract them (Haring & McCormick, 1990).

Students experiencing difficulties focusing attention may display inappropriate attention duration (poor sustained attention), short attention span (pay attention to very little), or high distractibility (pay attention to everything). Students with learning disabilities often are highly visually distractible and focus on trivial or irrelevant situations. Frequently, students with LD are auditorily distractible and experience trouble with focusing and sustaining listening for detail.

Selective Intention Problems. Many children and youth who have deficits in selective attention, also, exhibit deficits in selective intention. These students may experience difficulty with many aspects of self-regulation in academics and social behaviors. They may experience difficulty with social interactions because of verbal disinhibition (fail to monitor what they say) and display impulsive behavior (poorly planned, inappropriate action). Learning disabled students have difficulty with academic achievement because of impulsive performance (sacrifice accuracy for rapid completion), inconsistent performance (erratic academic performance and unpredictable test scores), impersistence (seldom completes projects or assignments and experiences difficulty with transitions), and reduced response to feedback (little if any quality control, numerous errors, resistant to proofreading and revising, failure to learn from experience) (Levine, 1987). Dysfunctions of selective attention and selective intention are probably the most common sources of underachievement and school related maladaptation (Levine, 1987).

Attention Deficit Hyperactivity Disorder. Although short attention span, hyperactivity, and other attention problems are frequently associated with learning disabilities and 15 percent to 20 percent of children and adolescents with learning disabilities have ADHD, they are not synonymous terms (Silver, 1990). The essential features of attention-deficit hyperactivity disorder (AD/HD) are inattention, impulsiveness, and hyperactivity (APA, 1994). The new AD/HD classifications include the following: (1) Attention-Deficit/Hyperactivity Disorder, Combined Type, (2) Attention-Deficit/Hyperactivity Disorder, Predominantly Inattentive Type, (3) Attention-Deficit/Hyperactive-Impulsive Type, and (4) Attention-Deficit/Hyperactivity Disorder, Not Otherwise Specified.

Language Processing Problems

Students with "true" learning disabilities experience underlying language processing problems including receptive language, inner language, and expressive language problems which interfere with acquisition and mastery of basic academics in reading, math, and oral and written expression (Polloway & Smith, 1992). Receptive language is an individual's ability to understand or decode spoken (listening) and written symbols (reading). Inner language or the language of thought is the cognitive processing element in communication. Students with learning disabilities may have difficulty remembering due to language processing problems and "poor language skills, which make verbal material particularly difficult for them to remember" (Hallahan & Kauffman, 1988, 120). Expressive language is the ability to encode or transform thoughts and ideas into verbal or written symbols. Encoding linguistic information is particularly difficult for students with learning disabilities.

Deficits in the Rules of Language

All languages are rule-governed and share the same basic structure with rules in form, content, and use (Polloway & Smith, 1992). Each language contains rules for dealing with form including a system of sounds (phonology), a system of building meaning into words (morphology), and a system of forming grammatical sentences (syntax). Each language contains rules for dealing with content including a system for deriving meaning from words and sentences (semantics). Additionally, each language contains rules for dealing with use, essentially a system governing communication among people (pragmatics) (Polloway & Smith, 1992). Students with learning disabilities frequently experience difficulties in all aspects of language.

Deficits in Language Form. Three systems of rules that comprise the form of any language are phonology, morphology, and syntax (Polloway & Smith, 1992). **Phonology** is the system of sounds in a language and phonemes are the smallest units of sound that have linguistic meaning. Children and youth who experience difficulties in phonology, also, experience difficulty in learning phonics and in using those skills in decoding unknown words. A student with deficits in phonology may experience problems with correct speech articulation. A definite relationship exists between phonological (sound) discrimination, and reading disorders (Myers & Hammill, 1990).

Phonology, also, includes the study of prosodic features in speech including stress (loudness and softness on specific syllables), juncture (pauses within sentences), and intonation (rise and fall of pitch in the voice which indicates the type of sentence—declarative or question) (James, 1990). By two years of age, most children have mastered the adult intonation system (Jones, 1992). Thus, they can listen to subtle tone changes and can predict if adults and other children feel angry, happy, or sad even if they cannot understand the words they may say. Many children with learning disabilities lack mastery of the intonation system and experience difficulty interpreting emotions by listening to vocal intonation. These children may have difficulty adjusting language and tone of voice to a specific social situation. They may fail at integrating accurate feelings or emotions with expressive language. "Their intonation and word choice, for example, might suggest anger and hostility when this is not actually the case, leading to misunderstanding and sometimes rejection by peers" (Levine, 1987, 158).

Morphology is a system for building meaning in words including the rules for indicating tense, person, and number in verbs and for forming adjectives and adverbs from root words (Polloway & Smith, 1992). Morphology forms the basis for structural analysis in reading. Disabled students who experience difficulty with morphology may experience difficulty with decoding unknown words and with the acquisition of new vocabulary words. The lack of efficient use of structural analysis will significantly effect understanding what the student is reading in content areas.

Syntax is the grammatical rules system that specifies the appropriate word orderings for intended meaning (Oyer et al., 1987). Grammatical rules provide information on how to transform one sentence construction into another so that compound sentences, negatives, questions, imperatives, passives, and sentences with embedded clauses can be produced (Oyer et al., 1987). Children and youth with learning disabilities experience delays or deficits in language acquisition, often by as much as 3 to 4 years or more (Shames & Wiig, 1990). Sentences that express comparison, passive, spatial, temporal, or familial relationships also convey a sequence in time or space which is very difficult for youngsters with learning disabilities to understand (Lovitt, 1989). Students with learning disabilities often experience difficulty understanding pronouns and pronoun antecedents, and complex sentences.

Deficits in Language Content. Semantics deals with the meanings of words (including multiple meanings) and word combinations (Oyer et al., 1987). Children with language disabilities have trouble with interpreting figurative language (e.g., idioms, proverbs, metaphors, similes, puns, jokes), implied information, ambiguous sentences, words with multiple meanings, synonyms, verbal opposites, and verbal analogies (Wiig & Semel, 1984). Often figurative language is interpreted literally (Oyer et al., 1987).

Youngsters with language disabilities have less well-developed meaning systems and poorer comprehension of language than their nondisabled peers (Robinson & Deshler, 1988). Children with language disabilities have smaller vocabularies, use fewer words to express themselves, and communicate fewer concepts in comparison to their peers (Oyer et al., 1987). Word finding problems are common. Students with learning disabilities experience difficulty in understanding humor and do not exhibit the increase in understanding humor at the intermediate or middle school grade levels that non-LD students demonstrate (Bruno, Johnson, & Simon, 1987).

Deficits in Language Usage. Pragmatics refers to the use of language in a social context for a particular purpose or communicative competence (Oyer et al., 1987). Communicative incompetence reduces the social effectiveness of children who are learning disabled. They appear to experience difficulties in (1) imparting intentions to listeners in specific situations, (2) conveying and understanding information, and (3) initiating, and sustaining conversation (Levine, 1987). Learning disabled boys appear to experience significant difficulty in adapting messages to the needs of the listener and in interpreting and responding to subtle nonverbal feedback (Knight-Arest, 1984). The language disabled tend not to speak in polite terms or to show consideration for others in conversation. Thus, in addition to being widely misunderstood, they unintentionally commit many faux pas.

As children approach adolescence, increasing social demands are made by their peers. Language disabilities may prevent students from meeting these demands (e.g., appropriate use of slang terms or coy, flirting behaviors with the opposite sex), resulting in social maladjustment (Oyer et al., 1987). Preteens and adolescents must develop metalinguistic competence, one's ability to think about language, which enables them to decide whether a message is acceptable or successful in its intent, and to determine the meanings of unfamiliar expressions, ambiguous messages, and linguistic ambiguity (Nippold, 1988).

ACADEMIC LEARNING PROBLEMS

Academic problems are the most widely accepted characteristics of individuals with learning disabilities (Mercer, 1987). Academically, students with learning disabilities bring a configuration of skills and abilities to instructional negotiations that is more like that of younger normally achieving children than that of their peers (Reid, 1988). The cognitive and language deficits of students with learning disabilities significantly impact acquisition of academic skills and social/emotional developmental skills.

Preschool "At-Risk" Students

It is difficult to identify young children as learning disabled because they have not as yet failed academically. Since P.L.99-457 does not require that preschool disabled children be labeled a categorical label, they are frequently labeled "developmentally delayed" or "at-risk" for educational problems. Preschool children who may eventually be labeled learning disabled often experience a developmental delay in one or more of the developmental milestones. These developmental areas include the following: (1) sensory acuity and perception: auditory and visual; (2) motor development; fine, gross, and perceptual-motor integration; (3) cognitive development: attention, memory, and concepts; (4) speech/language skills: expressive language, receptive language, and speech development; (5) social and affective development: interactions with adults, children, the environment, and play skills; (6) adaptive skills: eating, dressing, toileting. A young child is frequently diagnosed and provided special education services if one or more developmental areas are significantly delayed (i.e., 50% delayed in one area or 25% delayed in two areas).

Preschool children who are mildly developmentally delayed may eventually be labeled learning disabled if preschool intervention programs and/or maturation do not lead to near average-range functioning. Speech and/or language problems of preschool disabled students include speech disorders, language delays, and language disorders. Children with language delays may experience a limited vocabulary, lack names for concrete items in the environment, and lack relationship terms such as big-little. They may experience receptive and expressive language problems, reduced listening comprehension ability; and prereading, prewriting, and premath deficits. Developmentally delayed preschool students frequently lack mathematics prerequisites in classification (function, color, size, shape), matching sets 1–10 objects, one-to-one correspondence, and spatial relationships. Children may be delayed in fine motor skills (i.e., putting together puzzles, tracing templates, drawing and coloring), and/or delayed in gross motor skills (i.e., catching and throwing a ball, running, jumping, hopping). Visual-motor integration skills are often very difficult for disabled preschool-aged children.

Social skills problems of preschool children may include delays in acquiring parallel play, domestic make-believe, symbolic play, and sharing toys. Social developmental delays are evidenced when the child functions similar to a younger child. Children who experience speech and language delays may also experience deficits in pragmatics or social communication.

Elementary Students with Learning Disabilities

"In many children, learning disabilities first become apparent when they enter school and fail to acquire academic skills" (Lerner, 1993, 23). Children with learning disabilities in elementary schools experience difficulty with listening comprehension, reading comprehension, basic prereading skills, math calculation and reasoning, written expression (handwriting, spelling, composition skills, written composition), receptive and expressive language, and social-emotional skills.

Kindergarten and First Grade

During kindergarten and first grade, "at-risk" and mildly disabled students frequently experience difficulty in the following areas: (1) Academic Readiness Skills: alphabet knowledge, quantitative concepts, directional concepts; (2) Language Skills: receptive and expressive; (3) Perception: visual, auditory, and perceptual-motor integration; (4) Gross and fine motor skills; (5) Attention; (6) Hyperactivity; and (7) Social skills (Mercer, 1987).

Math Deficits. Young children frequently experience difficulty in math due to lack of acquisition of math cognitive prerequisite skills. The ability to count, match, sort, compare, and understand one-to-one correspondence hinges on the child's experiences in manipulating objects (Lerner, 1993). The student with attention problems and perceptual-motor problems may experience significant difficulty with understanding space, form, order, time, distance, and quantity (Lerner, 1993).

If young children are not provided math readiness in terms of daily use and real-life problem-solving, math calculation will have very little meaning for them (Krogh, 1995). Most primary grade children are gaining competence in conservation, classification, seriation, and ordering of numbers, however, children who possess significant deficits in these areas will experience difficulty with acquisition of math concepts.

Lack of understanding of cognitive concepts and language terminology such as "up-down, over-under, top-bottom, more-less, larger-smaller, add-take away, minus-plus" will hinder progress in mathematics processes (addition, subtraction, multiplication, and division). Children with math disabilities have been observed to have difficulty with activities that require motor and visual-perception association (Lerner, 1993).

Reading Deficits. Young children frequently experience difficulty in skills prerequisites for reading. The kindergarten child who does not discriminate letters (especially those in his/her name), lacks left-to-right orientation, has an inadequate conceptual background, and lacks age appropriate language development skills will probably experience difficulty in learning to read without remediation. A lack of adequate auditory skill development in phonological awareness of letter sounds, auditory attending, discrimination, sound counting, and memory will probably result in difficulty in learning to read. Additionally, the kindergarten child who experiences difficulty in reading letters and numbers, in copying geometric patterns, and in matching printed letters and words, will probably experience difficulty in learning to read. Children who have not had a rich language and experiential background and a broad vocabulary (i.e., names for colors, names for common concepts, household items) will probably experience difficulty in learning to read and with all language-based subject areas.

Elementary Grades (2nd–6th)

Language Deficits. Language problems of one form or another are the underlying basis for many learning disabilities. Oral language disorders or delays (previously discussed) include problems in the areas of phonology, morphology, syntax, semantics, and pragmatics. Language problems hamper progress in all academic areas. By 1st or 2nd grade, language impaired students may already be functioning 3–4 years deficit. This gap in language facility continues to grow during elementary and secondary school years.

Elementary school students with language problems frequently function at the literal level in receptive language (reading and listening) and expressive language (talking and writing). This becomes a severe deficit when understanding receptive and expressive language require higher level cognitive functioning. Many students with learning disabilities do not do well in situations requiring extensive language interactions and conversations, and they are less skillful than their non-learning disabled peers in maintaining a conversation (Pearl et al., 1986).

Math Deficits. Problems in math are frequently noted if the child lacks math cognitive prerequisite skills including classification, ordering and seriation, one-to-one correspondence, and conservation. A disturbance in spatial relationships can interfere with the visualization of the entire number system (Lerner, 1993). A student with an auditory or visual memory deficit may be unable to recall number facts quickly, and may experience difficulty remembering the steps in computing the basic arithmetic processes (addition, subtraction, multiplication, division) (Lerner, 1993).

Intermediate grade LD students frequently experience difficulty understanding place value, regrouping, fractions, multiplication, division, decimals, percent, estimating, and reasoning problems (Mercer, 1987). Math reasoning problems pose extreme difficulty for students with learning disabilities functioning at the literal level in academics and cognition because they require problem-solving skills, language proficiency, comprehending math vocabulary and automaticity in using algorithms and basic facts. Thus, elementary learning disabled students may be functioning 2–3 years behind age-grade expectations in mathematics.

Reading Deficits. About 80 percent of the students with learning disabilities have difficulty in reading (Lyon, 1985). Reading deficits are classified into two areas: basic reading skills and reading comprehension. Basic reading skills include reading vocabulary words (sight words) and word analysis skills (phonetic analysis, structural analysis, syllabication, contextual analysis, and dictionary skills). Facility in language is the foundation for word analysis or decoding skills. Thus, a language disabled child with deficits in phonology will experience difficulty learning phonics and syllabication; deficits in morphology will cause significant difficulty in learning structural analysis. Language deficits in syntax and semantics result in deficits in reading comprehension. Listening comprehension, also, has a foundation in language competency.

Children and youth with reading disabilities generally fall into one of several categories: (1) problems with basic reading skills including acquisition of adequate sight vocabulary and/or decoding skills especially phonics, (2) problems in reading comprehension especially with inference, evaluation, and appreciation levels, or (3) problems in both basic reading skills and reading comprehension. It is not uncommon for a reading disabled 6th grade student to be reading on the third grade level experiencing difficulty with basic reading skills and comprehension. Obviously, a reading deficit severely hampers a student's efforts in the content subject areas such as science and social studies.

A reader who must exert a great deal of effort to recognize words has little processing capacity remaining for comprehension (Lerner, 1993).

Reading comprehension can also be hindered if the child lacks an adequate conceptual background and if the child does not get actively involved and thinking during the reading process.

Written Expression Deficits. The lack of automaticity in written expression prerequisites make creative writing and report writing almost impossible. Written expression is composed of four basic areas of skills: handwriting, spelling, composition skills (grammar, word usage, sentence and paragraph construction, capitalization, punctuation), and written composition. In order for a student to be fluent in written composition (i.e., creative stories, reports), handwriting, spelling, composition skills, and language fluency must be at an automatic level, so the student can focus on the content of the story or report she/he is writing. Almost all students with learning disabilities experience severe written expression deficits of 3 to 4 years for grade expectancy.

Secondary Level: 7th to 12th Grades

The tougher demands of the junior and senior high school curriculum and teachers, the turmoil of adolescence, and the continued academic failure, all combine to intensify the effects of the learning disability. Adolescents with learning disabilities frequently experience problems in reading and listening comprehension, basic reading skills, math calculation and reasoning, written and oral expression, study skills, attention, motivation, metacognition, and social and emotional skills.

The most common academic functioning range for adolescents with LD in reading and math is the 4th to 6th grade range (Deshler et al., 1980). The most common academic disability of students with LD is a pervasive reading disability which adversely affects all subject areas. Problems in learning phonics and word analysis skills adversely effect acquiring a fluent reading vocabulary. Difficulty in understanding sequence, predicting outcomes, analyzing cause and effect, and finding the main idea adversely effect comprehension. The lack of higher level content vocabulary impedes progress in content area subjects.

It has been estimated that 50% of individuals with learning disabilities have language and speech problems (Marge, 1972). "Language and speech difficulties reflect deficient skills in oral expression and listening comprehension" (Haring & McCormick, 1990, 121). Adolescents with learning disabilities have poorer language and communication skills than their counterparts who are achieving normally (Johnson & Blalock,

1987). Language disorders may also take the form of written language disabilities in reading and written expression. Many students with severe reading problems have underlying disabilities in oral language (Lerner, 1993).

SOCIAL AND EMOTIONAL LEARNING PROBLEMS

"Social success with peers is of paramount importance to most school children. The avoidance of humiliation at all costs is a relentless campaign, as is the quest for friendship and popularity" (Levine, 1987, 240). Since a deficit in social skills implies a lack of sensitivity to people and a poor perception of social situations, the deficit affects almost every aspect of the student's life and is one of the most crippling disabilities a student can have (Lerner, 1993).

Social Skills Problems

When students with learning disabilities are compared to their non-disabled peers, their social behaviors are less acceptable because they demonstrate less ability to predict the consequences for their behaviors, greater misinterpretation of social cues, more difficulty adapting their behaviors to the characteristics of their listeners, and more frequently perform inappropriate social behaviors (Schumaker & Hazel, 1984). Interactions with peers, teachers, parents, and siblings are frequently marred by the inappropriate behavior of the student with learning disabilities.

Numerous explanations for the social skills problems of students with learning disabilities have been postulated including the following: (1) cognitive and social cognition deficits, (2) communication deficits, (3) social imperceptiveness, (4) lack of empathy and role-taking ability. Children and youth with learning disabilities experience a wide variety of cognitive and communication deficits which make understanding social situations very difficult. These cognitive deficits include (1) concrete level thinking, (2) problems with cause and effect reasoning, (3) difficulty learning from imitation and modeling, (4) delayed logical reasoning, (5) lack of motivation, (6) inability to self-monitor (metacognition), and (7) lack of automatic generalization abilities. Additionally, children with learning disabilities often experience attention deficits, hyperactivity, and impulsiveness which result in problems drawing social inferences and in social metacognitive deficits.

Social Imperceptiveness

The social and emotional problems of some youngsters with learning disabilities are due to their social imperceptions, their inability to perceive accurately the feelings and subtle responses of others (Bryan, 1977). For many students with learning disabilities, attention deficits, impulsivity, and hyperactivity interfere with socialization efforts. Children with hyperactivity experience difficulty in social situations due to their purposeless excessive motor activity and lack of attention. They have frequent accidents from running recklessly, and sometimes they unintentionally hurt a classmate when playing too rough on the playground (Mercer, 1987). Hyperactive children are also impulsive, acting quickly without considering the consequences. "Children who are impulsive may also have trouble predicting social consequences, generating appropriate interactional strategies, and controlling aggressive outbursts. All of these shortcomings are apt to predispose children to rejection" (Levine, 1987, 262).

Youngsters with learning disability experience significant difficulties in interpersonal exchange and in understanding the affective states of others because of an inability to interpret nonverbal and verbal communication (Bryan & Pflaum, 1978). Some students with learning disabilities do not "react appropriately to others' facial expressions, hand and arm gestures, posture, tone of voice, or general moods" (Mercer, 1987, 447). Students with learning disabilities often do not grasp the significance of nonverbal communication including judging emotions and assessing affective expressions (Bryan, 1977). They are unable to infer emotions from verbal and nonverbal communication, also have difficulty taking the perspective of others.

> Students with social perception problems may not be able to anticipate . . . , they may be unable to confirm whether the action matches what is anticipated, and they may be unable to adjust their behavior in the light of the results. For these reasons they appear to lack tact and sensitivity (Lerner, 1989, 470).

"Some children with language processing problems may have real difficulty drawing appropriate social inferences from what is said" (Levine, 1987, 263). "People with social disabilities appear to be less attuned than their peers to the feelings of others. They may use inappropriate behavior or language because they do not know if the person to whom they are reacting is sad or happy, approving or disapproving, accepting or rejecting" (Lerner, 1989, 471). "Thus, failure to appreciate detail, impulsiveness, and impaired sensitivity to feedback may combine to make it hard for children to read a relationship, to take the appropriate initiative based on that reading, and to monitor the effectiveness of the action" (Levine, 1987, 261).

Social Disability

Students with learning disabilities may behave inappropriately because of social cognition problems. "Social cognition generally refers to a child's ability to understand social interaction processes" (Pullis, 1988, 86). "Children with learning disabilities often have social and emotional behavior problems. The child with social problems may be unable to behave appropriately with peers in social situations (teasing, withdrawing, interrupting conversations)" (Mercer & Mercer, 1989, 146). They may show aggressive behavior toward a victim, throw temper tantrums, and use inappropriate language as a result of frustration over lack of academic success (Mercer, 1987). There is increasing evidence that children with learning disabilities experience problems in social relationships whether interacting with parents, teachers, peers, or strangers (Bryan & Bryan, 1986).

Many students with learning disabilities are said to have a social disability. "Students with such deficits have been described in general as performing poorly in the kinds of independent activities expected of students of the same chronological age, inept in judging moods and attitudes of people, insensitive to the atmosphere of a social situation, displaying inappropriate behaviors, and making inappropriate remarks" (Lerner, 1989, 470).

Peer relationships are difficult for individuals with learning disabilities and the social life of LD youngsters is different from that of other students. They are more often ignored when attempting to initiate a social interaction. Their socially different behavior is even noted by strangers, who are able to reliably detect differences between learning disabled and non-learning disabled youngsters after viewing interactions for only a few minutes (Bryan & Bryan, 1986). Children and youth with conceptual and spatial disabilities (e.g., inadequate verbal expression skills, poor body image) have more problems acquiring positive peer relationships than youth with sequential disabilities (e.g., sequencing or auditory and visual memory problems); and the more severe the learning disability, the more difficulty with peer relationships (Weiner, 1979).

Several authorities believe that children with learning disabilities elicit negative reactions from others because they lack social comprehension skills (Weiss, 1984). "Learning disabled children tend to be either rejected or ignored by their peers" (Mercer, 1987, 449) "and evidence indicates that learning-disabled girls are even more at risk for social rejection and isolation than are learning-disabled boys" (Hallahan & Kauffman, 1988, 122). Some of the negativeness emitted toward youngsters with learning disabilities may be due to not making eye contact with other people during conversations (Bryan, Sherman, & Fisher, 1980). In the classroom setting, they behave differently in that they are more 'off-task', more distractible, initiate more interactions with the teacher, and engage in more nonproductive activity (Lerner, 1993).

In conversation, students with learning disabilities make more nasty and competitive statements and receive more rejections than non-learning disabled youngsters. When working with a partner, they tend to resist the initiatives of the partner for cooperative work. Youngsters with learning disabilities have been described as both deferential and hostile (Lerner, 1993).

Although many adolescents with learning disabilities are not social isolates, they tend to engage in fewer activities related to extracurricular events and go out with friends less frequently than non-learning disabled adolescents (Deshler & Schumaker, 1983).

> Even adolescents who have had opportunities for peer interactions and modeling as children may have failed to learn social skills. Many learning disabled youngsters have as much difficulty learning social skills as they have with reading, writing, and arithmetic. They reach adolescence with inadequate social tools to choose the right clothes to wear, the right things to say, the right things to do (Silverman et al., 1983, 168).

Adolescents with learning disabilities do not seem to develop a broad enough repertoire of social behaviors to react differently to different situations (Zigmond, 1978). They seem to lack social judgment, so are continuously getting themselves and their peers into trouble, both in school and in the community. Students with LD do not seem to understand the role they play in influencing the consequences that accrue to them. They need to be taught explicitly that their classroom behaviors have an impact on how the teacher responds to them and that, depending on the behaviors they display, the teacher's response will be positive or negative" (Silverman et al., 1983).

Some adolescents with learning disabilities use egocentric reasoning strategies and are less able than their peers to make moral decisions based on group norms and expectations (Derr, 1986). Even though students with LD are aware of social norms, they appear more willing than nondisabled peers to violate the social norms by committing antisocial acts (Bryan et al., 1982). Adolescents with learning disabilities do not appear to have the skills of social metacognition which would allow them to analyze and reflect consciously on personal social ability; analyze themselves, the social scene, and its requirements (Flavell, 1985).

Parents and teachers view students with learning disabilities more negatively than they do children without learning disabilities (Lerner, 1993). Teachers, parents, and peers rated mainstreamed students with LD as deficient in task related, interpersonal, and self-related social skills (e.g., accepting authority, helping others, expressing feelings, and having positive attitudes); and that children with LD were more poorly accepted by peers in play and work situations (Gresham & Reschly, 1986). Youngsters with LD are likely to be rejected by parents, teachers, and peers due to their numerous problems in social behavior, language, and temperament (Bryan, 1986).

Students with LD have been described as having emotional lability (frequent changes in mood) which can be viewed as a particular aspect of personality and social maladjustment. "The learning disabled child frequently exhibits behaviors characteristic of emotional disturbance. There are at least four sources of evidence for the notion that learning-disabled individuals exhibit signs of social maladjustment: ratings by peers, teachers, parents, and learning-disabled students themselves" (Hallahan & Kauffman, 1988, 121).

Sense of Personal Control

Metacognitive Deficits

Metacognition involves two processes: (1) cognitive self-awareness (knowledge about one's own cognitions), and (2) the regulation and control of the strategic aspects of cognition (one's ability to control his/her cognitions) (Mann & Sabatino, 1985).

Qualitative and quantitative differences exist between mildly disabled and average children and youth on a variety of information processing variables, including (1) efficiency of learning (capacity), (2) availability of prior knowledge (knowledge base), (3) strategies for processing information, and (4) metacognitive operations used by the learner to direct the learning process (Reschly, 1987; Reid, 1988). Students with learning disabilities often fail to develop efficient and effective strategies for learning (Reid, 1988). The memory deficits of youngsters with learning disabilities appear to be a production deficit or mediation deficit in which they do not automatically produce appropriate strategies for learning (Robinson & Deshler, 1988).

There appear to be a number of reasons why children with learning problems may not use strategies effectively: (1) lack a problem-solving plan or hypothesis (lack awareness of alternate methods, problem-solving and production difficulties); (2) weak metacognition (inactive learners, difficulty becoming active strategists in learning situations, rarely monitor their progress); (3) deficient inferential reasoning; (4) poor appreciation and/or application of rules; (5) tenuous formation of concepts (imprecise about concepts they form, difficulty with categories); (6) ineffective abstraction and/or symbolism (problems dealing with abstract concepts or systems of symbols) (Levine, 1987, 192–194).

"The impulsive behavior of learning-disabled students may be basically due to a lack of alternative cognitive strategies. These students respond impulsively because they do not have other ways readily at hand for coping with the learning task" (Mercer, 1987, 189). A characteristic of students with learning disabilities is that they lack functional cognitive strategies. They do not know how to control and direct their thinking to learn, how to gain more knowledge, or how to remember what they learn (Mercer, 1987, 190).

Metacognition can be divided into categories according to specific cognitive processes including metalistening, metacomprehension, and meta-attention (Hallahan et al., 1985). These specific categories of metacognitive skills continue to involve the student's specific knowledge of his/her abilities in that area and the strategies necessary for organizing, planning, and learning the specific skills involved in memory, listening, reading comprehension, etc. and controlling one's attention for better task focus. Children with learning disabilities frequently experience difficulty in all areas of metacognition.

Students with learning disabilities are deficient in metacomprehension strategies used in reading: (1) clarifying the purpose of reading, (2) focusing on the important content of passages, (3) monitoring one's understanding of the material, (4) rereading and scanning, and (5) using external sources (e.g., dictionary). It has also been found that while many poor readers lack effective cognitive strategies, others may be fully capable of exercising strategies but do not know when or how to best use them (Hallahan et al., 1985). These readers are metacognitively deficient. They do not understand that different strategies are needed to achieve different goals (Mann & Sabatino, 1985). Metacognition distinguishes good readers from poor readers. Poor readers acquire skills, but they seldom apply them independently in reading contexts. Poor readers lack the self-management skills that help them regulate the flow among knowledge sources and know when to use a strategy and how to adapt it to ever-changing situations (Reid, 1988).

Students with learning disabilities tend to produce poorly organized compositions and recalls because they have difficulty organizing their expository ideas, sustaining their expository writing, and summarizing information from single or multiple sources (Englert & Thomas, 1987). The performance gaps found in students' reading and writing perform-ance were also found in their metacognitive knowledge about text organizations. Students with learning disabilities demonstrate little or no awareness of the broader conceptual categories related to text structures that could be used to predict, generate, and monitor text ideas. When planning questions, students with LD focused exclusively on details rather than categories or groups of ideas.

Motivation Deficits

Recent research has established significant differences in motivation, attention, social skills, and locus of control between mildly disabled and average learners (Reschly, 1987). "Teachers and parents often note that learning-disabled students do not have the motivation needed for learn-ing academic tasks" (Lerner, 1989, 475).

Cognitive Prerequisite Deficits. Motivation can be viewed as goal-directed activity that involves different ways of thinking (Ames, 1984a). From a quantitative perspective, goal-directed activity is translated into time-on-task or academic engaged time (Ames, 1984a). From a qualita-tive perspective, goal-directed activity involves specific cognitive-media-tional processes such as information processing, metacognitive processes, and attributions (Ames, 1984b, 236). Thus, motivation is a complex, multifaceted entity.

The literature is replete with information regarding students with learning disabilities lack of task focus and attention difficulties. Young-sters with learning disabilities experience information processing difficulties including reduced speed or efficiency in elementary information processing operations and in problems integrating knowledge from previous learning. Students with LD experience difficulty using strategies in acquisition, memory, and problem-solving, and lack automaticity in metacognitive processes (Palinesar & Brown, 1987). Thus, LD youngsters may lack the cognitive prerequisites to maintain or increase academic engaged time (quantitative perspective of motivation) or to utilize cognitive-mediational processes (qualitative perspective of motivation) in sustaining motivation.

Inconsistent Motivation. Children and youth with learning disabilities frequently experience difficulties in consistently maintaining motivation and often experience a loss of motivation. "Like all humans, children with deficits of attention and intention have little difficulty performing under conditions of high motivation" (Levine, 1987, 32).

> The real issue is how effectively a child concentrates and produces under moderately motivating conditions. This is indeed what separates children with intention problems from those without such problems. The former are less able to be productive unless the content and/or potential rewards are intensely compelling (Levine, 1987, 32). Thus, inconsistent performance may relate to variations in levels of motivation (Douglas, 1983).

Lack Independence. "One characteristic of children with learning disabilities is that they do not develop a schema that promotes active, independent learning" (Beckman & Weller, 1990, 26). Due to lack of automaticity in metacognitive skills, children with learning disabilities are frequently unable to plan and organize for task completion whether a daily assignment or a term paper. They lack the ability to monitor their progress toward task completion and plan needed time allotments. They frequently are unable to monitor their own errors, and to evaluate the accuracy of task performance once the assignment is completed. This lack of metacognitive skills often results in a student who is dependent on others to plan and organize academic tasks and to depend on others to determine if the finished product is accurate. Many learning disabled individuals lack the motivation needed to complete tasks and reach goals independently, thus, they frequently must rely on others for motivation, direction, and approval (Beckman & Weller, 1990).

Visual Image Deficits. Students with learning disabilities frequently do not appear to be motivated by the rewards associated with appropriate academic behavior. "Verbal descriptions of motivational systems are often ineffective because exceptional learners are unable to maintain a mental image of them. To perform at their maximum potential, these students need concrete, visible examples of the contingency arrangement" (Raschke & Dedrick, 1989, 62).

Lack or Loss of Motivation. This lack of motivation may be the consequence of chronic academic failure. When students learn to doubt their intellectual abilities, they come to view their achievement efforts as futile" (Lerner, 1989). "Each LD student, by definition, has experienced significant and often prolonged academic failure" (Pullis, 1988, 78). Negative feelings about the self in the student role are often manifested in two areas—lack of motivation on tasks and classroom misbehavior (Pullis, 1988). Children who have developed negative feelings about their academic performance often will not be very task-oriented because their school experiences cause them to anticipate failure, feelings of incompetence, and embarrassment (Pullis, 1988).

Children who appear to lack motivation may engage in numerous avoidance behaviors to prevent failure and feelings of incompetence such as not starting tasks without several reminders, asking many questions about the quality of their work, or looking busy without actually finishing any academic tasks (Pullis, 1988). Some students' avoidance behaviors may involve withdrawal in terms of "excessive daydreaming, psychosomatic illnesses, truancy, or even fear of school," while other students may resort to acting out behaviors "such as excessive talking during work periods, out-of-seat behavior, aggression toward peers, and conflicts with the teacher concerning compliance with rules or assignments" to such a degree that the student is removed from the classroom (Pullis, 1988, 82).

Personal priorities can affect motivation. For some learning disabled children and youth, completing academic tasks in school rank low in their priorities. "Their perception that what they are being asked to memorize is irrelevant, remote from their current interests and future plans, makes it especially hard for them to consolidate such data in a meaningful manner" (Levine, 1987, 123). Some children may be motivated to strive for success in one subject area or situation and not in others, which may also be a coping strategy to avoid failure. "If a particular goal requires too much effort or too much delay of gratification, or if it greatly exceeds the capacity of a child's attention, it may be abandoned" (Levine, 1987, 424). Thus, it is not unusual for children who have experienced continual frustration in the classroom to merely "give up" trying to meet the demands of the school situation.

Attribution Deficits

Studies of motivation in students with learning disabilities often involve an analysis of the students' style of attribution or their ideas concerning the causes of their academic successes and failures (Lerner, 1989). Good students attribute their successes and failures to their own efforts or actions (reflecting an internal locus of control). They persevere on difficult tasks, are actively involved in the learning situation, and delay gratification (Lerner, 1993).

"There is considerable evidence that children's causal attributions (personal analyses of reasons) for failure are good predictors of their responses to difficulties in achievement situations" (Levine, 1987, 425). Learning-disabled "students often attribute their successes and failures to factors outside of their control (reflecting an external locus of control). They attribute success to luck or to the teacher, and they blame failures on their lack of ability or the difficulty of the task" (Lerner, 1989, 475). Children "who believe somehow that uncontrollable forces, such as their innate inability, caused them to fail are likely to respond in a helpless fashion. This is typically accompanied by a loss of motivation, a sense of diminished expectancy from goals" (Levine, 1987, 425). LD children and youth have been labeled "at risk for developing learned helplessness" (Hallahan & Kauffman, 1988, 125), a belief "that one simply does not have the ability to succeed and therefore any intensification of effort would be doomed to failure" (Levine, 1987, 425).

The locus of control orientation may effect the success of specific teaching strategies. Students with internal locus of control made greater progress using the low structure independent teaching strategy, while the students with external locus of control made greater reading progress using high structure and a direct-teaching strategy (Pascarella et al., 1983).

Children with learning disabilities have external orientations for achievement outcomes in school and significantly lower achievement expectations than non-learning disabled children (Chapman, 1988). Children with LD, therefore, have relatively little confidence in their ability and expect to achieve at lower levels, but when success does occur, they see it as being caused by a teacher's assistance or easy work (Chapman, 1988).

Self-Concepts of Students with Learning Disabilities

Recent research and literature focusing on the affective characteristics of students with learning disabilities specify the need to consider a number of affective characteristics rather than just a general self-concept. These affective characteristics include general and academic self-concepts, locus of control, performance expectations, and social characteristics.

General Self-Concept

Self-concept, the general way in which one sees oneself, has been investigated in numerous studies comparing learning disabled students to other disabled and nondisabled students. "In general, the investigation of self-concept differences between learning disabled and normally achieving children has yielded inconsistent results" (Gresham, 1988, 294). Numerous researchers have reported that learning disabled students have significantly lower or more negative self-concept scores than nondisabled or normally achieving peers and other researchers reported no significant differences.

The self-concept is currently viewed as complex and multifaceted. A number of factors are considered relevant to the development of the student's self-concept including athletic skill, personal physical attractiveness, social attractiveness, special aptitudes, intelligence, academic performance, peer acceptance, moral code, and leadership qualities. Thus, individuals may simultaneously have positive and negative perceptions regarding various aspects of their personality and their abilities to function in their world. More consistent research results may be achieved by analyzing the separate factors of self-concept rather than trying to determine a generalized self-concept.

Self-Concept of Academic Achievement

Success and failure in school is influenced not only by cognitive abilities, but also by various affective and motivational variables (Dweck, 1986). Several researchers have revealed that the correlations between intelligence test performance and scholastic achievement account for only 25 to 50 percent of the variance associated with predicting achievement from intelligence quotients alone (Zigler, 1968). Thus, the effect of noncognitive variables on academic achievement accounts for 50 to 75 percent of the variance. At the kindergarten level a self-concept evaluation is a more accurate predictor of second grade reading achievement than a mental age evaluation (Wattenberg & Clifford, 1964).

Academic Self-Concept

The cognitive-motivational characteristics of children with learning disabilities include academic self-concept, locus of control, and achievement expectations appear to be significantly related to success and failure in school (Chapman, 1988). The academic self-concept is formed before the end of the third grade and it quickly stabilizes as patterns of school success and failure are established (Battle, 1981). Children with learning disabilities acquire a negative academic self-concept by age 8 or 9 years (around Grade 3) and it remains relatively stable through at least Grade 10 (Chapman, 1987).

Children with learning disabilities tend to report significantly lower academic self-concepts than do non-learning disabled or normally achieving peers (Bryan & Bryan, 1986). Academic self-concept appears to be consistently stronger in predicting grades and academic achievement than academic locus of control and achievement expectations for both learning disabled and nondisabled students (Chapman, 1988).

Locus of Control

The nondisabled child is external for both success and failure at the age of 4 to 5 years, becomes internal for success by age 6 to 7 years, and finally becomes internal for both success and failure by the age of 10 to 11 years (Lawrence & Winschel, 1975). Children with learning disabilities do not follow this typical pattern and are more external in their orientation than same-aged nondisabled peers (Rogers, 1983). When internality does develop for learning disabled children, it is internality for failure (a result of their behavior) and not for success (chance or action of others) (Chapman & Boersma, 1979). Learning disabled children take significantly less responsibility for their academic successes and failures than normal achievers (Rogers & Saklofske, 1985).

Achievement Expectations

Children with learning disabilities have been portrayed as lacking confidence in their ability to positively influence learning outcomes (Bryan, 1986) as having more negative perceptions of their ability (Chapman, 1988), and as having relatively low expectations for future successful achievement outcomes (Chapman, 1988). It seems likely that negative self-concepts, external locus of control beliefs, and low academic performance expectations would have a negative effect on persistence and effort in learning situations, leading to failure experiences (Rogers & Saklofske, 1985). The relationship between academic failure experiences and negative affective characteristics is likely one of reciprocal interaction (Rogers & Saklofske, 1985).

Social Deficits

"Deficits in academic self-concept usually co-exist with poor peer acceptance/rejection, deficits in positive social behaviors, and excessive negative social interaction patterns" (Gresham, 1988, 295). Collectively, this suggests that students with learning disabilities are paying a high social-psychological price for their poor academic achievement (Hiebert et al., 1982).

Gresham & Reschly (1986) studied perceptions of teachers, parents, and peers for learning disabled and non-learning disabled youngsters using rating scales. The results indicated that teachers, parents, and peers rated mainstreamed students with learning disabilities as deficient in task-related, interpersonal, and self-related social skill domains. "LD children's social interaction problems may exacerbate their academic problems. If they are not able to interact effectively with their classmates or teachers, their school experiences (which may already be marked by severe academic failure can become even more negative)" (Pullis, 1988, 86).

Anxiety

One of the few characteristics that all students with learning disabilities have in common is failure in school. The failure to learn leads to adverse emotional responses including feelings of self-derision, poor ego perception, and anxiety which augment the failure to learn syndrome (Lerner, 1996). "Within the social learning theory, anxiety is often viewed as a series of responses indicative of low-expectancy of success in a valued-need area" (Margalit & Zak, 1984, 537). High anxiety levels are considered to be related to low self-concept scores (McCandles, 1967), and to reduced efficiency of the cognitive processes (Tobias, 1979).

Children with learning disabilities demonstrate higher levels of anxiety as compared to nondisabled peers related to their feelings that events beyond their control happen to them (Margalit & Zak, 1984). The children with learning disabilities expressed lower levels of self-concept related to their feelings of self-dissatisfaction, and they tended to attribute negative self-reference items to themselves. Students with LD experienced significantly more negative self-concepts in comparison to other disabled and nondisabled children, high anxiety levels due to their perceived intelligence deficits and reduced school status, and negative physical characteristics and attributes (Jones, 1985).

Various studies of children with learning disabilities have suggested that a loss of self-esteem, high levels of performance anxiety, and even clinical depression are further complications of learning disabilities (Levine, 1987). Childhood depression is a common psychiatric complication of developmental dysfunction as between 10 percent and 20 percent of children with learning disabilities have been found to have significant depression (Stevenson & Romney, 1984).

SUMMARY

The major characteristics of elementary and secondary learning disabled students can be categorized into three areas: (1) academic deficits, (2) cognitive deficits (attention, perceptual, motor, memory, problem-solving, metacognition), (3) social and emotional problems (hyperactivity, self-concept, learned helplessness, social imperception, distractibility, motivation). It is difficult to identify preschool children as learning disabled because they have not as yet failed academically. However, preschool-aged children who are at high risk for developing learning disabilities frequently demonstrate inadequate motor development, language delays, speech disorders, and poor cognitive and concept development. During kindergarten and first grade potential learning disabled students frequently experience difficulty in academic readiness skills, language, perceptual skills, motor, attention, and social skills.

The social-emotional problems of students with learning disabilities may be their most serious weakness. The social behaviors of many students with learning disabilities are less acceptable than their nondisabled peers as they evidence (1) less ability to predict the consequences for their behaviors, (2) greater misinterpretation of social cues, (3) more difficulty adapting their behaviors to the characteristics of their listeners, and (4) more frequent performance of inappropriate social behaviors. Explanations for the social skills problems of students with learning disabilities have been postulated including the following: (1) cognitive and social cognition deficits, (2) communication deficits, (3) social imperceptiveness, (4) lack of empathy and role-taking ability. Adolescents with learning disabilities do not seem to develop a broad enough repertoire of social behaviors to react differently to different situations.

Youngsters with learning disabilities demonstrate a reduced sense of personal control in all aspects of their lives as compared to nondisabled peers. Their metacognitive deficits render them less aware of their own cognitive abilities, and unable to regulate and control strategic aspects of their cognition. They often fail to develop efficient and effective strategies for learning. They do not know how to control and direct their thinking to learn, to gain more knowledge, or how to remember what they learn. Youngsters with learning disabilities frequently experience difficulties in consistently maintaining motivation and often experience loss of motivation.

Children with learning disabilities who have developed negative feelings about their academic performance often will not be very task-oriented because their school experiences cause them to anticipate failure, and experience feelings of incompetence and embarrassment. Youngsters with LD often attribute their successes and failures to factors outside of their control (reflecting an external locus of control), thus, they do not believe in their own abilities and do not understand the role of their effort in the success or failure. In summary, children with learning disabilities report significantly lower academic self-concepts, less responsibility for their academic successes and failures, lower expectations for future successful achievement outcomes, more peer rejection and deficits in social interaction skills, and higher anxiety than normally achieving peers.

UNIT 4
COMPARATIVE ASPECTS

Chapter 11

CATEGORICAL COMPARISONS

Clearly, there are differences between the mildly handicapped groups in certain variables (IQ and behavior are two examples)... (Bender, 1995, 339).

Cognitive Learning Characteristics
    Intelligence/Learning Rates
    Information Processing
    Language Processing
Social/Emotional Learning Characteristics
Academic Learning Characteristics
    Preschool Age/Grade Level
    Elementary Age/Grade Level
    Secondary Age/Grade Level

A number of authors have indicated that students with mild disabilities are not that much different from their regular classroom peers (Lilly, 1979). Henley et al. (1993) indicated that students with mild disabilities are often unrecognizable before entering school and after exiting school; and regardless of the category in which students are receiving services, they have similar learning needs and may be indistinguishable.

This chapter will consider the validity of the previous statements regarding students with mild disabilities functioning at similar levels, often indistinguishable from nondisabled peers.

COGNITIVE LEARNING CHARACTERISTICS

Intelligence/Learning Rates

"Individuals with mild learning and behavior disorders exhibit academic and/or social-interpersonal performance deficits that range from one to two standard deviations below average on normative and criterion-referenced assessments" (Hardman et al., 1990, 217). Thus, the IQ or intelligence level of students categorized as mildly behavior disordered

(BD) generally falls within the low average range (IQ 70–85+). Though the definition of learning disabilities (LD) requires average range intellectual functioning (IQ 85–115), many students currently labeled LD function within the low–average cognitive range (IQ 70–85). Students with mild mental retardation (MMR) function within the IQ 50–70/75 cognitive range or between two and three standard deviations below the mean IQ 100 on norm referenced intelligence tests.

The general learning rates of students with LD and BD can be expected to range from ¾th average rate to average learning rates. Students with MMR cognitively function within the mild range of mental retardation, but they do not function within the mild range of human intelligence. The learning rates of students with mild mental retardation are ½ to ¾th the average learning rate.

Information Processing

Research studies indicate that students with mild mental retardation are deficient in most aspects of information processing. MMRs experience deficits in attention span, focus, and selective attention due to developmental delays. Students with behavior disorders and learning disabilities experience significant attention deficits in the areas of sustained attention, selective attention, selective intention, and perhaps ADHD which interferes with academic productivity. The definition of learning disabilities indicates a disorder in information processing skills which include attention deficits.

Students with mild behavior disorders generally experience intact perceptual and perceptual-motor integration skills. Students with mild mental retardation experience perceptual and perceptual-motor processing deficits due primarily to developmental delay, so function similarly to a younger child. "True" learning disabled students, by definition, experience perceptual and/or perceptual-motor integration deficits. Students with LD often experience significant difficulties with tasks requiring auditory memory with a written response or visual memory with a written response.

Students with mild disabilities (MMR, BD, and LD) experience deficits in memory skills (see Characteristics Table). The major source of the memory problem for mildly retarded students is a small short-term memory capacity which limits the amount of information placed in long-term memory. BDs may experience memory problems due to attention deficits. Students with learning disabilities experience significant memory problems due to perceptual and language processing problems.

Students with mild disabilities lack automaticity among prerequisite skills which significantly interferes with learning, and either cannot generalize (MMRs) or do not spontaneously generalize (BD and LD). Students with learning disabilities and/or behavior disorders can be taught to use metacognition and learning strategies to facilitate learning and behavior control and to generalize to new situations, whereas MMRs cannot.

Language Processing

Students with mild disabilities function on the literal level experiencing difficulties with both receptive and expressive language: MMRs due to developmental delay, BDs because of failure to acquire skills, and LDs because of language processing problems. MMRs have difficulties with all aspects of language including restricted vocabulary development, incorrect grammatical structure and usage, pragmatics or social communication, and language-based academics. BD students experience significant difficulties with pragmatics, as aggressive students often utilize vulgar language as a weapon against peers and adults. Students with LD often experience deficits with the rules of language (phonology, morphology, syntax); semantics or the content of language (complex or abstract language such as figurative language, implied information, words with multiple meanings, and verbal analogies); and pragmatics (the social use of language).

SOCIAL/EMOTIONAL LEARNING CHARACTERISTICS

Students with mild disabilities all experience social learning problems: MMRs due to developmental delays; BDs due to aggression or withdrawal, and lack of social evaluative ability; and LDs due to language and nonverbal processing problems. They experience negative self-concepts, external locus of control, high anxiety levels regarding their inabilities. Social and emotional problems of students with mild disabilities include the following: lack of social sensitivity, lack of perspective-taking, difficulty with social problem solving, and poor interpersonal relationships. The major differences have to do with degree of the problem. MMRs function as younger children; BDs are hostile and aggressive or withdrawn and painfully shy; and LDs reveal high frustration. Again, students with LD and BD can be taught to use their metacognitive skills automatically to improve social behaviors and to generalize to other situations. MMRs cannot be taught to generalize, but can be taught social skills in each context relevant to the student. Differences among the marginal or borderline students with IQs 70–80 may be few, the major differences are among average to above-average functioning students who can be taught generalization of social skills, self-control, and motivation.

ACADEMIC LEARNING CHARACTERISTICS

The academic functioning of children and youth with mild disabilities depends significantly on many factors including the student's cognitive ability, socioeconomic background and experiences, health problems, and the success of previous developmental and remediation interventions. By virtue of definition, children and youth with mild disabilities experience learning problems that result in deficit academic functioning.

Preschool Age/Grade Level

At the preschool level, children with MMR (IQ 75), BD and LD (IQ 70–85) will also show developmental delays and function similarly. However, the functioning level of the preschool child with MMR (IQ 50) functioning like a 1½ to 2½-year-old will be significantly lower in all areas than that of MMRs (IQ 70–75), and minimally functioning BDs and LDs (IQ 75–85); and much significantly lower than BDs and LDs with IQs 85–115. The child with behavior disorders will display severe aggression or withdrawal as compared to other children with and without disabilities. The problems of the child with LD may center around naming deficits, and perceptual-motor integration deficits. However, unlike the child with MMR, children with LD may have age and ability appropriate behaviors in some developmental areas and experience deficits in others.

Elementary Age/Grade Level

By the end of elementary school, students labeled MMR, BD, and LD are functioning significantly below grade level, lacking automaticity with prerequisite academic skills. The child with MMR (IQ 75) may function about the 3rd grade level in math calculation, but not math reasoning; in reading vocabulary words, but not in reading comprehension. The child with MMR (IQ 50) may be just beginning formal academics. The average intelligence student with LD may experience wide intra-individual differences with 3rd grade functioning in some areas and 6th grade level functioning in other areas. Low cognitive level LD students (IQ 75–85) may function on the 3rd grade level by the end of elementary years and may seem to function similarly academically to the child with MMR (IQ 70–75). Students with BD (IQ 75–85) may function on the 3rd to 4th grade level by the end of elementary school years. All students with mild disabilities (MMR, BD, LD) may be overage compared to peers due to grade retention which is very commonly used as a remediation strategy.

Secondary Age/Grade Level

During senior high school years, 15-to-18 year-old students with MMR (IQ 75) may function similar to 11-to-13 year-old nondisabled students in some areas such as math calculation and some basic reading skills, however, they seldom function higher than 3rd grade level in math reasoning and reading comprehension. Much of their secondary years will be spent on prevocational and transition skills rather than basic academics. Secondary level students with MMR (IQ 50) may function at the beginning 2nd grade literal level in some academics (e.g., math calculation, but not math reasoning). Their curriculum will focus on prevocational, life skills, and transition skills.

Secondary level students with BD often drop out of school. Students with BD of average intellectual functioning perform about the 5th to 6th grade levels in reading and mathematics by the 10th to 11th grade levels, about five to six years behind expectancy. Their inappropriate behavior (aggressive or withdrawn) continues to interfere with academic progress. Lack of academic prerequisites for the secondary academic curriculum often results in failure.

Students with learning disabilities (IQ 80–90) at the secondary level function about 4th to 5th grade level in reading and 6th grade level in mathematics. The pervasive reading problem interferes with academic functioning in all content subject areas. They experience severe language deficits in oral and written expression, thus, report writing is an almost impossible task.

SUMMARY

It must be noted that students of similar cognitive ability levels may function on similar academic and social levels. Low level cognitive ability LDs and BDs (IQs 70–85) may function cognitively similar to high functioning MMRs (IQ 70–75); at this level the primary differences may be in adaptive behavior. LDs and BDs with average to above-average cognitive ability will show much more intraindividual differences than students with mild retardation.

Though MMRs (IQ 70/75), BDs and LDs (IQs 75–85) have many seemingly similar characteristics, the reasons for that level of functioning is different, so teaching strategies and expectations for learning may need to be different. Low level MMRs (IQ 50) function much lower than BDs and LDs in all areas. Higher ability LDs and BDs may function significantly differently with greater degrees of intraindividual differences.

CHARACTERISTICS OF STUDENTS
WITH MILD DISABILITIES

Mild Retardation	Learning Disabilities	Behavior Disorders
Cognitive and Psychomotor Functioning		
•IQs 50–70/75	•IQs 75–115	•IQs 75–90
•*Attention Problems:*	•*Attention Problems:*	•*Attention Problems:*
Short attention span.	Coming to attention, sustaining attention, intermittent attention.	Short attention span.
•*Perception Problems:*	•*Perception Problems:*	•*Perception Problems:*
Developmentally delayed in all areas.	Auditory memory with written response and Visual memory with written response most severe problems.	No specific problems.
•*Memory Problems:*	•*Memory Problems:*	•*Memory Problems:*
Experience small capacity STM. Reduced amount of information in	Perception & integration may interfere with memory. Fails to integrate information in LTM with new information	No basic deficits. Poor behavior and attention problems may interfere with

Mild Retardation	*Learning Disabilities*	*Behavior Disorders*
LTM. No incidental learning.	**Retrieval problems due to language processing deficits.**	**STM and LTM.**
•*Learning Strategies:* Cannot generate and use learning strategies automatically and cannot be taught.	•*Learning Strategies:* Does not automatically use learning strategies but can be taught these skills.	•*Learning Strategies:* Does not automatically use learning strategies but can be taught these skills.
•*Lacks Metacognitive* skills due to reduced cognitive abilities and cannot be taught.	•*Lacks Metacognitive* skills: organization, error-monitoring, project planning, academics.	•*Lacks Metacognition* for self-management of behavior control and academics.
•*Generalization:* Cannot generalize to new settings, must be taught skill in each separate setting.	•*Generalization:* Do not automatically generalize, but can be taught these skills.	•*Generalization:* Do not automatically generalize, but can be taught these skills.
•*Language Deficits:* Developmentally delayed. Function on literal, concrete level. Pragmatics problems. Problems with complex and abstract language. Difficulty interpreting nonlinguistic aspects of communication.	•*Language Deficits:* Word finding problems. Fails to label concepts. 3–4 years delayed in language skills. Lack skills in understanding tenses, negatives, humor, sarcasm, pronouns, etc. Functions on literal level. Difficulty interpreting nonlinguistic aspects of communication. Deficits in rules of language. Deficits in pragmatics.	•*Language Deficits:* Depends on degree of behavior interference. Deficits in pragmatics, often use socially inappropriate language (cursing). Deficits in interpreting nonlinguistic aspects of communication.
•*Speech:* Frequent articulation problems. Developmentally delayed.	•*Speech:* Few Articulation problems.	•*Speech:* No specific concerns.
•*Gross Motor Skills:* Developmentally delayed, one of higher skills.	•*Gross Motor Skills:* Clumsy, poor eye-foot coordination, balance problems.	•*Gross Motor Skills:* No specific concerns.
•*Fine Motor Skills:*	•*Fine Motor Skills:*	•*Fine Motor Skills:*

Mild Retardation	Learning Disabilities	Behavior Disorders
Developmentally delayed, commensurate with IQ.	Poor eye-hand coordination. Problems in handwriting, all written work.	No specific concerns.
•*Coordination of Motor Skills:* Developmentally delayed.	•*Coordination of Motor Skills:* Poor eye and foot coordination skills.	•*Coordination of Motor Skills:* Depends on behavior.

Social Functioning

Mild Retardation	Learning Disabilities	Behavior Disorders
•*Affective Deficits:* Negative Self-Concept. High anxiety. External locus of control. Negative academic self-concept. Expectations of failure. Low self-motivation. Lack of self-responsibility. Lack of self-confidence.	•*Affective Deficits:* Negative Self-Concept. High anxiety. External locus of control. Negative academic self-concept. Expectations of failure. Low self-motivation. Lack of self-responsibility. Lack of self-confidence.	•*Affective Deficits:* Negative self-concept. High anxiety. External locus of control. Negative academic self-concept. Expectations of failure. Low self-motivation. Lack of self-responsibility. Lack of self-confidence.
•*Social/Behavioral Concerns:* Developmentally delayed. Egocentric. Deficits in social sensitivity and insight. Socially imperceptive. Lack empathy and role-taking. Deficits with social problem-solving. *Poor interpersonal relationships.* Lack insight into reciprocal nature of interactions. Poor comprehension of social situations. Cannot predict	•*Social/Behavioral Concerns:* Immature. Egocentric. Deficits in social sensitivity and insight. Socially imperceptive. Lack empathy and role-taking. Deficits with social problem-solving. *Poor interpersonal relationships.* Lack insight into reciprocal nature of interactions. Poor comprehension of social situations. Cannot predict	•*Social/Behavioral Concerns:* Severely Aggressive or withdrawn. Egocentric. Deficits in social sensitivity and insight. Socially imperceptive. Lack empathy and role-taking. Deficits with social problem-solving. *Poor interpersonal relationships.* Lack insight into reciprocal nature of interactions. Poor comprehension of social situations. Cannot predict

Mild Retardation	*Learning Disabilities*	*Behavior Disorders*
consequences of behavior. Lack social evaluation ability to modify behaviors.	consequences of behavior. Lack social evaluation ability to modify behaviors.	consequences of behavior. Lack social evaluation ability to modify behaviors.

Academic Functioning

Mild Retardation	*Learning Disabilities*	*Behavior Disorders*
•Preschool Level: Developmental delays in all areas. Immature socially.	*•Preschool Level:* Developmental delay in perception, motor skills, language, immature socially.	*•Preschool Level:* Developmental delay social/emotional skills. Severely aggressive or severe withdrawal. Severe tantrums. Noncompliance.
•Elementary Level: Primary: IQ 50—functions at preschool levels. IQ 75—functions at 1st grade level. *Intermediate:* Primary academic skills. 9–12 yr. old (IQ 50)— pre-K level 9 yr. old (IQ 75)— 1st grade. 12 yr. old (IQ 75)— 3rd grade level. *High School:* IQ 75— Reading: 3rd grade. Math calculation: 4th–5th grade	*•Elementary Level: Primary:* Problems with math prerequisites: 1:1, direction concepts. Problems with reading prerequisites: alphabet, letter discrimination. *Intermediate:* Math problems: place value, regrouping, fractions. Reading problems: sight words, word attack, comprehension. 6th grade: reading 3rd grade level. *High School:* Ave. IQ— Reading: 4th grade. Math: 6th grade Often dropout.	*•Elementary Level:* Not a participant in education. Lacks many prerequisite skills. Refuses to complete assignments. *Intermediate:* Self-Contained Classroom: Begins to make academic progress and behavior control. *High School:* Ave. IQ— Reading: 5–6th grade level Math: 5–6th grade level. Often dropout.

BIBLIOGRAPHY

Abel, E. & Sokol, R.: A revised conservative estimate of the incidence of FAS and its economic impact. *Alcoholism: Clinical and Experimental Research,* 15 (3): 514–524, May/June 1991.

Agency for Toxic Substances and Disease Registry: *The Nature and Extent of Lead Poisoning in Children in the United States: A Report to Congress.* Washington, DC: U.S. Department of Health and Human Services, 1988.

American Psychiatric Association: *The Diagnostic and Statistical Manual of Mental Disorders, Fourth Ed.* (DSM–IV). Washington, D.C.: Author, 1994.

Ames, L., Ilg, F. & Haber, C.: *Your One-Year-Old.* New York: Dell, 1985.

Ames, L. & Ilg, F.: *Your Two-Year-Old.* New York: Dell, 1976.

Ames, L. & Ilg, F.: *Your Three-Year-Old.* New York: Dell, 1976.

Ames, L. & Ilg, F.: *Your Four-Year-Old.* New York: Dell, 1976.

Ames, L. & Ilg, F.: *Your Five-Year-Old.* New York: Dell, 1976.

Andrews, R.: The self-concepts of good and poor readers. *Slow Learning Child: The Australian Journal of Education of Backward Children,* 18: 160–167, 1971.

Anokhin, P.: Ivan Pavlov and Psychology. In B. Whoman (Ed.), *Historical Roots of Contemporary Psychology.* New York: Harper & Row, 1968.

Ariel, A.: *Education of Children and Adolescents with Learning Disabilities.* New York: Merrill, 1992.

Arnold, J. & Dodge, H.: Room for all. *The American School Board Journal,* 181 (10): 22–26, 1994.

Asher, S. & Renshaw, P.: Children Without Friendships: Social Knowledge and Social Skill Training. In S.R. Asher & J. Gottman (Eds.), *Development of Children's Friendships.* New York: Cambridge University Press, 1981.

Ayres, A.: *Southern California Sensory Integration Tests.* Los Angeles: Western Psychological Services, 1969.

Bagnato, S. & Neisworth, J.: Normal and Exceptional Early Development. In J. Neisworth & S. Bagnato (Eds.) *The Young Exceptional Child Early Development and Education.* New York: Macmillan, 1987.

Bandura, A.: Self-efficacy: Toward a unifying theory of behavioral change. *Psychological Review,* 84: 191–195, 1977.

Barresi, J.G.: Educating handicapped migrants: Issues and options. *Exceptional Children,* 48: 473–488, 1982.

Bateman, B.D.: Learning disabilities: Yesterday, today, and tomorrow. *Exceptional Children,* 31: 167, 1964.

Battle, J.: *Enhancing Self-Esteem and Achievement.* Seattle: Special Child Publications, 1982.

Batshaw, M. & Perret, Y.: *Children With Handicaps: A Medical Primer* (2nd ed.). Baltimore: Paul H. Brookes, 1986.

Baumeister, A. (Ed.): *Mental Retardation: Appraisal, Education, and Rehabilitation.* Chicago: Aldine, 1967.

Beckman, P. & Weller, C.: Active independent learning for children with learning disabilities. *Teaching Exceptional Children,* 22 (2): 26–27, Winter 1990.

Bedell, F.: Testamony delivered at hearings conducted by the National Council on the Handicapped, June 7 and 8, Washington, D.C., 1989.

Beery, K. & Buktenica, N.: *Developmental Test of Visual-Motor Integration.* Novato, CA: Academic Therapy Publications, 1989.

Beirne-Smith, M., Patton, J. & Ittenback, R.: *Mental Retardation,* (4th Ed.). New York: Merrill, 1994.

Bender, W.: *Learning Disabilities Characteristics, Identification, and Teaching Strategies.* Boston: Allyn & Bacon, 1995.

Bieler, R. & Snowman, J.: *Psychology Applied to Teaching* (5th ed.). Boston: Houghton Mifflin, 1986.

Bijou, S.: *Child Development: The Basic Stage of Early Childhood.* Englewood Cliffs, NJ: Prentice-Hall, 1976.

Bijou, S. & Ribes-Inesta, E. (Eds.): *Behavior Modification: Issues and Extensions.* New York: Academic Press, 1972.

Bijou, S. & Ruiz, R. (Eds.): *Behavior Modification: Contributions to Education.* Hillsdale, NJ: Earlbaum, 1981.

Blackman, L., Burger, A., Tan, N. & Weiner, S.: Strategy training and the acquisition of decoding skills in EMR children. *Education and Training of the Mentally Retarded,* 17, 83–87, 1982.

Bley, N. & Thornton, C.: *Teaching Mathematics to the Learning Disabled.* Austin, TX: Pro-ed, 1989.

Bloom, R., Shea, R. & Eun, B.: The Piers-Harris Self-Concept Scale: Norms for behaviorally disordered children. *Psychology in the Schools,* 16(4): 483–486, 1979.

Boca, L. & Cervantes, H.: *The Bilingual Special Education Interface.* Columbus, OH: Merrill, 1989.

Borkowski, J. & Varnhagan, C.: Transfer of Learning Strategies: Contrast of Self-Instructional and Traditional Formats With EMR Children. *American Journal of Mental Deficiency,* 83: 369–379, 1984.

Borys, S.: Factors influencing the interrogative strategies of mentally retarded and nonretarded students. *American Journal of Mental Deficiency,* 84: 280–288, 1979.

Bowerman, M.: Semantic factors in the acquisition of rules for word use and sentence construction. In D. Morehead & A. Morehead (Eds.), *Directions in Normal and Deficient Child Language.* Baltimore: University Park Press, 1976.

Bray, N.: Strategy production in the retarded. In N.R. Ellis (Ed.), *Handbook of Mental Deficiency: Psychological Theory and Research* (2nd ed.). Hillside, NJ: Erlbaum, 1979.

Brigance, A.: *BRIGANCE Diagnostic Inventory of Early Development.* Allen, TX: Teaching Resources/Developmental Learning Materials, 1983.

Brody, J.: Lead is everywhere—and so is its threat to children's brains. *The New York Times* reprinted in *The Stars and Stripes* (p. 20), Feb. 23, 1993.

Brolin, D.: *Life-Centered Career Education: A Competency-Based Approach* (Rev. ed.). Reston, VA: The Council for Exceptional Children, 1986.

Brown, A.: The Role of Strategic Behavior in Retardate Memory. In N.R. Ellis (Ed.), *International Review of Research in Mental Retardation,* Vol. 7. New York: Academic Press, 1974.

Brown, L. & Hammill, D.: *Behavior Rating Profile.* Austin, TX: pro-ed, 1983.

Bruno, R., Johnson, J. & Simon, S.: Perception of humor by regular class students and students with learning disabilities or mild mental retardation. *Journal of Learning Disabilities,* 20: 568–570, 1981.

Bryan, T.: Learning disabled children's comprehension of nonverbal communication, *Journal of Learning Disabilities,* 10: 501–506, 1977.

Bryan, T. & Bryan, J.: *Understanding Learning Disabilities (3rd ed.).* Palo Alto, CA: Mayfield, 1986.

Bryan, T. & Pflam, S.: Social interactions of learning disabled children: A linguistic, social, and cognitive analysis, *Learning Disabilities Quarterly,* 1: 70–79, 1978.

Bryan, T., Sherman, R. & Fisher, A.: Learning disabled boys' nonverbal behaviors with a dyadic interview, *Learning Disability Quarterly,* 3: 65–72, 1980.

Bryan, T., Werner, M. & Pearl, R.: Learning disabled students' conformity responses to prosocial and antisocial situations, *Learning Disability Quarterly,* 5: 344–352, 1982.

Burgess, D. & Streissguth, A.: Fetal alcohol syndrome and fetal alcohol effects: Principles for educators. *Phi Delta Kappan,* 74(1): 24–30, Sept. 1992.

Burns, S. (Ed.): *Homelessness demographics, causes and trends: Homewords,* 3 (4): 1–3, 1991.

Bush, W. & Giles, M.: *Aids to Psycholinguistic Teaching.* Columbus, OH: Merrill, 1977.

Campbell, K.: *The New Science: Self-Esteem Psychology.* Lanham, MD: University Press of America, 1984.

Campione, J. & Brown, A.: Memory and Metamemory Development in Educable Retarded Children. In R.V. Kail, Jr. & J.W. Hagen (Eds.), *Perspectives on the Development of Memory and Cognition.* Hillsdale, NJ: Erlbaum, 1977.

Cantrell, M. & Cantrell, R.: Assessment of the natural environment. *Education and Treatment of Children,* 8: 275–295, 1985.

Cartwright, G., Cartwright, C. & Ward, M.: *Educating Special Learners* (3rd ed.). Belmont, CA: Wadsworth, 1989.

Center for the Study of Social Policy: *Kids Count Data Book.* Washington, D.C.: Author, 1993.

Chapman, J.: Cognitive-motivational characteristics and academic achievement of learning disabled children: A longitudinal study. *Journal of Educational Psychology,* 80 (3): 357–365, 1988.

Chapman, J. & Boersma, F.: *Projected Academic Self-Concept Scale.* Unpublished instrument, University of Alberta, Edmonton, Alberta, Canada, 1978.

Charles, C.: *Building Classroom Discipline From Models to Practice (3rd ed.).* New York: Longman, 1989.

Cheek, H. Jr., Flippo, R. & Lindsey, J.: *Reading for Success in Elementary Schools.* Fort Worth, TX: Holt, Rinehart & Winston, 1989.

Cline, R.: A description of self-esteem measures among educable mentally retarded children and their nonretarded peers. *Dissertation Abstracts International,* 36: 2133A, 1975.

Cohen, S. & Warren, R.: Preliminary survey of family abuse of children served by United Cerebral Palsy Centers. *Developmental Medicine and Child Neurology,* 29: 12–18, 1987.

Combs, A. & Snygg, D.: *Individual Behavior* (2nd ed). New York: Harper & Row, 1959.

Combs, A., Avila, A. & Purkey, W.: *Helping Relationships: Basic Concepts for the Helping Professions* (2nd ed.). Boston: Allyn & Bacon, 1978.

Conger, J.: *Adolescence and Youth: Psychological Development in a Changing World* (4th ed). New York: HarperCollins, 1991.

Cook, J. "Quiet Area". In C. Jones *Enhancing Self-Concepts and Academic Achievement of Mildly Handicapped Students.* Springfield, IL: Thomas, 1992.

Coopersmith, S.: *The Antecedents of Self-Esteem.* San Francisco: W.H. Freeman, 1967.

Craft, M. (Ed.): *Tredgold's Mental Retardation* (12th ed.). London: Bailliere Tindall, 1979.

Cromwell, R.L.: Personality evaluation. In A. Baumeister (Ed.) *Mental Retardation Appraisal, Education, and Rehabilitation.* Chicago: Aldine, 1967.

Cruickshank, W.: *The Brain-Injured Child in Home, School, and Community.* Syracuse, NY: Syracuse University Press, 1967.

Cullinan, D. & Epstein, M.: Behavior Disorders. In N. Haring & L. McCormick (Eds.) *Exceptional Children and Youth: An Introduction to Special Education (5th ed.),* Columbus, OH: Merrill, 1990.

Derr, A.: How learning disabled adolescent boys make moral judgments, *Journal of Learning Disabilities,* 19: 160–164, 1986.

Deshler, D. & Schumaker, J.: Social skills of learning disabled adolescents: A review of characteristics and intervention, *Topics in Learning and Learning Disabilities,* 3: 15–23, 1983.

Deshler, D., Schumaker, J., Alley, G., Warner, M. & Clark, F.: An epidemological study of learning disabled adolescents in secondary schools: Academic self-image and attributions. (Research Report No. 14), Lawrence: University of Kansas, Institute for Research in Learning Disabilities, 1980.

Dodge, K. & Frame, C.: Social cognitive biases and deficits in aggressive boys, *Child Development,* 53: 620–635, 1982.

Douglas, V.: Attentional and cognitive problems. In M. Rutter (Ed.), *Developmental Neuropsychiatry.* New York: Guilford Press, 1983.

Drew, C., Logan, D., Hardman, M.: *Mental Retardation: A Life Cycle Approach* (5th ed.). Columbus, OH: Merrill, 1995.

Dudek, S., Strobel, M. & Thomas, A.: Chronic learning problems and maturation. *Perceptual and Motor Skills,* 64: 407–429, 1987.

Dunn, L. & Dunn, L.: *Peabody Picture Vocabulary Test-Revised.* Circle Pines, MN: American Guidance Service, 1981.

Dweck, C.: Motivational processes affecting learning. *American Psychologist,* 41: 1040–1048, 1986.

Edwards, J. & Edwards, D.: Rate of Behavior Development: Direct and Continuous Measurement. *Perceptual & Motor Skills,* 31: 633–634, 1970.

Ellis, N.: Memory processes in retardates and normals. *International Review of Research in Mental Retardation,* 4, 1970.

Englert, C. & Thomas, C.: Sensitivity to text structure in reading and writing: A comparison of learning disabled and nondisabled students, *Learning Disabilities Quarterly,* 10: 93–105, 1987.

Environmental Protection Agency: Secondhand smoke report leads to widespread curbs. *The Stars and Stripes,* p. 6, March 2, 1993.

Epanchin, B.: Aggressive behavior in children and adolescents. In B. Epanchin & J. Paul (Eds.) *Emotional Problems of Childhood and Adolescence: A Multidisciplinary Perspective.* Columbus, OH: Merrill, 1987.

Epanchin, B. & Paul, J. (Eds.): *Emotional Problems of Childhood and Adolescence: A Multidisciplinary Perspective.* Columbus, OH: Merrill, 1987.

Epstein, M. & Cullinan, D.: Academic performance of behaviorally disordered and learning disabled pupils, *The Journal of Special Education,* 17: 303–307, 1983.

Epstein, M., Polloway, E., Patton, J., & Foley, R.: Mild Retardation: Student characteristics and services. *Education & Training of the Mentally Retarded,* 24 (1): 7–16, 1989.

Evans, R.: Psychoneurological Theory and Practice. In J. Paul and B. Epanchin, *Educating Emotionally Disturbed Children and Youth: Theories and Practices for Teachers* (2nd ed.). New York: Merrill, 1991.

Fallen, N. & Umansky, W.: *Young Children With Special Needs* (2nd ed.). Columbus, OH: Merrill, 1985.

Famighetti, R. (Ed.): *World Almanac 1995.* Mahwah, NJ: Funk & Wagnalls, 1994.

Federal Register: Implementation of Part B of the Education of All Handicapped Children Act, 42, August, 23, 1977.

Fernald, G.: *Remedial Techniques in Basic School Subjects.* New York: McGraw-Hill, 1943.

Feuerstein, R.: *Instrumental Enrichment: An Intervention Program for Cognitive Modifiability.* Baltimore: University Park Press, 1980.

Fine, R.: Psychoanalysis. In R. Corsini (ed.) *Current Psychotherapies.* Itasca, IL: Peacock, 1973.

Finnegan, L.: Smoking and its effects on pregnancy and the newborn. In S. Harel & N. Anastasiow (Eds.), *The At-Risk Infant: Psycho/Socio/Medical Aspects.* Baltimore: Paul H. Brookes, 1985.

Flavell, J.H.: *Cognitive Development* (2nd ed.). Englewood Cliffs, NJ: Prentice-Hall, 1985.

Forness, S. & Knitzer, J.: *A New Proposed Definition and Terminology to Replace "Serious Emotional Disturbance: In the Education of Handicapped Act"* (Report of the Workgroup on Definition, National Mental Health and Special Education Coalition). Alexandria, VA: National Mental Health Association, 1990.

Frostig, M., Lefever, D., Whittlesey, J.: *Frostig Developmental Test of Visual Perception* (3rd ed.). Palo Alto, CA: Consulting Psychologists, 1961.

Frostig, M. & Horne, D.: *The Frostig Program for the Development of Visual Perception.* Chicago: Follett, 1964.

Frymier, J. & Gansneder, B.: The Phi Delta Kappa Study of Students At Risk. *Phi Delta Kappan,* 71(2): 142–146, 1989.

Garrett, P., Ng'andu, N. & Ferron, J.: Is rural residency a risk factor for childhood poverty? *Rural Sociology,* 59(1): 66–83, 1994.

Garrison, K. & Force, D. Jr.: *The Psychology of Exceptional Children* (4th ed.). New York: Ronald Press, 1965.

Gelfand, D. & Hartman, D.: Behavior therapy with children: A review and evaluation of research methodology. In S. Bijou, L. Elliot, V. Armbruster, et al., *The Exceptional Child: Conditioned Learning and Teaching Ideas.* New York: MSS Information Corp., 1971.

Golden, G.: A hard look at fad therapies for developmental disorders. *Contemporary Pediatrics,* 40–60, 1987.

Goldman, S. & Pellegrino, J.: Information processing and educational microcomputer technology: Where do we go from here? *Journal of Learning Disabilities,* 20: 144–154, 1987.

Goldstein, A., Sprafkin, R., Gershaw, N. & Klein, P.: *Skillstreaming the Adolescent.* Champaign, IL: Research Press, 1980.

Gomby, D. & Shiono, P.: Drug exposed infants. *Future of Children,* i(i): 17–25, Spr. 1991.

Gredler, M.: *Learning and Instruction: Theory into Practice* (6th ed.). New York: Macmillan, 1992.

Greenspan, S.: Defining Childhood Social Competence: A Proposed Working Model. In B.K. Keogh (Ed.), *Advances in Special Education,* 3: 1–39. Greenwich, CT: JAI Press, 1981.

Gresham, F.: Social Competence and Motivational Characteristics of Learning Disabled Students. In M. Wang, M. Reynolds & H. Walberg (Eds.), *Handbook of Special Education: Research and Practice, Vol. 2, Mildly Handicapped Conditions.* New York: Pergamon, 1988.

Gresham, F. & Reschly, D.: Social skills and peer acceptance differences between learning disabled and nonhandicapped students. *Learning Disability Quarterly,* 9: 23–32, 1986.

Griffin, G.: Childhood predictive characteristics of aggressive adolescents. *Exceptional Children,* 54 (3): 246–252, 1987.

Griffith, D.: Prenatal exposure to cocaine and other drugs: Developmental and educational prognoses. *Phi Delta Kappan,* 74(1): 30–34, Sept. 1992.

Grossman, H. (Ed.): *Manual on Terminology and Classification in Mental Retardation.* Washington, D.C.: American Association on Mental Deficiency, 1973.

Grossman, H. (Ed.): *Classification in Mental Retardation.* Washington, D.C.: American Association on Mental Deficiency, 1983.

Guetzloe, E.: *Depression and Suicide: Special Education Students At Risk.* Reston, VA: The Council for Exceptional Children, 1991.

Guralnick, N. & Groom, J.: The peer relations of mildly delayed and nonhandicapped preschool children in mainstreamed play groups. *Child Development,* 58: 1556–1579, 1987.

Hallahan, D., Kauffman, J. & Lloyd, J.: *Introduction to Learning Disabilities* (2nd ed.). Englewood Cliffs, NJ: Prentice-Hall, 1985.

Hallahan, D. & Kauffman, J.: *Exceptional Children: An Introduction to Special Education.* Boston: Allyn & Bacon, 1988 and 1994.

Hammill, D.: On defining learning disabilities: An emerging consensus. *Journal of Learning Disabilities,* 23: 74–84, 1990.

Hammill, D.: *Detroit Tests of Learning Aptitude-3.* Austin, TX: Pro-ed, 1991.

Hansen, J. & Maynard, D.: *Youth: Self-Concept and Behavior.* Columbus, OH: Merrill, 1973.

Hardman, M., Drew, C., Egan, M. & Wolf, B.: *Human Exceptionality.* Boston: Allyn & Bacon, 1990.

Hardt, J.: How passive-aggressive behavior in emotionally disturbed children affects peer interactions in a classroom setting. (ERIC Documents ED297518), 1988.

Haring, N. & McCormick, L. (Eds.): *Exceptional Children and Youth* (5th ed.). Columbus, OH: Merrill, 1990.

Haring, N., McCormick, L. & Haring, T. (Eds.): *Exceptional Children and Youth* (6th ed.). New York: Merrill/Macmillan, 1994.

Haring, N. & Phillips, E.: *Educating Emotionally Disturbed Children.* New York: McGraw-Hill, 1962.

Heber, R.: A Manual on Terminology and Classification in Mental Retardation. *American Journal of Mental Deficiency,* 64 (Monograph Supplement), 1959.

Hegge, T., Kirk, S. & Kirk, W.: *Remedial Reading Drills.* Ann Arbor, MI: George Wahr, 1936.

Helge, D.: *A National Study Regarding At-Risk Students.* Bellingham, WA: National Rural Development Institute, 1990.

Helge, D.: *Rural, Exceptional, At Risk.* Reston, VA: The Council for Exceptional Children, 1991.

Henley, M., Ramsey, R. & Algozzine, R.: *Characteristics of and Strategies for Teaching Students with Mild Disabilities.* Boston: Allyn & Bacon, 1993.

Hetherington, E. & Parke, R.: *Child Psychology: A Contemporary Viewpoint* (3rd ed.). New York: McGraw-Hill, 1986.

Heward, W.: *Exceptional Children* (5th ed.). Columbus, OH: Merrill, 1996.

Hewett, F.: *The Emotionally Disturbed Child in the Classroom.* Boston: Allyn & Bacon, 1968.

Hewett, F. & Taylor, F.: *The Emotionally Disturbed Child in the Classroom: The Orchestration of Success (2nd ed.).* Boston: Allyn & Bacon, 1980.

Hickson, L., Blackman, L. & Reis, E.: *Mental Retardation: Foundations of Educational Programming.* Boston: Allyn & Bacon, 1995.

Hiebert, B., Wong, B. & Hunter, M.: Affective influences on learning disabled adolescents. *Learning Disability Quarterly,* 5: 334–343, 1982.

Hobbs, N.: Helping disturbed children: Psychological and ecological strategies. *American Psychologist,* 21 (12): 1105–15, 1966.

Hobbs, N.: Perspectives on re-education. *Behavioral Disorders,* 3: 65–66, 1978.

Hoffman, M. (Ed.): *The World Almanac and Book of Facts 1993.* New York: World Almanac, 1992.

Horney, K.: *Neurosis and Human Growth.* New York: Norton, 1950.

Hresko, W. & Parmar, R.: The educational perspective. In D.K. Reid, W. Hresko & H.L. Swanson (Eds.): *A Cognitive Approach to Learning Disabilities* (2nd ed.). Austin, TX: Pro-ed, 1991.

Humphrey, G.: Wilhelm Wundt: The Great Master. In B. Wolman (Ed.) *Historical Roots of Contemporary Psychology.* New York: Harper & Row, 1968.

Inhelder, B.: *The Diagnosis of Reasoning in the Mentally Retarded.* New York: John Day, 1968.

James, S.: *Normal Language Acquisition.* Austin, TX: Pro-ed, 1990.

Jensen, M.: The young child's rudimentary self. In T. Yawkey (Ed.) *The Self-Concept of the Young Child.* Salt Lake City: Brigham Young University Press, 1980.

Johnson, D. & Blalock, J.: *Young Adults with Learning Disabilities.* New York: Grune & Stratton, 1987.

Johnson, D. & Myklebust, H.: *Learning Disabilities: Educational Principles and Practices.* New York: Grune & Stratton, 1967.

Jones, C.J.: *Enhancing Self-Concepts and Achievement of Mildly Handicapped Students: Learning Disabled, Mildly Mentally Retarded, and Behavior Disordered.* Springfield, IL: Charles C Thomas, 1992.

Jones, C.J.: Analysis of the self-concepts of handicapped children. *Remedial and Special Education,* 6: 32–36, Sept./Oct. 1985.

Jurkovic, G. & Selman, R.: A developmental analysis of intrapsychic understanding: Treating emotional disturbances in children. In R.L. Selman & R. Yando (Eds.), *New Distinctions for Child Development, No. 7, Clinical-Developmental Psychology.* San Francisco: Jossey-Bass, 1980.

Kanner, L.: *A History of the Care and Study of the Mentally Retarded.* Springfield, IL: Thomas, 1964.

Kauffman, J., Cullinan, D. & Epstein, M.: Characteristics of students placed in special programs for the seriously emotionally disturbed. *Behavior Disorders,* 12: 175–184, 1987.

Kazdin, A.E.: *Conduct Disorders in Childhood and Adolescence.* Beverly Hills, CA: Sage, 1987.

Kehle, T. & Barclay, J.: Social and behavioral characteristics of mentally handicapped children. *Journal of Research and Development in Education,* 12 (4): 46–56, 1979.

Keogh, B.: Learning disabilities: In defense of a construct. *Learning Disabilities Research,* 3 (1): 4–9, 1987.

Kephart, N.: *The Slow Learner in the Classroom.* Columbus, OH: Merrill, 1960 and 1971.

Kerr, M. & Nelson, C.: *Strategies for Managing Behavior Problems in the Classroom* (2nd ed.). New York: Merrill/Macmillan, 1989.

Kidd, J.: An open letter to the committee on terminology and classification of AAMD from the committee on definition and terminology of CEC–MR. *Education and Training of the Mentally Retarded,* 14: 74–76, 1979.

Kids Count: See Center for Study of Social Policy.

Kimball, S.: The influence of lead exposure and toxicity to children's neurological development and school performance. In Montgomery, D. (Ed), *Rural Partnerships Working Together.* Proceedings of the Annual National Conference of the American Council on Rural Special Education (ACRES) (ED 369 630). Austin, TX, March, 1994.

King, R.: Differentiating conduct disorder from depressive disorders in school-age children. Paper presented at the Annual Meeting of the American Educational Research Association, 70th, San Francisco, CA, April 16–20, 1986. (ERIC Document Number: ED269683).

Kirk, S.: *Teaching Reading to Slow Learning Children.* Cambridge, MA: Houghton-Mifflin, 1940.

Kirk, S. & Gallagher, J.: *Educating Exceptional Children* (6th ed.). Boston: Houghton-Mifflin, 1989.

Kirk, S., Gallagher, J. & Anastasiow, N.: *Educating Exceptional Children* (7th ed). Boston: Houghton Mifflin, 1993.

Kirk, S. & Kirk, W.: *Psycholinguistic Learning Disabilities: Diagnosis and Remediation.* Urbana, IL: University of Illinois Press, 1971.

Kirk, S., McCarthy, J. & Kirk, W.: *Illinois Test of Psycholinguistic Abilities* (Rev. Ed.). Urbana: University of Illinois Press, 1961 and 1968.

Knight-Arest, I.: Communicative effectiveness of learning disabled and normally achieving 10-to-13-year old boys. *Learning Disability Quarterly,* 7: 237–245, 1984.

Knobloch, H. & Pasamanick, B.: *Developmental Diagnosis.* New York: Harper & Row, 1974.

Koetting, J. & Rice, M.: Influence of the Social Context on Pragmatic Skills of Adults with Mental Retardation, *American Journal on Mental Retardation,* 95, 435–443, 1991.

Kominski, R. & Adams, A.: School Enrollment—Social and Economic Characteristics of Students, Oct. 1991. Washington, D.C.: U.S. Department of Commerce, Economics and Statistics Administration, Bureau of Census, April 1992.

Kramer, J. & Engle, R.: Teaching Awareness of Strategic Behavior in Combination with Strategy Training: Effect on Children's Memory Performance. *Journal of Experimental Child Psychology,* 32: 513–530, 1981.

Kramer, J., Piersel, W. & Glover, J.: Cognitive and social development of mildly retarded children. In M. Wang, M. Reynolds, & H. Walberg (Eds.), *Handbook of Special Education: Research and Practice, Volume 2, Mildly Handicapped Conditions.* Oxford: Pergamon, 1988.

LaBenne, W. & Green, B.: *Educational Implications of Self-Concept Theory.* Pacific Palisades, CA: Goodyear, 1969.

LSA Newsbriefs: A Guide to Section 504: How it Appears to Students with Learning Disabilities and ADHD. Author, 1995.

Lawrence, E. & Winschel, J.: Self-Concept and the Retarded: Research and Issues. *Exceptional Children,* 39: 310–319, 1973.

Lenz, B., Clark, F., Deshler, D. & Schumaker, J.: *The Strategies Intervention Model Training Package.* Lawrence, KS: The University of Kansas Institute for Research in Learning Disabilities, 1988.

Lerner, J.: *Learning Disabilities: Theories, Diagnosis, and Teaching Strategies.* Boston: Houghton-Mifflin, 1976, 1989, 1993.

Lerner, J., Mardell-Cudnowski, C. & Goldenberg, D.: *Special Education for the Early Childhood Years* (2nd ed.). Englewood Cliffs, NJ: Prentice Hall, 1987.

Levanthal, T. & Sills, M.: Self-image in school phobia. *American Journal of Orthopsychiatry,* 34 (4): 685–689, 1964.

Levine, M.: *Developmental Variations and Learning Disorders.* Cambridge, MA: Educators Publishing Service, 1987.

Levitt, E.: *The Psychology of Anxiety* (2nd ed.). Hillsdale, NJ: Earlbaum, 1980.

Linehan, M.: Children who are homeless: Educational strategies for school personnel. *Phi Delta Kappan,* 74(1): 61–66, Sept. 1992.

Logan, D. & Rose, E.: Characteristics of the Mentally Retarded. In P.T. Cegelka & H.J. Prehm (Eds.), *Mental Retardation: From Categories to People.* Columbus, OH: Merrill, 1982.

Long, N., Morse, W., Newman, R. (Eds.): *Conflict in the Classroom: The Education of Emotionally Disturbed Children.* Belmont, CA: Wadsworth, 1965.

Loper, A.: A Metacognitive Development: Implications for Cognitive Training. *Exceptional Education Quarterly,* 1: 1–8, 1980.

Lovitt, T.: *Introduction to Learning Disabilities.* Boston: Allyn & Bacon, 1989.

Lyon, G.: Educational validation studies. In B. Rourke (Ed.), *Neuropsychology of Learning Disabilities.* New York: Guilford, 1985.

Luckasson, R. (Ed.): *Mental Retardation: Definition, Classification, and Systems of Supports* (9th Edition). Washington, D.C.: American Association on Mental Retardation, 1992.

Luftig, R.: *Assessment of Learners with Special Needs.* Boston: Allyn & Bacon, 1988.

MacMillan, D.: Mild Mental Retardation: Emerging Issues. In G. Robinson, J. Patton, E. Polloway, & L. Sargent (Eds.), *Best Practices in Mild Mental Disabilities.* Reston, VA: CEC–MR, 1989.

MacMillan, D.L.: *Mental Retardation in School and Society* (2nd ed.). Boston: Little, Brown, 1982.

MacMillan, D., Balow, I., Wideman, K.: *A Study of Minimum Competency Tests and Their Impact: Final Report.* Riverside, CA: University of California, Riverside, 1991.

MacMillan, D., Hendrick, I. & Watkins, A.: Impact of Diana, Larry P., and PL 94-142 on minority students. *Exceptional Children,* 54: 426–432, 1988.

MacMillan, D. & Morrisson, G.: Correlates of social status among mildly handicapped learners in self-contained classes. *Journal of Educational Psychology,* 72: 437–444, 1980.

Mann, L. & Sabatino, D.: *Foundations of Cognitive Process in Remedial and Special Education.* Rockville, MD: Aspen, 1985.

Margalit, M. & Zak, I.: Anxiety and self-concept of learning disabled children. *Journal of Learning Disabilities,* 17(9): 537–539, Nov. 1984.

Marge, M.: The general problem of language disabilities in children. In J.V. Irwin & M. Marge (Eds.) *Principles of Childhood Language Disabilities.* Englewood Cliffs, NJ: Prentice-Hall, 1972.

Matson, J. & Andrasik, F. (Eds.): *Treatment Issues and Innovations in Mental Retardation.* New York: Plenum, 1983.

McCandless, B.: *Children: Behavior and Development.* New York: Holt, Rinehart & Winston, 1967.

McCarney, S. & Leigh, J.: *Behavior Evaluation Scale.* Austin, TX: Pro-Ed, 1983.

McCormick, L.: Cultural diversity and exceptionality. In N. Haring and L. McCormick (Eds.), *Exceptional Children and Youth* (5th ed.). Columbus: OH: Merrill, 1990.

McDonald, D.: A special report on the education of Native Americans: Stuck in the horizon. *Education Week,* 7(4): 1–16, 1989.

McGinnis, E. & Goldstein, A.: *Skill Streaming the Elementary School Child: A Guide for Teaching Prosocial Skills.* Champaign, IL: Research Press, 1984.

McKown, R.: *Pioneers in Mental Health.* New York: Dodd, Mead & Co., 1961.

McLaren, J. & Bryson, S.: Review of recent epidemiological studies of mental retardation: Prevalence, associated disorders, and etiology. *American Journal of Mental Retardation,* 92: 243–254, 1987.

Mehring, T. & Colson, S.: Motivation and mildly handicapped learners. In Meyen, E., Vergason, G. & Whelan, R. (Eds.) *Educating Students with Mild Disabilities.* Denver: Love, 1993.

Meichenbaum, D.: *Cognitive-Behavior Modification: An Integrative Approach.* New York: Plenum, 1977.

Mercer, C.: *Students with Learning Disabilities* (3rd ed.). Columbus, OH: Merrill, 1987.

Mercer, C. & Mercer, A.: *Teaching Students with Learning Problems* (4th ed.). Columbus, OH: Merrill, 1993.

Mercer, C. & Snell, M.: *Learning Theory Research in Mental Retardation: Implications for Teaching.* Columbus, OH: Merrill, 1977.

Minskoff, E., Wiseman, D. & Minskoff, J.: *The MWN Program for Developing Language Abilities.* Ridgefield, NJ: Educational Performance Associates, 1972.

Monson, L. & Simeonsson, R.: Normal Child Development. In B. Epanchin & J. Paul (Eds.) *Emotional Problems of Childhood and Adolescence.* Columbus, OH: Merrill, 1987.

Morgan, S. & Reinhart, J. (Eds.): *Interventions for Students with Emotional Disorders.* Austin, TX: pro-ed, 1991.

Morrison, G.: Relationship Among Academic, Social, and Career Education in Programming for Handicapped Students. In M. Wang, M. Reynolds, and H. Walberg

(Eds.) *Handbook of Special Education Research and Practice. Vol. I. Learner Characteristics and Adaptive Education.* Oxford: Pergamon, 1987.

Morrison, G.: Mentally Retarded. In E. Meyen & T. Skrtic (Eds.) *Exceptional Children and Youth: An Introduction* (3rd ed.). Denver: Love, 1988.

Muccigrosso, L., Scavarda, M., Simpson-Brown, R. & Thalacker, B.: *Double Jeopardy: Pregnant and Parenting Youth in Special Education.* Reston, VA: Council for Exceptional Children, 1991.

Mussen, P., Conger, J., Kagan, J. & Huston, A.: *Child Development and Personality* (Seventh Edition). New York: Harper & Row, 1990.

Myers, D.: *Social Psychology* (3rd ed.). New York: McGraw-Hill, 1990.

Myers, P. & Hammill, D.: *Learning Disabilities: Basic Concepts, Assessment Practices, and Instructional Strategies* (4th ed.). Austin, TX: pro-ed, 1990.

National Clearing House for Alcohol Information: *Fetal Alcohol Syndrome.* Rockville, MD: National Institute on Alcohol Abuse and Alcoholism, 1985.

National Commission of Migrant Education: *Invisible Children: A Portrait of Migrant Education in the U.S.: A Final Report.* Washington D.C.: Author, 1992.

NJCLD: National Joint Committee on Learning Disabilities. Letter from NJCLD to member organizations. Topic: Modifications to the NJCLD definition of learning disabilities, Sept. 18, 1989.

Needleman, H.: Childhood exposure to lead: A common cause of school failure. *Phi Delta Kappa,* 74(1): 35–37, Sept. 1992.

Needleman, H. & Bellinger, D.: The health effects of low level exposure to lead. *Annual Review of Public Health,* 12: 111–140, 1991.

Neisworth, J. & Bagnato, S.: *The Young Exceptional Child: Early Development and Education.* New York: MacMillan, 1987.

Nelson, R., Cummings, J. & Boltman, H.: Teaching Basic Concepts to Students Who Are Educable Mentally Handicapped. *Teaching Exceptional Children,* 23(2), 12–15, 1991.

Newcomer, P.: *Understanding and Teaching Emotionally Disturbed Children and Adolescents* (2nd ed.). Austin, TX: Pro-Ed, 1993.

Newcomer, P. & Hammill, D.: *Test of Language Development: Primary-2.* Austin, TX: Pro-Ed, 1982.

Nippold, M.: Comprehension of figurative language in youth. *Topics in Language Disorders* 5(3): 1–2, 1985.

Nowicki, S. & DiGirolamo, A.: The association of external locus of control, nonverbal processing difficulties, and emotional disturbance. *Behavioral Disorders,* 15(1): 28–34, 1989.

Office of Special Education (OSEP), U.S. Department of Education: *Sixteenth Annual Report to Congress on the Implementation of Individuals with Disabilities Act.* Washington, D.C.: Author, 1994.

Ollendick, H., Balla, D. & Zigler, E.: Expectancy of success and the probability learning performance of retarded children. *Journal of Abnormal Psychology,* 77: 275–281, 1971.

Osborne Jr., A. & Dimattia, P.: Counterpoint: IDEA's LRE Mandate: Another Look. *Exceptional Children,* 61 (6): 582–584, May 1994.

Oyer, H., Crowe, B. & Hass, W.: *Speech, Language, and Hearing Disorders: A Guide for the Teacher.* Boston: Little, Brown, 1987.

Palincsar, A. & Brown, D.: Enhancing instructional time through attention to metacognition. *Journal of Learning Disabilities,* 20(2): 66–75, 1984.

Pallas, A., Natriello, G. & McDill, E.: The changing nature of the disadvantaged population: Current dimensions and future trends. *Educational Research,* 18: 16–22, 1986.

Pascarella, E., Pflaum, S., Bryan, T. & Pearl, R.: Interaction on internal attribution for effort and teacher response mode in reading instruction: A replication note. *American Educational Research Journal,* 5: 173–176, 1983.

Patton, J., Beirne-Smith, A. & Payne, J.: *Mental Retardation* (3rd ed.). Columbus, OH: Merrill, 1990.

Patton, J. & Polloway, E.: Mild Mental Retardation. In N. Haring & L. McCormick (Eds.). *Exceptional Children and Youth* (5th ed.). Columbus, OH: Merrill, 1990.

Paul, J.: Defining behavioral disorders in children. In B. Epanchin & J. Paul (Eds.) *Emotional Problems of Childhood and Adolescence: A Multidisciplinary Perspective.* Columbus, OH: Merrill, 1987.

Paul, J.: Emotional and Behavior Disorders in Children. In J. Paul & B. Epanchin (Eds.) *Educating Emotionally Disturbed Children and Youth: Theories and Practices for Teachers* (2nd ed.). New York: Merrill, 1991.

Paul, J. & Epanchin, B.: *Educating Emotionally Disturbed Children and Youth* (2nd ed.). New York: Merrill, 1992.

Pearl, R., Donahue, M. & Bryan, T.: Social relationships of learning disabled children. In J. Torgensen & B. Wong (Eds.) *Psychological and Educational Perspectives on Learning Disabilities.* New York: Academic, 1986.

Peterson, C.: *Introduction to Psychology.* New York: Harper Collins, 1991.

Peterson, N.: *Early Intervention for Handicapped and At-Risk Children.* Denver: Love, 1987.

Phelps, M. & Prock, G.: Equality of educational opportunity in rural America. In A. DeYoung (Ed.), *Rural Education Issues and Practice.* New York: Garland, 1991.

Phelps-Terasaki, D. & Phelps-Gunn, T.: *Test of Pragmatic Language.* Austin, TX: Pro-Ed, 1992.

Piers, E. & Harris, D.: *Piers-Harris Children's Self-Concept Scale (The Way I Feel About Myself).* Los Angeles: Western Psychological Services, 1969 & 1984.

Pindus, N., O'Reilly, F., Schulte, M. & Webb, L.: *Services for migrant children in the health, social services, and educational systems.* Washington, D.C.: The Urban Institute, March, 1993.

Platt, J., Cranston-Gingras, A. & Scott, Jr., J.: Understanding and educating migrant students. *Preventing School Failure,* 36 (1): 41–46, Fall 1991.

Podell, D., Tournaki-Rein, N. & Lin, A.: Automatization of mathematics skills via computer assisted instruction among students with mild mental handicaps. *Education and Training in Mental Retardation,* 27(3): 200–206, Sept. 1992.

Polatajko, H.: A critical look at vestibular dysfunction in learning disabled children. *Developmental Medicine and Child Neurology,* 27: 283–292, 1985.

Politino, V.: Attitude toward physical activity and self-concept of normal and emotionally disturbed children. *Dissertation Abstracts International,* 40(8A): 4476, Feb. 1980.

Polloway, E., Epstein, M. & Cullinan, D.: Prevalence of behavior problems among educable mentally retarded students. *Education and Training of the Mentally Retarded,* 20: 3–13, 1985.

Polloway, E., Epstein, M., Patton, J., Cullinan, D. & Luebke, J.: Demographic, social and behavioral characteristics of students with educable mental retardation. *Education and Training of the Mentally Retarded,* 21: 27–34, 1986.

Polloway, E., Patton, J., Payne, J. & Payne, R.: *Strategies for Teaching Learners with Special Needs* (4th ed.). Columbus, OH: Merrill, 1989.

Polloway, E. & Smith, T.: *Language Instruction for Students with Disabilities,* (2nd ed.). Denver: Love, 1992.

Poplin, S.: The reductionistic fallacy in learning disabilities: Replicating the past by reducing the present. *Journal of Learning Disabilities,* 21 (7): 389–400, 1989.

Powell, M.: An Interpretation of Effective Management and Discipline of the Mentally Retarded Child. In S. Bijou, L. Elliot, V. Armbruster et al., *The Exceptional Child: Conditioned Learning and Teaching Ideas.* New York: MSS Information Corp., 1971.

Poulsen, M.: *Schools Meet the Challenge: Educational Needs of Children At Risk Due to Substance Exposure.* Sacramento: Resources in Special Education, 1991.

Pullis, M.: Affective and motivational aspects of learning disabilities. In D.K. Reid (Ed.), *Teaching the Learning Disabled: A Cognitive Developmental Approach.* Boston: Allyn & Bacon, 1988.

Purkey, W.: *Self-Concept and School Achievement.* Englewood Cliffs, NJ: Prentice-Hall, 1970.

Purkey, W. & Novak, J.: *Inviting School Success.* Belmont, CA: Wadsworth. 1984.

Quay, H.C.: Classification. In H.C. Quay & J.S. Weery (Eds.) *Psychopathological Disorders of Childhood* (3rd ed.). New York: Wiley, 1986.

Quay, H. & Peterson, D.: Manual for the revised Behavior Problem Checklist. Coral Gables, FL: University of Miami, 1987.

Quay, H. & Weery, J.: *Psychopathological Disorders of Childhood* (3rd ed.). New York: Wiley, 1986.

Ramirez, B.: Culturally and linguistically diverse children. *Teaching Exceptional Children,* 20(4): 45–46, 1988.

Raschke, D. & Dedrick, C.: Earn your fortune: A system to motivate reluctant learners. *Teaching Exceptional Children,* 62–63, Spring 1989.

Recer, P.: 12% of kids mentally troubled, study says. *Associated Press,* 1–2, June 8, 1989.

Reid, D.K.: *Teaching the Learning Disabled: A Cognitive Developmental Approach.* Boston: Allyn & Bacon, 1988.

Reinert, H.: *Children in Conflict* (2nd ed.). St. Louis: Mosby, 1980.

Reschly, D.: Incorporating adaptive behavior deficits into instructional programs. In G.A. Robinson, J.R. Patton, E.A. Polloway & L.R. Sargent (Eds.) *Best Practices in Mild Mental Retardation.* Reston, VA: Division on Mental Retardation, The Council for Exceptional Children, 1989.

Reschly, D.: Learning characteristics of mildly handicapped students: Implications for Classification, Placement, and Programming. In M. Wang, M. Reynolds, & H. Wolberg (Eds.), *Handbook of Special Education Research and Practice. Vol. 1, Learner Characteristics and Adaptive Education.* New York: Pergamon, 1987.

Restak, R.: *The Brain.* Toronto: Bantam, 1984.

Ringness, T.: Emotional reactions to learning situations as related to the learning efficiency of mentally retarded children. ED022782, 1959.

Rizzo, J. & Zabel, R.: *Educating Children and adolescents with Behavior Disorders: An Integrative Approach.* Boston: Allyn & Bacon, 1988.

Roberts, C. & Zubrick, S.: Factors influencing the social status of children with mild academic disabilities in regular classrooms. *Exceptional Children,* 59(3): 192–202, 1992.

Robinson, S. & Deshler, D.: In E. Meyen & T. Skrtic (Eds.), *Exceptional Children and Youth: An Introduction* (3rd ed.). Denver: Love, 1988.

Robinson, H. & Robinson, N.: *The Mentally Retarded Child: A Psychological Approach.* New York: McGraw-Hill, 1976.

Rogers, C.: *Client Centered Therapy.* Boston: Houghton Mifflin, 1951.

Rogers, H. & Saklofske, D.: Self-concepts, locus of control and performance expectations of learning disabled children. *Journal of Learning Disabilities* 18(5): 273–278, 1985.

Saccuzzo, D. & Michael, B.: Speed of information processing and structural limitations of mentally retarded and dual-diagnosed retarded-schizophrenic persons. *American Journal of Mental Deficiency,* 89: 187–194, 1984.

Scheerenberger, R.: *A History of Mental Retardation.* Baltimore: Brookes, 1983.

Scheerenberger, R.C.: *A History of Mental Retardation: A Quarter of a Century of Promise.* Baltimore: Brookes, 1987.

Schloss, P.: Dimensions of student behavior disorders: An alternative to medical model classification. *Diagnostique,* 11 (11): 21–30, Fall, 1985.

Schroeder, C. & Riddle, D.: Behavior Theory and Practice. In J. Paul & B. Epanchin (eds.) *Educating Emotionally Disturbed Children and Youth: Theories and Practices for Teachers* (2nd ed.). New York: Merrill, 1991.

Schultz, E.: Depth of Processing by Mentally Retarded and MA Matched Nonretarded Individuals, *American Journal of Mental Deficiency,* 88, 307–313, 1983.

Schumaker, J. & Hazel, J.: Social skills assessment and training for the learning disabled: Who's on first and what is on second? Part I. *Journal of Learning Disabilities,* 17: 422–431, 1984.

Seligman, M. & Peterson, C.: A learned helplessness perspective on childhood depression. In M. Rutter, C. Izard & P. Read (Eds.) *Depression in Young People: Developmental and Clinical Perspectives.* New York: Guilford, 1986.

Siegel, M.: *Psychological Testing from Early Childhood Through Adolescence.* Madison, CT: International University Press, 1987.

Shames, G. & Wiig, E.: Language disorders in preschool children. In L. Leondard, *Human Communication Disorders.* Columbus, OH, 1990.

Shea, T.: *Teaching Children and Youth With Behavior Disorders.* St. Louis: Mosby, 1978.

Shea, T. & Bauer, A.: *Teaching Children and Youth with Behavior Disorders* (2nd ed.). Englewood Cliffs, NJ: Prentice Hall, 1987.

Shea, T. & Bauer, A.: *Learners with Disabilities: A Social Systems Perspective of Special Education.* Madison, WI: Brown & Benchmark, 1994.

Sheinker, A., Sheinker, J. & Stevens, L.: Cognitive strategies for teaching the mildly handicapped. In E.L. Meyen, G. Vergason & R. Whelan (Eds.) *Effective Instructional Strategies for Exceptional Children.* Denver: Love, 1988.

Sherman, T.: *Exceptional Children.* Denver: Love, 1992.

Silver, L. (Ed.): *The Assessment of Learning Disabilities: Preschool Through Adulthood.* Boston: Little, Brown, 1989.

Silver, L.: *The Misunderstood Child.* Blue Ridge Summit, PA: Tab Books, 1992.

Silverman, R., Zigmond, N. & Sansone, J.: Teaching coping skills to adolescents with learning problems. In E. Meyen, G. Vergason & R. Whelan (Eds.) *Promising Practices for Exceptional Children: Curriculum Implications.* Denver: Love, 1983.

Silverstein, A.: Anxiety and the quality of human figure drawings. *American Journal of Mental Deficiency,* 70: 607–608, 1966.

Simeonsson, R.: Social competence. In J. Wortis (Ed.) *Mental Retardation and Developmental Disabilities: An Annual Review* (Vol. 10). New York: Brunner/Mazel, 1978.

Slavin, R.: *Educational Psychology.* Englewood Cliffs, NY: Prentice-Hall, 1994.

Sloan, W. & Stevens, H.: *A Century of Concern: A History of the American Association on Mental Deficiency 1876–1976.* Washington, D.C.: AAMR, 1976.

Smith, D. & Luckasson, R.: *Introduction to Special Education: Teaching in an Age of Challenge* (2nd ed.). Boston: Allyn & Bacon, 1995.

Smith, M., Schloss, P. & Hunt, F.: Differences in social and emotional development. In J. Neisworth & S. Bagnato, *The Young Exceptional Child: Early Development and Education.* New York: Macmillan, 1987.

Smith, S. & Pennington, B.: Genetic influences. In K. Kavale, S. Forness & M. Bender (Eds.) *Handbook of Learning Disabilities Vol. 1: Dimensions and Diagnosis.* San Diego, CA: College-Hill, 1987.

Smith, T., Finn, D. & Dowdy, C.: *Teaching Students with Mild Disabilities.* Orlando, FL: Harcourt Brace Jovanovich, 1993.

Snell, M.: Functional Reading. In M. Snell (Ed.), *Systematic Instruction of the Moderately and Severely Handicapped* (2nd Ed.). Columbus, OH: Merrill, 1983.

Sparrow, S., Balla, D. & Cicchetti, D.: *Vineland Adaptive Behavior Scales.* Circle Pines, MN: American Guidance Service, 1984.

Spitz, H.: The role of input organization in the learning and memory of mental retardates. In N.R. Ellis (Ed.) *International Review of Research in Mental Retardation Vol. 2.* New York: Academic Press, 1966.

Spitz, H.: Beyond field theory in the study of mental deficiency. In N.R. Ellis (Ed.) *Handbook of Mental Deficiency: Psychological Theory and Research* (2nd ed.). Hillside, NJ: Erlbaum, 1979.

Sprinthall, R. & Oja, S.: *Educational Psychology: A Developmental Approach* (6th ed.). New York: McGraw-Hill, 1994.

Stangvik, G.: Self-Concept and School Segregation. Goteborg, Sweden: *ACTA, UNIVERSITATIS GOTHOBURGENESIS,* 1979.

Stanovich, K.: Cognitive processes and the reading problems of learning-disabled children: Evaluating the assumption of specificity. In J.K. Torgesen & B. Wong (Eds.) *Psychological and Educational Perspectives on Learning Disabilities.* New York: Academic Press, 1986.

Stennett, R.: Emotional handicaps in the elementary years: Phase or disease? *American Journal of Orthopsychiatry,* 36: 444–449, 1966.

Stephens, W.: Equivalence formation by retarded and nonretarded children at different mental ages, *American Journal of Mental Deficiency,* 71: 311–313, 1972.

Stevens, L. & Price, M.: Meeting the challenge of educating children at risk. *Phi Delta Kappan,* 74(1): 18–23, Sept. 1992.

Stevenson, D. & Romney, D.: Depression in learning disabled children. *Journal of Learning Disabilities,* 17: 579, 1984.

Stronge, J. & Tenhouse, C.: *Educating Homeless Children: Issues and Answers.* Bloomington, IN: Phi Delta Kappa Educational Foundation, 1990.

Swanson, H.L.: Learning disabilities and memory. In D.K. Reid, W. Hresko & H.L. Swanson (Eds.) *A Cognitive Approach to Learning Disabilities* (2nd ed.). Austin, TX: Pro-Ed, 1991.

Swanson, M. & Bray, N.: Learning Disabilities: The medical view. In D.K. Reid, W. Hresko & H.L. Swanson (Eds.) *A Cognitive Approach to Learning Disabilities* (2nd ed.). Austin, TX: Pro-Ed, 1991.

Swap, S.: Disturbing classroom behaviors: A developmental and ecological view. *Exceptional Children,* 41, 163–172, 1974.

Sweeney, M. & Zionts, P.: The "Second Skin": Perceptions of disturbed and nondisturbed early adolescents on clothing, self-council, and body image. *Adolescence,* 24 (94): 411–420, Sum. 1990.

Taylor, R.: Psychological intervention with mildly retarded children: Prevention and remediation of cognitive skills. In M. Wang, M. Reynolds, & H. Walberg (Eds.) *Handbook of Special Education Research and Practice, Vol. 2, Mildly Handicapped Conditions.* New York: Pergamon, 1988.

The Chronicle of Higher Education: *Almanac.* Washington D.C.: Author, 1992.

The Stars and Stripes: Health Notes. Author, Feb. 1993. (News Release of an Environmental Protection Agency study.)

Thomas, C. & Patton, J.: Mild and Moderate Retardation. In J. Patton, M. Beirne-Smith & J. Payne (Eds.), *Mental Retardation.* Columbus, OH: Merrill, 1990 and 1994.

Tobias, S.: Anxiety research in educational psychology. *Journal of Educational Psychology,* 11: 573–582, 1979.

Turnbull III, R.: *Free Appropriate Public Education* (4th ed.). Denver: Love, 1993.

Turnbull III, R. & Turnbull, A.: *Free Appropriate Public Education Law and Implementation.* Denver: Love, 1982.

Turner, R.: Helmholtz, Sensory Physiology, and the Disciplinary Development of German Psychology. In W. Woodward & Mitchell Ash (Eds.), *The Problematic Science: Psychology in Nineteenth-Century Thought.* New York: Praeger, 1982.

U.S. Bureau of the Census: *Statistical Abstract of the United States: 1990* (110th ed.). Washington, D.C.: U.S. Government Printing Office, 1990.

U.S. Dept. of Health and Human Services: National Center on Child Abuse and Neglect, National Child Abuse and Neglect Data System, Working Paper 2, 1991, Summary Data Component, May 1993.

U.S. Dept. of Education: *To Assure the Free Appropriate Public Education of All Children with Disabilities.* Fifteenth Annual Report to Congress on the Implementation of the Individuals with Disabilities Education Act. Washington, D.C.: Author, 1993.

U.S. Dept. of Education: *To Assure the Free Appropriate Public Education of All Children with Disabilities.* Sixteenth Annual Report to Congress on the Implementation of the Individuals with Disabilities Education Act. Washington, D.C.: Author, 1994.

Wade, C. & Travis, C.: *Psychology* (2nd ed.). New York: Harper & Row, 1990.

Wagner, M.: Environmental interventions in emotional disturbance. In W.C. Rhodes & M.L. Tracey (Eds.), *A Study of Child Variance. (Vol. II): Intervention.* Ann Arbor: University of Michigan Press, 1972.

Wahler, R., House, K. & Stambaugh, E.: *Ecological Assessment of Child Problem Behavior: A Clinical Package for Home, School, and Institutional Settings.* New York: Pergamon, 1976.

Wallace, G., Cohen, S. & Polloway, E.: *Language Arts: Teaching Exceptional Students.* Belmont, CA: Wodsworth, 1990.

Wallace, P. & Goldstein, J. & Nathan, P.: *Introduction to Psychology* (2nd ed.). Dubuque, IA: Wm. C. Brown, 1987.

Walker, J. & Shea, T.: *Behavior Management: A Practical Approach for Educators.* St. Louis: Mosby, 1984.

Warger, C., Tewey, S. & Megivern, M.: *Abuse and Neglect of Exceptional Children.* Reston, VA: The Council for Exceptional Children, 1991.

Warren, S. & Abbeduto, L.: The Relation of Communication and Language Development to Mental Retardation, *American Journal of Mental Retardation,* 97 (2), 125–130, 1992.

Wattenburg, W. & Clifford, C.: Relation of self-concept to beginning achievement in reading. *Child Development,* 35: 461–467, 1964.

Wechsler, D.: *Wechsler Intelligence Scale for Children* (3rd ed.). New York: Psychological Corporation, 1992.

Weiner, B.: A theory of motivation for some classroom experiences. *Journal of Educational Psychology,* 71: 3–25, 1979.

Weiss, E.: Learning disabled children's understanding of social interactions of peers. *Journal of Learning Disabilities,* 17: 612–615, 1984.

Wepman, J.: *Wepman Test of Auditory Discrimination.* Chicago, IL: Language Research Association, 1958.

Whelan, R.: Emotionally Disturbed. In E. Meyen and T. Skrtic (Eds.) *Exceptional Children and Youth: An Introduction* (3rd ed.). Denver: Love, 1988.

Whitman, T.L.: Self-regulation and mental retardation. *American Journal on Mental Retardation,* 94(4) 347–362, 1990.

Whorton, J. & Algozzine, R.: Comparison of intellectual, achievement, and adaptive behavior levels for students who are mentally retarded. *Mental Retardation,* 16: 320–321, 1978.

Widerstrom, A., Mowder, B. & Sandall, S.: *At-Risk and Handicapped Newborns and Infants Development, Assessment, and Intervention.* Englewood Cliffs, NJ: Prentice Hall, 1991.

Wiederholt, J.: Historical Perspectives on the Education of the Learning Disabled. In L. Mann & D. Sabatino (Eds.) *The Second Review of Special Education.* Philadelphia, PA: JSE Press, 1974.

Wood, F. & Lakin, K.: *Punishment and Aversive Stimulation in Special Education: Legal, Theoretical and Practical Issues in Their Use with Emotionally Disturbed Children and Youth.* Minneapolis, MN: University of Minnesota, 1978.

Woodcock, R. & Johnson, M.: *Woodcock-Johnson Psychoeducational Battery Revised Tests of Achievement:* Standard and Supplemental Batteries. Dallas: DLM Teaching Resources, 1989.

Woodward, W. & Ash, M. (Eds.): *The Problematic Science: Psychology in Nineteenth-Century Thought.* New York: Praeger, 1982.

World Almanac, 1995: See Famighetti (Ed.).

World Almanac, 1993: See Hoffman (Ed.).

Wyne, M. & O'Connor, D.: *Exceptional Children: A Developmental View.* Lexington, MA: Heath, 1979.

Youniss, J.: The nature of social development: A conceptual discussion of cognition. In H. McGurk (Ed.) *Issues in Childhood Social Development.* London: Methuen, 1978.

Ysseldyke, J. & Algozzine, B.: *Introduction to Special Education* (2nd ed.). Boston: Houghton Mifflin, 1990.

Zigler, E.: Research on personality structure in the retardate. In N. Ellis (Ed.) *International Review of Research in Mental Retardation, Vol. 1.* New York: Academic Press, 1966.

Zigmond, N.: A prototype of comprehensive service for secondary students with learning disabilities: A preliminary report. *Learning Disability Quarterly,* 1: 39–49, 1978.

Zirkel, P.: Courtside W(h)ither Full Inclusion? *Phi Delta Kappan,* 76 (5): 415–417, Jan. 1995.

Zirpoli, T.: *Understanding and Affecting the Behavior of Young Children.* Englewood Cliffs, NJ: Merrill/Prentice Hall, 1995.

INDEX